"WHEN IN THE COURSE OF HUMAN EVENTS"

1776 AT HOME, ABROAD, AND IN AMERICAN MEMORY

THE McDONALD
CENTER FOR
AMERICA'S FOUNDING
PRINCIPLES

MERCER
UNIVERSITY

THE A. V. ELLIOTT CONFERENCE SERIES

The Thomas C. and Ramona E. McDonald Center
for America's Founding Principles

Guided by James Madison's maxim that "a well-instructed people alone can be permanently a free people," the McDonald Center exists to promote the study of the great texts and ideas that have shaped our regime and fostered liberal learning.

Directors
Will R. Jordan and Charlotte C. S. Thomas

Published Volumes

Charlotte C. S. Thomas, ed., *No Greater Monster nor Miracle than Myself: The Political Philosophy of Michel de Montaigne* (2014)

Charlotte C. S. Thomas, ed., *Of Sympathy and Selfishness: The Moral and Political Philosophy of Adam Smith* (2015)

Will R. Jordan and Charlotte C. S. Thomas, ed., *The Most Sacred Freedom: Religious Liberty in the History of Philosophy and America's Founding* (2016)

Will R. Jordan, ed., *Promise and Peril: Republics and Republicanism in the History of Political Philosophy* (2017)

Will R. Jordan, ed., *When in the Course of Human Events: 1776 at Home, Abroad, and in American Memory* (2018)

Forthcoming

Charlotte C. S. Thomas, ed. *Essays on Thucydides* (2019)

Will R. Jordan, ed., *Essays on the Federalist and Anti-Federalist Papers* (2020)

“When in the Course of Human Events”

1776 at Home, Abroad, and in American Memory

Edited by Will R. Jordan

MERCER UNIVERSITY PRESS | *Macon, Georgia*
2018

MUP/ P568

Published by Mercer University Press
1501 Mercer University Drive
Macon, Georgia 31207

9 8 7 6 5 4 3 2 1

Books published by Mercer University Press are printed on acid-free paper that meets the requirements of the American National Standard for Information Sciences—Permanence of Paper for Printed Library Materials.

ISBN 978-0-88146-660-7
Cataloging-in-Publication Data is available from the Library of Congress

CONTENTS

MERCER UNIVERSITY

MERCER UNIVERSITY PRESS

Endowed by

TOM WATSON BROWN
and
THE WATSON-BROWN FOUNDATION, INC.

CONTRIBUTORS

W.B. Allen—Professor Emeritus of Political Science, Michigan State University, East Lansing, Michigan

Jane E. Calvert—Associate Professor of History, University of Kentucky, Lexington, Kentucky

Will R. Jordan—Associate Professor of Political Science, Co-Director of the McDonald Center for America's Founding Principles, Mercer University, Macon, Georgia

Adam Potkay—William R. Kenan, Jr. Professor of Humanities and Professor of English, The College of William & Mary, Williamsburg, Virginia

Dennis C. Rasmussen—Associate Professor of Political Science, Tufts University, Medford, Massachusetts

James H. Read—Professor of Political Science, College of Saint Benedict / Saint John's University, Collegeville, Minnesota

Diana Schaub—Professor of Political Science, Loyola University Maryland, Baltimore, Maryland

Scott Philip Segrest—Assistant Professor of Political Science, The Citadel, Charleston, SouthCarolina

Brian Steele—Associate Professor of History, University of Alabama at Birmingham, Birmingham, Alabama

ACKNOWLEDGMENTS

Many people are deserving of thanks for their contributions to this volume. The essays in the book were originally presented at Mercer University's 2016 A.V. Elliott Conference on Great Books and Ideas, sponsored by the Thomas C. and Ramona E. McDonald Center for America's Founding Principles. Neither the Center nor the Conference would be possible without the generous support of the Elliott and McDonald families. We truly cannot thank them enough. The McDonald Center is also very fortunate to have strong institutional support, and I would like to thank Mercer University President William D. Underwood and successive College of Liberal Arts Deans Lake Lambert, Keith Howard, and Anita Gustafson for their efforts to nurture and promote the Center over the years. I also especially thank Charlotte Thomas, my co-director at the McDonald Center. It takes a good team to make the Center work, and I am very fortunate to have Charlie as a partner.

I am very grateful to Bill Allen, Jane Calvert, Adam Potkay, Dennis Rasmussen, Jim Read, Diana Schaub, Scott Segrest, and Brian Steele for attending the Elliott Conference and for contributing their essays to this volume. It is a bit nerve-wracking to bring together a group of scholars from different disciplines and areas of expertise in hopes that they will unite around a theme as vague as "1776". This group was wonderful to work with throughout the process. I especially thank them for the attention they lavished on our students while on campus. I would also like to acknowledge the Mercer undergraduate students who were willing to share their excellent papers at the Elliott Conference; so, thanks to Anna Bates, Maggie Callahan, Samuel Moses, and Maurilia Oldham. Gordon Lloyd, Peter McNamara, and Thomas Merrill are also to be commended for the scholarly contributions they made to the 2016 Elliott Conference.

To prepare for the Elliott Conference, the McDonald Center spent much of the 2015-16 school year exploring the theme of "1776". Central to this preparation were two faculty-student reading groups. The fall group met weekly to discuss J. Hector St. John de Crevècoeur's remarkable *Letters from an American Farmer*. The spring group read some Plutarch, Shakespeare, and Joseph Addison in order to evaluate the competing lives of Julius Caesar and Cato the Younger (in case anyone is wondering, the tie to 1776 here is that Addison's *Cato* was a favorite of George Washington). I enjoyed learning from this delightful group of faculty and students. So, many thanks to Charlotte Thomas, Garland Crawford, Sarah Gardner, Kevin Honeycutt, Mark Jones, Eric O'Dell, J. Thomas Scott, Andrew Silver, Anna Bates, Kyle Bligen, Maggie Callahan, Preston Earle, Gabrielle Hale, Jacob Harvey, Anna Johnson, Justin Kasian, Samuel Moses, Maurilia Oldham, Heidi Park, Yash Patel, Teal Baker St. Nicklaus, and David Wildes. I am also grateful to the Apgar Foundation for providing a generous grant that was used to support these reading groups.

Marc Jolley and Mercer University Press have been wonderful to work with. I thank them for their patience and for catching my mistakes. They have done a wonderful job on all of the books in this series.

I also thank my wife, Anissa, and my sons, Evan and Alex, for their constant love and support. I couldn't do any of this without them, and I've even forgiven them for being underwhelmed by Washington's Crossing when we drove through Trenton last summer.

Finally, I would like to remember two great friends of the McDonald Center, Michael Novak and Peter Augustine Lawler, who we lost during the past year. They will be missed.

INTRODUCTION

Will R. Jordan

The essays in this volume were originally prepared for the 2016 A.V. Elliott Conference on Great Books and Ideas at Mercer University. Our theme was "1776," and we sought to reflect not only on the significance of the Declaration of Independence, but to recognize some of the other important events of that fateful year. The proceedings in America are well known: the publication of Thomas Paine's *Common Sense*, the creation of the first revolutionary flag, the writing and signing of the Declaration of Independence, the formal naming of the United States of America, and the dispiriting series of military setbacks checked only by Washington's famous crossing of the Delaware River on Christmas night and subsequent victory at the Battle of Trenton. Meanwhile, on the other side of the Atlantic Ocean, 1776 saw the publication of Edward Gibbon's *The History of the Decline and Fall of the Roman Empire*, of Adam Smith's *Inquiry into the Nature and Causes of the Wealth of Nations*, and the death of Scottish philosopher David Hume. Given Hume and Smith's contributions to the theoretical development of large and free commercial republics, 1776 looks to be a watershed moment, a year when the Americans would begin putting into practice what the Scots had largely developed in theory. Of course, 1776 has also loomed large in American memory, as succeeding generations appeal to its principles and contest its significance. This book attempts to bring together some of these diverse ideas and events into one volume. What unites the essays is an attempt to better understand the core principles of free societies, principles for which human beings might even be willing to sacrifice their lives, their fortunes, and their sacred honor.

The book is divided into three parts. In the first part, we explore the thoughts and lives of two of the great heroes of the American Revolution—John Adams and John Dickinson—in order to elucidate the founders' commitment to the ideas articulated in the Declaration of Independence. The second part takes us abroad. It includes two essays on the major thinkers of the Scottish Enlightenment—Hume and Smith—and one on German diplomat Friederich von Gentz's comparison of the American and French Revolutions. The book's final section moves forward in time, considering how the spirit of 1776 has been remembered and applied in American history. The central figure here is Abraham Lincoln, perhaps the greatest ever student and teacher of the Declaration.

The book opens with W.B. Allen's thoughtful reading of a little-known document written by John Adams: the January 19, 1776 "Proclamation by the General Court." Comparing Adams's argument to both Aristotle and Thomas Hobbes, Allen suggests that the happiness envisioned by the founders as the end of government—the pursuit of which is enshrined in the Declaration—is closer in spirit to the ancients than it is to the Enlightenment. The decisive factor here is the necessary role that character of a certain sort, formed by habit and religion, plays in securing the end of happiness. Allen's reading of Adams suggests that many scholars err in reading the Declaration as a full-throated defense of modern—that is, of Hobbesian or Lockean—liberty. If Allen is correct, recapturing the true spirit of 1776 requires more careful attention to the moral prerequisites necessary for the responsible exercise of freedom.

Jane E. Calvert's "An Expansive Conception of Rights: The Quakerly Abolitionism of John Dickinson" also seeks to correct the record with respect to our understanding of the principles of 1776. She argues that modern advocates of an expansive, universal doctrine of human rights are sure to be unsatisfied by the more limited theories of rights prevailing in 18th century America, and yet more unsatisfied by the restrictive practices which denied even those rights to large segments of the population. One exception, however, can be found in an unlikely source: in the life and thought of John Dickinson, the founder whose caution led him to abstain from voting for independence and from signing the Declaration. Calvert dispels the myth of Dickinson's "conservatism," and shows that in thought and practice he did more than any other founder to expand the concept of rights. She carefully details Dickinson's actions taken with respect to the emancipation of slaves, and attributes his singular achievements here to the influence of Quaker theology. Calvert's Dickinson stands out, against the common view, as one of the most forward thinking figures of 1776.

Moving across the Atlantic, Dennis Rasmussen's "An Apology for Adam Smith, Friend of David Hume" weighs in on one of the most vexing private controversies of the Scottish Enlightenment. David Hume died on August 25, 1776. In the months leading up to his death, he had asked his close friend Adam Smith to take responsibility for posthumously publishing Hume's *Dialogues Concerning Natural Religion*. Smith refused, forcing Hume to make other arrangements. While most scholars conclude that this episode casts a pall over their friendship, and reflected poorly on Smith, Rasmussen argues persuasively that Smith was both justified in his caution and did not damage his relationship with Hume. He does so, in part, by combing through their 1776 correspondence. Though it exceeds the scope of Rasmussen's essay, we might wonder what the *Dialogues* controversy teaches us about the role of friendship in the kind of society Hume and Smith envisioned.

Focusing more narrowly on Hume, Adam Potkay's essay examines another of Hume's posthumous publications, the essay "Of Suicide." Potkay suggests that Hume—followed by his French acquaintances d'Holbach and Diderot—carved out a unique defense of suicide. Not only did it, obviously, break with traditional Christian teaching—by arguing that suicide did not violate any duty to God, community, or self—but it also rejected the classical and German idealist glorification of suicide as an heroic "assertion of rational autonomy over external causes and the vagaries of *fortuna*." According to Potkay, what distinguishes Hume's account is its radical determinism. The only real freedom at work here is the negative freedom to be left alone to end unbearable misery. Potkay's Hume provides a perfect example of the modern Enlightenment philosophy that is described by Allen in the first essay. We do well to consider the extent to which that philosophy, with all of its implications, is necessarily embedded in the spirit of 1776.

The final essay of the book's middle section is Scott Philip Segrest's "Lawful Return vs. Will to Transformation." Here, we have moved from Scotland to the continent of Europe and the writings of Friedrich von Gentz (1764-1832). The first half of Segrest's essay describes in detail Gentz's remarkable comparison between the American and French revolutions. Strongly influenced by Edmund Burke, Gentz criticizes the French revolutionaries for their passions, lack of restraint, and zeal for fantastical abstract principles; he commends the Americans for their relative moderation, dedication to law, and political pragmatism. Although he finds Gentz's account largely compelling, Segrest turns to Aristotle and Alexis de Tocqueville to refine Gentz's conclusions. Appealing to Aristotle, Segrest suggests that Gentz perhaps underestimates the importance of appeals to universal principles of right, such as those contained in the Declaration of Independence. And Segrest uses Tocqueville to correct Gentz's insufficient appreciation for the role religion played in the development of American liberty. In the end, Segrest contends that Gentz is indispensable for understanding why so many modern revolutions fail: they take their bearings from 1789 rather than 1776.

Brian Steele's "'Fame Is a Form of Incomprehension': How We Read 1776" calls our attention to the inherent difficulty of describing the true significance of any historical event, let alone something as complex and contentious as 1776. Although he sympathizes with the historians of the "Cambridge School" and their efforts to recover original meaning, he suggests that even this might prove an impossible task. Steele makes his case by considering the 20th century Argentinian writer Jorge Luis Borges and his story "Pierre Menard, Author of the *Quixote*." Borges's fictional Menard spent a whole lifetime in writing "a few pages which would coincide—word for word and line for line—with those of Miguel de Cervantes," yet at the same time be richer and more subtle than the original. Steele's point in appealing to Borges is that any reader, translator, or historian can only approach a text from his own time and place. For this reason, the most significant accomplishment of 1776 was the creation of a nation, an interpretive community, that can keep 1776 alive by giving it ever new meanings in the present.

While Steele's essay gives us little direction for distinguishing between better and worse interpretations of 1776, our final two essays make a strong case that Abraham Lincoln captures what is best and truest in the spirit of that year. James Read's "The Public Mind Shall Rest" makes the case that Lincoln possessed a viable strategy for abolishing slavery peacefully, democratically, and constitutionally. Read's account centers on Lincoln's role as party builder, as strengthening the fledgling Republican Party was a necessary first step in changing public discourse, and therefore public opinion, about the institution of slavery. Read also describes the chain of political measures (described as a "long slow squeeze") that the Republicans might have been able to enact once public opinion had been adequately prepared. Read's strongest evidence in favor of his thesis is that the "slow squeeze" scenario is exactly what Southern leaders feared most during their secession debates. Read's essay is important both for showing the capacity of our constitutional system to accommodate meaningful change without resort to violence, and for reminding us of the deep incompatibility between slavery and the pure spirit of 1776.

Diana Schaub develops this last point in her lovely essay "Lincoln and the Daughters of Dred Scott." In a careful reading of Lincoln's June 26, 1857 speech on the *Dred Scott* decision, Schaub compares Lincoln's reading of the Declaration to that offered by Stephen Douglas and Roger Taney. She shows the superiority of Lincoln's argument both as a piece of theory and for its rhetorical power. Focusing on Lincoln's several references to women in the speech, Schaub details how Lincoln turns on its head his opponents' fear of racial amalgamation by proving that it was slavery, with its rapacious violation of "not only the right to the fruit of one's labor but the right to the integrity of one's body," that accounted for the presence of racial mixing in the South. Schaub's piece reminds us of the importance of the doctrine of consent, a bedrock principle of the Declaration, in establishing a free society.

In the end, we hope that these essays will be useful to citizens and scholars alike. If W.B. Allen's essay is correct, an important part of developing the character required to secure happiness is studying the types of questions posed by this book. How do we protect and enlarge the freedoms envisioned in 1776? And what kinds of lives should we lead to make the best use of those freedoms? There is a strong case to be made that America has been at its best when it has fully embraced and lived up to the Declaration's self-evident truths. Diana Schaub's essay reminds us of Lincoln's elegant description of the founders' true purpose:

> They meant to set up a standard maxim for free society, which should be familiar to all, and revered by all; constantly looked to, constantly labored for, and even though never perfectly attained, constantly approximated, and thereby constantly spreading and deepening its influence, and augmenting the happiness and value of life to all people of all colors everywhere.[1]

This volume reminds us, however, that 1776 cannot be reduced to just one moment or one idea. We need to study it with eyes open to all of its variety, risk, and contingency. It is our hope that such an approach allows us to better understand and appreciate both the wonder of 1776 and the elementary conditions of human freedom.

[1] "The *Dred Scott* Decision, Speech at Springfield, June 26, 1857," in *Abraham Lincoln: his Speeches and Writings*, ed. Roy P. Basler (Cambridge, MA: Da Capo Press, 2001) 361.

PART I

1776 IN AMERICA

1

HAPPINESS THE END; CONSENT THE FOUNDATION; CHARACTER THE MEANS

W.B. Allen

Happiness is a fundamental political principle. I will here set forth three things related to it. In 1776 John Adams opened the deliberations prefiguring the lineaments of the Declaration of Independence and in such a way as to focus our attention on what was sought in the Revolution and the founding. Further, John Adams in that prefiguring was prepared in some ways by Aristotle's *Politics*. I will lay out that very brief argument that Aristotle made, which intersects so well with the deliberations of the American founding. Then I shall discuss how Thomas Hobbes addressed the same question, though not in the same manner, and therefore lays out for us the necessity to make a choice as to what we think to be the foundations of this political order. After relating those three things, I will close with the signature that George Washington impressed upon the overall conversation.

I begin with Aristotle, the most ancient source. Aristotle's *Politics*, Book 7, relates in a series of passages (1323b21–1325b31) that happiness is fundamental for the individual and the *polis* (city or state). Aristotle writes:

> Now let us acknowledge that the extent to which we become happy corresponds to the extent to which our virtues and prudence and the *actions* according to these are present, and let us acknowledge as a witness also God, who is happy and blessed not because of any external goods but because of Himself and His kind of nature.[1]

---

[1] Aristotle, *Politics*, translated by Hippocrates G. Apostle and Lloyd P. Gerson (Grinnell, IA: The Peripatetic Press, 1986) 1323b21.

> ...let us assume that the best way of life, for each individual separately as well as for what is common to states, is the virtuous life which is supplied with as many external goods as to make *actions* according to virtue possible.[2]

> ...the best form of government must be the one whose arrangement makes it possible for anyone to *act* best and live blessedly.[3]

Aristotle did not finish with those observations. He also laid out the end, the circumstances and the means of acting toward the best life:

> ...although all military pursuits may be assumed to be noble, they are not the ultimate end of the state but only instrumental to [its happiness]. Thus, the function of a virtuous lawgiver is to have in view a state and a race of men in it and every other association and see how those men can partake of a good life and the happiness that is possible for them.[4]

> ...for happiness is an *action* [of a certain kind], and the *actions* of just and temperate men have many noble ends.[5]

> ... among peers, the noble and the just should be shared by turns, as this is fair and alike to all.[6]

> ...if happiness should be posited as being *actions* well performed, then the best way of life for every state as well as for every citizen would be the practical life [i.e., a life of *action*]... and practical *thoughts*, too are not only those occurring for the sake of what follows from *acting*, but much more those which are complete in themselves and are speculations and acts of *thinking* for their own sake... the best way of life is of necessity the same for both the state and for each individual.[7]

---

[2] Ibid., 1324a1.
[3] Ibid., 1324a25.
[4] Ibid., 1325a5.
[5] Ibid., 1325a32.
[6] Ibid., 1325b8.
[7] Ibid., 1325b15-31.

Aristotle has made clear that in the famous choice between the life of speculation or contemplation and the life of action that the life which is most centered on human happiness is the life of action. But in speaking of the life of action he does not exclude the important concept that thinking is also an action. So Aristotle focuses our attention on the question of just what this happiness is in the form of an accomplished act, an act of virtue. To state it still more generically, what is an act of excellence?

We could reflect at length about Aristotle and the account of human nature that leads us to understand why the life of excellence describes the preeminent human possibility. But what we focus on in this essay is not so much the full development or elaboration of Aristotle's *Ethics* or *Politics* but just this central concept that happiness is the end for state and individual alike. Happiness is not to be produced by policy but by certain dispositions of the soul, which dispositions come to be prominent, centered in, instrumental to, and decisive for the life of politics as well as for each individual.

With this observation in mind, we next attend to remarks of John Adams, delivered January 19, 1776 in a proclamation that he authored for the General Court of Massachusetts.[8] At that point the colonies had been at war with the mother country some nine months, and during this time of warfare they had undergone the disorienting effects of dissolving government and being uncertain at least for the instant of what the replacement should be. They marched inexorably though not without division toward the Declaration of Independence

[8] "IV. A Proclamation by the General Court, 19 January 1776," *Founders Online*, National Archives (https://founders.archives.gov/documents/Adams/06-03-02-0195-0005). Original source: *The Adams Papers*, Papers of John Adams, vol. 3, *May 1775–January 1776*, ed. Robert J. Taylor (Cambridge, MA: Harvard University Press, 1979) 383–388. I owe the discovery of this document to Danielle Allen, who identified it as a key data-point overlooked in Pauline Maier's discussion (in *American Scripture: The Making of the Declaration of Independence* [Knopf, 1997]) of the rivalry between Paine's *Common Sense* and Adams's *Thoughts on Government*. The publication of her research findings is pending. All of the passages attributed to Adams on the next few pages are taken from this document.

in July and toward the establishment of constitutions within the respective states that they were to become and, of course, for the confederation itself. Early in these deliberations, the following proclamation, written by Adams, was sent to the people:

> The frailty of human Nature, the Wants of Individuals, and the numerous Dangers which surround them, through the Course of Life, have in all Ages, and in every Country impelled them to form Societies, and establish Governments.
>
> As the Happiness of the People <*alone*>, is the sole End of Government, So the Consent of the People is the only Foundation of it, in Reason, Morality, and the natural Fitness of things: and therefore every Act of Government, every Exercise of Sovereignty, against, or without, the Consent of the People, is Injustice, Usurpation, and Tyranny. It is a Maxim, that in every Government, there must exist Somewhere, a Supreme, Sovereign, absolute, and uncontroulable Power: But this power resides always in the Body of the People, and it never was, or can be delegated, to one Man, or a few, the great Creator having never given to Men a right to vest others with Authority over them, unlimited either in Duration or Degree.

Here we pause before concluding these passages to note that what we encounter is an advance explanation of the terms of the Declaration of Independence. We recognize the centrality of the principle of consent, but we also see its derivation from the notion of equality when equality is understood as the principle that no one human being is born by nature the ruler of any other human being. Here, of course, Adams derives that from the relationship to the Creator (and thus obligations of conscience) when he indicates that the Creator has never given to men a right to invest others with authority over them. Thus, he proceeds to the following observation:

> The present Generation, therefore, may be congratulated on the Acquisition of a Form of Government, more immediately in all its Branches under the Influence and Controul of the People, and therefore more free and happy than was <*ever*> enjoyed by their Ancestors. But as a Government so popular can be Supported only by universal Knowledge and Virtue, in the Body of the People, it is

> the Duty of all Ranks, to promote the Means of Education, for the rising Generation as well as true Religion, Purity of Manners, and Integrity of Life among all orders and Degrees.

Three things are laid out. First, there is the end, the only end: happiness. Then there is the foundation, explicitly stated as such: consent of the people. Finally, we have the means: character. I use the general expression *character*, whereas Adams invokes the acquisition of knowledge and of virtue, the development of habits, manners, religion and integrity, all of which is to say that people acting in a certain way and under certain constraints can alone express that informed consent that gives rise to the government that seeks the end of happiness.

This is a formula, but is it a mere formula? That is the question. Is it an affectation on the part of John Adams, an affectation of the American Revolution, or is it foundational in our understanding of human nature? John Adams adds, in the Proclamation by the General Court:

> That Piety and Virtue, which alone can Secure the Freedom of any People may be encouraged and Vice and Immorality suppress'd, the great and general Court have thought fit to issue this Proclamation, commending and enjoining it upon the good People of this Colony, that they lead sober, religious and peaceable Lives, avoiding all Blasphemies, Contempt of the holy Scriptures and of the Lords Day and all other Crimes and Misdemeanors, all Debauchery, Prophaneness, Corruption, Venality all riotous and tumultuous Proceedings and all Immoralities whatever: and that they decently and reverently attend the public Worship of God at all Times acknowledging with Gratitude his merciful Interposition in their Behalf, devoutly confiding in Him, as the God of Armies, by whose Favour and Protection alone they may hope for Success, in their present Conflict.

So Adams has wound together in a complete tapestry the full weight of moral and political obligation in an argument that they are inseparable, such that the unfolding of the Revolution may be understood in this context as an unfolding of these intertwined layers of obligation for human beings. Whence these obligations? Where are they derived? The text seems to make clear that they are derived not just from reason and nature but from reason, nature, and God. That is not incompatible with what Aristotle said at the outset, when he averred that these things are to be considered in light of God and God's particular nature. But this leads to certain conclusions and recommendations in the hands of Adams and which seem to lead directly to the next steps in the way of political formation or political foundation. The proclamation concludes as follows:

> [And all Judges, Justices, Sheriffs, Grand Jurors, Tythingmen, and all other] civil Officers, within this Colony, are hereby Strictly enjoined and commanded that they contribute all in their Power, by their Advice, Exertions, and Example towards a general Reformation of Manners, and that they bring to condign Punishment, every Person, who shall commit any of the Crimes or Misdemeanors aforesaid, or that shall be guilty of any Immoralities whatsoever; and that they Use their Utmost Endeavours, to have the Resolves of the Congress, and the good and wholesome Laws of this Colony duly carried into Execution.

And in the final clause, the proclamation invokes the assistance of the ministers of the Gospel within the colony, who,

> have during the late Relaxation of the Powers of civil Government, exerted themselves for our Safety, it is hereby recommended to them, still to continue their virtuous Labours for the good of the People, inculcating by their Public Ministry and private Example, the Necessity of Religion, Morality, and good order.

We have not space to explore the depths of these projected relationships. But we should be able to understand the emphasis with which they are introduced to the community at large. This was a public, not a private expression, occurring in the depths of the crisis of deliberation and judgment about what to do when faced with war with the mightiest power on the earth and being at sea with respect to the understanding of civil and political relations. That the instinct is to turn to a knitting together of powerful religious, moral, and political principles suggests something about the order, about the manner in which the founding itself was undertaken.

Let us re-emphasize that term, character, that we have identified as the means for carrying into effect the principles and foundations of the founding. It may mean something as relaxed as habits. We acquire habits that produce for us settled dispositions to act in a certain way. But certain habits conform to the ends in view, ends approved by nature itself, the ends that are appropriate to produce human happiness. Other habits are contra-indicative. Thus, in deciding which habits are needed in this crucible of construction, deliberation and reflection settle the case of the Proclamation by the General Court on building up the sources of moral and religious support that will sustain the notion of consent and direct it toward happiness. Or, to put it differently, consent of the people stands upon the bulwark of information, of knowledge, of understanding; it is informed consent. What is to inform the consent are religion, morality, manners—good habits.

Now, that is a different way of thinking about the Revolution and, potentially, the Declaration of Independence than we are perhaps familiar with. We are often inclined to derive them strictly from the Enlightenment and, in doing so, to distinguish the political philosophical principles from any moral principles. So, the underlying question is whether that approach is legitimate. Or, must we at least entertain the notion that a moral foundation is essential not only to the expression but to the achievement of the ends of the Revolution?

In light of the Enlightenment challenge, it may be urged that Adams's proclamation notwithstanding, the Revolution stood more firmly on the ground of the Declaration of Independence as primarily authored by Thomas Jefferson, and in which no such connections and allusions as those developed by Adams appear. Such an argument, however, would misrepresent the drafting of the Declaration of Independence, as Danielle Allen has demonstrated. She argues that "The story of the writing of the Declaration presents a case of the human mind at work on a scale larger than that of a single individual."[9] More importantly, she identifies the major influence of John Adams in shaping the text not only through his editorial and political influence but also by the direct influence of his preceding pamphlet, *Thoughts on Government*. As Allen shows, that widely-read text expatiates on the twin themes of happiness as the end of society and happiness as the end of the individual man, tying those foundations to the "science of politics" as "the science of social happiness." As Allen expresses it, "The purpose of government is, he argues, 'in one word, happiness.'"[10]

It follows, therefore, that we do not establish Adams in place of Jefferson in order to arrive at an interpretation of "the pursuit of happiness" that conforms to broad moral requisites. The point is not to distinguish Adams from Jefferson, but to discern a substantive understanding of happiness that we do not derive from Jefferson alone. It was the sustained development of a moral-philosophical understanding that eventuated in the language of the Declaration of Independence. That understanding, moreover, directly challenges attempts to narrow the application of "the pursuit of happiness" to mere euphemism for property interests. Nowhere in either Adams's Proclamation or his *Thoughts on Government* is the property interest instrumental in developing the concept of happiness, although prosperity is an expected result from institutions wisely devised to produce "social happiness."

In order to place this question in context, it is necessary to review Thomas Hobbes's political philosophy in his *Leviathan* as an example of the pure Enlightenment position:

> The finall Cause, or End, or Designe of men (who naturally love liberty, and Dominion over others,) is the introduction of that restraint upon themselves (in which we see them live in Commonwealths), is the foresight of their own preservation, and of a more contented life thereby; that is to say, of getting themselves out from

---

[9] Danielle Allen, *Our Declaration: A Reading of the Declaration of Independence in Defense of Equality* (New York: W. W, Norton, 2014) 47.

[10] Ibid., 60.

> that miserable condition of Warre, which is necessarily consequent (as hath been shown) to the naturall Passions of men, when there is no visible Power to keep them in awe, and tye them by feare of punishment to the performance of their Covenants, and observation of those Lawes of Nature set down in the fourteenth and fifteenth Chapters.[11]
>
> But the Right of Nature, that is the naturall Liberty of man, may by the Civill Law be abridged, and restrained: nay, the end of making Lawes, is no other but such Restraint; without the which there cannot possibly be any Peace. And Law was brought into the world for nothing else, but to limit the naturall liberty of particular men, in such manner, as they might not hurt, but assist one another, and joyn together against a common Enemy.[12]

Interestingly, Hobbes saw a need for restraint in civil government, and that restraint assumed the form of tamping down the passions of men and preventing them from falling at odds with one another. But he says further,

> those qualities of man-kind, that concern their living together in Peace, and Unity. To which end we are to consider, that the Felicity of this life, consiseth not in the repose of a mind satisfied. For there is no such *Finis ultimus,* nor *Summum Bonum,* (greatest good,) as is spoken of in the Books of the old Morall Philosophers... Felicity is a continuall progresse of the desire, from one object to another; the attaining of the former, being still but the way to the latter. The cause whereof is, That the objet of mans desire, is not to enjoy once onely, and for one instant of time, but assure for ever, the way of his future desire. And therefore the voluntary actions, and inclinations of all men, tend, not only to the procuring, but also to the assuring of a contented life.[13]

The word, felicity, of course, means happiness, and Hobbes elsewhere uses the term happiness in addition to felicity. We take

---

[11] Thomas Hobbes, *Leviathan, or The Matter, Forme, & Power of a Common-Wealth Ecclesiasticall and Civill,* edited by Richard E. Flathman and David Johnston (New York: W. W. Norton & Company, 1997) chapter xvii, p. 93.

[12] Ibid., chapter xxvi, p. 134.

[13] Ibid., chapter xi, p. 55.

note, however, of his definition of felicity: a continual progress of the desire from one object to another. Previously in *Leviathan* Hobbes had defined deliberation as a "succession of appetites" and will as "the last appetite." He has, therefore, combined the definition of happiness with the definition of deliberation. The rational process, he intends, is not a process independent of desire or the experience of appetite. Hobbes provides all that is needed to ground the modern concept of the uncoordinated expressions of subjective preferences (or values) as the natural foundation of human conduct. In short, happiness or felicity in Hobbes's account is only transient; it is the satisfaction of a given desire, and that is only momentary. For new appetites shall form and we shall move on to satisfy them. Indeed, Hobbes, says,

> there is no other Felicity of Beasts, but the enjoying of their quotidian Food, Ease, and Lusts… man which looks too far before him, in the care of future time, hath his heart all the day long, gnawed on by feare of death, poverty, or other calamity; and has no repose, nor pause of his anxiety, but in sleep.[14]

In other words, man is but a beast with forethought. Politics is but the means to satisfy the most powerful of appetites, which is the fear of death. Felicity or happiness, then, is nothing more than the moment of security, the contentedness that Hobbes described. Nor is it produced by any specific character, but rather by the restraints of civil government.

Hobbes does not sound like Aristotle. The question is, does he sound like the John Adams who did, after all, call for civil restraint upon "any immoralities whatsoever"? Does America sound like Hobbes? Or, does America sound like Aristotle? Does John Adams sound like Hobbes? Does John Adams sound like Aristotle?

Perhaps the way to respond to that question is to put in still broader context, such as that established by George Washington in his "Farewell Address," where he said:

---

[14] Ibid., chapter xii, p. 60.

> Of all the dispositions and habits which lead to political prosperity, Religion and morality are indispensable supports. In vain would that man claim the tribute of Patriotism, who should labour to subvert these great Pillars of human happiness, these firmest props of the duties of Men and citizens. The mere Politician, equally with the pious man ought to respect and to cherish them. A volume could not trace all their connections with private and public felicity. Let it simply be asked where is the security for property, for reputation, for life, if the sense of religious obligation *desert* the oaths, which are the instruments of investigation in Courts of Justice? And let us with caution indulge the supposition, that morality can be maintained without religion. Whatever may be conceded to the influence of refined education on minds of peculiar structure, reason and experience both forbid us to expect that National morality can prevail in exclusion of religious principle.
>
> 'Tis substantially true, that virtue or morality is a necessary spring of popular government.[15]

Taken alone, Washington's brief word of praise for religion and morality may be considered rhetorical. Taken in the fuller context of the Revolution, and taken in the context of Adams's Proclamation, we can discern a pattern of affirmation that there are foundations of political happiness in the regime of modern liberty that do not derive from distinguishing modern liberty from moral and religious obligation.

Now, with that in mind, we can revisit the critical sentence in the Declaration of Independence, the one in which we too often supplant the emphasis required on the word happiness with an emphasis on the word pursuit, but which we can now perhaps hear differently:

> We hold these truths to be self-evident, that all men are created equal, that they are endowed by their Creator with certain unalienable Rights, that among these are life, Liberty and the pursuit of Happiness,—That to secure these rights, Governments are instituted among Men, deriving their just powers from the consent of the

---

[15] George Washington, *George Washington: A Collection*, ed. by W. B. Allen (Indianapolis: Liberty Fund, Inc., 1988) 521.

> governed,—That whenever any Form of Government becomes destructive of these ends, it is the Right of the People to alter or to abolish it, and to institute new Government, laying its foundation on such principles and organizing its powers in such form, as to them shall seem most likely to effect their Safety and Happiness.

I ask, then, whether it makes sense to think of happiness as the achievement of uncoordinated expressions of subjective preferences, in which light some pursuits will be crowned with success and some pursuits will meet with failure? Or is it more reasonable to conceive of happiness as the fruit of coordinated labors informed by moral purpose and thus always imperfectly attained until perfectly attained? It is perhaps unnecessary to elaborate that famous sentence with the observation that the Declaration's series of rights guarantees terminate in the collective agency that establishes government for "Safety and Happiness." We might say the drafters of the Declaration honored Hobbes in recognizing the necessity of "Safety" but went well beyond Hobbes when they superadded "and Happiness."

2

AN EXPANSIVE CONCEPTION OF RIGHTS: THE QUAKERLY ABOLITIONISM OF JOHN DICKINSON[1]

Jane E. Calvert

In 1783, as George Washington abdicated his military power to the Confederation government, he declared his age to be "an Epocha when the rights of mankind were better understood and more clearly defined, than at any former period."[2] If this was true, then Thomas Jefferson might also have been correct when he prognosticated in 1782 that "[f]rom the conclusion of this war we shall be going down hill" where rights were concerned.[3] Though the rhetoric of rights is the bedrock of American political discourse, today scholars still seek to understand precisely what the Founders meant by the very word "rights," where they originated, as well as the details of how and to what extent they ought to be exercised or limited, and by whom. On closer inspection, Washington's declaration notwithstanding, it is clear the leading figures of the Founding era neither fully understood nor agreed on these matters themselves. What seemed so apparent to some at the time became murkier and more complicated with every

---

[1] The author would like to thank Gary Nash, Nicholas Wood, Jonathan Clark, and Nathan Kozuskanich for their comments and sharing sources, as well as Gloria Henry and Vertie Lee at the John Dickinson Mansion in Dover, Delaware, for sharing their research on Dickinson's treatment of his slaves and former slaves.

[2] George Washington, "Circular to the States (1783)" in *The Sacred Rights of Conscience: Selected Readings on Religious Liberty and Church-State Relations in the American Founding*, ed. Daniel L. Dreisbach and Mark David Hall (Indianapolis: The Liberty Fund, Inc., 2009) 296–298, 296.

[3] Thomas Jefferson, "Query XVII" in *Notes on the State of Virginia* (Philadelphia: Prichard and Hall, 1788) 172.

passing decade, as the many stepped forward to claim what the few had already secured for themselves—and more.

Most scholars have assumed consensus among the leading figures[4] on their conception of rights and accepted the definitions that were put forth in America's "official" claims during the Founding.[5] They also agree that individual rights were not a central concern of the Founders. Although today Americans assume that the famous language in the Declaration of Independence refers to individual rights, as Jack Rakove has argued, it is a mistake "to assume that when Jefferson spoke of all men being created equal, he was primarily describing an equality of individuals rather than an equality of peoples."[6] Rather, as Rakove and others have found, in 1776, "modern conceptions of individual rights were rare;" they were generally "corporate in focus" rather than personal.[7] Whether corporate or individual, historians know that the rights the Founders lauded were protected in practice only for a narrow segment of society—white, mainline Protestant men with property. Equality was, as Jonathan Clark calls it, a "legal fiction."[8] Some scholars exploring the origins of the concept of "human rights," however, believe they have detected a

---

[4] By "leading figures" I mean mainly the seven most prominent men of the era: Franklin, Washington, Adams, Jefferson, Hamilton, Madison, and Dickinson (hereafter JD).

[5] John Phillip Reid, for example, argues that on the matter of rights, American colonists "were in general agreement about their definition and purpose." He also explicitly delineates his discussion to exclude those rights that were not "official," that is, those that were not listed by the Continental Congress or other representative body. See *Constitutional History of the American Revolution: The Authority of Rights* (Madison: University of Wisconsin Press, 1986) 4, 18.

[6] Jack N. Rakove, "Jefferson, Rights, and Freedom of Conscience," in *The Future of Liberal Democracy: Thomas Jefferson and the Contemporary World* (New York: Palgrave Macmillan, 2004) 49-64, 51. See also *The Nature of Rights at the American Founding and Beyond*, ed. Barry Shain (Charlottesville: University of Virginia Press, 2007).

[7] Barry A. Shain and Rogers Smith, "Introduction," in *The Nature of Rights at the American Founding and Beyond*, 2, 3.

[8] J. C. D. Clark, *Thomas Paine: Britain, America and France in the Age of the American Revolution* (Oxford: Oxford University Press, 2018, forthcoming).

shift in thinking in the late-eighteenth century away from bounded natural rights to something broader and more inclusive.[9] But, because Americans did not apply this understanding until, still others argue,[10] the late-twentieth century, scholarship on the eighteenth-century contains little or no discussion of their application to subordinated peoples.[11] For example, John Phillip Reid claims that "the rights of women...were unknown during the revolutionary era."[12] Although the matter of whether Native Americans and blacks possessed basic rights received more attention from leading thinkers, there was no consensus on realizing or protecting these rights.

Americans have in vain sought some redemption in the Founders' pantheon for our collective national sin of slavery. The search has been disappointing, if not repellant to modern sensibilities. "Having achieved *their* independence," writes historian Douglas Egerton, "most whites quickly retreated from the principles announced in the Declaration of Independence as they sought to rebuild their war-ravaged economy through the exploitation of black men and women."[13] We have therefore resigned ourselves to Jefferson's and Madi-

---

[9] In addition to the works noted above, see also Lynn Hunt, *Inventing Human Rights: A History* (New York: W. W. Norton: 2007); Peter de Bolla, *The Architecture of Concepts: The Historical Formation of Human Rights* (Brooklyn, NY: Fordham University Press, 2013); Clark, "Natural Rights Discourse," in *Thomas Paine.*

[10] Samuel Moyn argues that human rights as we know them did not arise until the 1970s. See *The Last Utopia: Human Rights in History* (Cambridge: Harvard University Press, 2010); Stefan-Ludwig Hoffmann pushed this timeline back to the 1990s in "Human Rights and History," *Past & Present*, vol. 232, no. 1 (2016): 279-310.

[11] One reviewer of Shain's volume expressed that "[i]t would have been ideal to have some recent scholarship on slaves, servants, Native Americans, or women at the founding brought into [the] conversation"; but she dismissed the idea as too ambitious. Kirsten Nussbaumer, Review of *The Nature of Rights at the American Founding and Beyond* by Barry Alan Shain, *Law and History Review*, vol. 29, no. 3 (2011): 906–08, 8.

[12] Reid, 4.

[13] Douglas R. Egerton, *Death or Liberty: African Americans and Revolutionary America* (New York: Oxford University Press, 2009) 13.

son's hypocrisy in preaching liberty while owning slaves and contented ourselves with the knowledge that Washington provided freedom for his slaves upon his death. Scholars generally disregard Adams, because, although he prided himself on never having owned slaves, he also never worked against the institution; indeed, he even killed an emancipation bill in Massachusetts.[14] Some have tried to enlist Paine as an abolitionist, but scholars have disproven the claim.[15] Of the leading Founders, Franklin once was considered *the* abolitionist. But recently, David Waldstreicher has debunked that myth, showing rather that Franklin's abolition activities were minimal, often depended on denigrating blacks to bolster foreign opinions of America, and were carefully calibrated for maximum political gain.[16] Recent scholarship has contested the claim of Hamilton's biographers that he was committed to abolitionism, arguing that the evidence is overstated or nonexistent.[17]

There was at least one prominent political leader who differed markedly from the prevailing philosophy on rights and pushed the

---

[14] David Waldstreicher, *Slavery's Constitution: From Revolution to Ratification* (New York: Hill and Wang, 2009) 50.

[15] James V. Lynch, "The Limits of Revolutionary Radicalism: Tom Paine and Slavery," *Pennsylvania Magazine of History and Biography,* 123, no. 3 (1999): 177–199.

[16] David Waldstreicher, *Runaway America: Benjamin Franklin, Slavery, and the American Revolution* (New York: Hill and Wang, 2004).

[17] Michelle DuRoss, "Somewhere in Between: Alexander Hamilton and Slavery," *The Early American Review: A Journal of People, Issues, and events in Eighteenth-Century America*, vol. 9, no. 4 (2011). (https://www.varsitytutors.com/earlyamerica/early-america-review/volume-15/hamilton-and-slavery); Phillip W. Magness, "Alexander Hamilton's Exaggerated Abolitionism," *History News Network*. June 27, 2015. (http://historynewsnetwork.org/blog/153639). John Jay was also an abolitionist, but scholars question the extent of his commitment. See William Pencak, "Jay Family," in *Encyclopedia of African American History, 1619-1895,* ed. Paul Finkleman (New York: Oxford University Press, 2006) 212-13; David N. Gellman, *Emancipating New York: The Politics of Slavery and Freedom, 1777–1827* (Baton Rouge: Louisiana State University Press, 2008) 58-59.

boundaries of their definition and applicability.[18] John Dickinson, the so-called Penman of the Revolution, whom scholars have dismissed as too timid and "conservative" to sign the Declaration of Independence, actually had a more expansive view of rights and how they should be protected than his colleagues.[19] While his peers ultimately could not reconcile themselves to applying rights to subordinated peoples, Dickinson suggested this course explicitly. From his earliest rhetoric of resistance to Britain around 1760 to his concrete ideas for legal provisions in the new Republic, Dickinson made plain, first, that his conception of fundamental rights differed from the "official" list; second, that those stated rights applied to not just a few, but all humans; and third, he attempted at each juncture of the Revolution to offer his alternative view as building blocks for the new nation. That he failed is the clearest sign that Americans were not yet ready for this kind of radicalism.

Dickinson was concerned with the rights of four main groups of subordinated peoples—the "lower sorts" (i.e., the ordinary working people, the poor, criminals and prisoners); Native Americans; women; and blacks, both free and enslaved. For the ordinary people (male and female) Dickinson sought religious liberty, education, political participation, justice under the law, and humane treatment. For women in particular, he sought religious liberty and freedom of speech (both religious and political).[20] For Native Americans he sought property

[18] Although most Americans—including many scholars—today do not know who Dickinson is, his celebrity during the Founding era was colony-wide and international. He was the leading figure, America's first political hero, before independence, and remained prominent through the Federal Convention and until his death in 1808. See Jane E. Calvert, *Quaker Constitutionalism and the Political Thought of John Dickinson* (New York: Cambridge, 2009) chapter 6.

[19] The usual interpretation of scholars who have not been able to understand JD's actions apart from his Quakerism is that he was a "conservative." See, for example, the only scholarly biography of JD, Milton E. Flower, *John Dickinson: Conservative Revolutionary* (Charlottesville: University of Virginia Press, 1983).

[20] See Jane E. Calvert, "The Friendly Jurisprudence and Early Feminism of John Dickinson," in *Great Christian Jurists in American History*, ed. Daniel L.

rights and dignified treatment. For blacks he sought personal physical liberty and a better quality of life, materially, intellectually, and spiritually. In each of these areas, Dickinson advocated legal arrangements—either constitutional or statutory—that were neither codified in the British constitution, recognized as English rights, nor accepted by most Americans at the time. The following pages will discuss his stance towards, and actions for, the rights and welfare of free and enslaved black people.

The evidence reveals that Dickinson was singular among the leading figures in his efforts for blacks' freedom and concern for their wellbeing, both before and after their manumission. The explanation for why he was singular leads back to the larger question of American rights discourse and when the concept expanded to include subordinated peoples in more than mere theory, but also in practice. His singularity was not because he was a leader among the Founders in his thinking about rights—one cannot be a leader if no one follows. Rather it was because he was a follower of the Religious Society of Friends. Elsewhere I have described in detail how his ideas of resistance were shaped by Quakerism.[21] This same ideological framework also distinguished his thinking from the ideas that informed his American colleagues, the British constitutionalist tradition and the natural rights tradition. Quakers' thinking went beyond these to what we today call "human rights." It is no coincidence that Quakers were the pioneers of the largest rights movements in America, not only abolition, women's rights/suffrage, and civil rights, but also rights for Native Americans, animals, prisoners and detainees, the sick and poor, refugees, and other un/disenfranchised populations. Yet scholars in the new field of human rights studies have ignored them, look-

Dreisbach and Mark David Hall (New York: Oxford University Press, forthcoming 2018). Work is also underway on JD's efforts to secure Native American rights.

[21] Calvert, *Quaker Constitutionalism.*

ing instead to their more secular contemporaries whose "rights talk" sounds more familiar to the modern ear.[22]

The place to begin an examination of rights is where their proponents believed they originated. For most Anglo-Americans, they came from their British heritage, by their birthright as Englishmen, and they were protected by the British constitution. During the resistance to Britain, Americans gradually adopted a more radical position, speaking of rights as natural, God-given, and self-evident. One might assume that because Dickinson objected to declaring independence and strongly desired reconciliation with Great Britain, he was satisfied with a narrower definition of rights, the one prescribed by the British legal tradition, than his more radical peers who agitated for revolution. Other superficial evidence would appear to support this assumption. For example, when Dickinson wrote the Olive Branch Petition (1775), Congress's last formal attempt to negotiate with the king, his language was highly circumscribed. He explained to Arthur Lee that "[w]e make no claim, and mention no right." Certainly this appears to be a cautious approach to rights advocacy. But we must not assume that Dickinson would express his true philosophy of rights in a political document designed to appeal to the opponent of American interests. "[T]his humility," he explained, "in an address to the Throne, is at present proper."[23] For his more candid language on rights, we must look for the times when he was speaking to his fellow countrymen and attempting to influence policy and practice at home.

Dickinson's primary aim was always to educate his countrymen on their rights and how to protect them. Far from finding American rights in the British constitution or any man-made legal apparatus, Dickinson was among the first to insist that rights came from a high-

---

[22] See, for example, Daniel Edelstein, "Enlightenment Rights Talk," *The Journal of Modern History*, vol. 86, no. 3 (2014): 530-65.

[23] JD to Arthur Lee, July 7, 1775. Transcription in the Papers of John H. Powell, American Philosophical Society. Original in Lee Mss., Harvard University Library.

er source. Writing in 1766 to the Committee of Correspondence in Barbados during the Stamp Act Crisis, he argued that

> Kings or parliaments could not *give* the *rights essential to happiness*, as you confess those invaded by the Stamp Act to be. We claim them from a higher source—from the King of kings, and Lord of all the earth. They are not annexed to us by parchments and seals. They are created in us by the decrees of Providence, which establish the laws of our nature. They are born with us; exist with us; and cannot be taken from us by any human power, without taking our lives. In short, they are founded on the immutable maxims of reason and justice. It would be an insult on the divine Majesty to say, that he has given or allowed any man or body of men a *right to make me miserable*. If no man or body of men has *such a right*, I have a *right to be happy*. If there can be no happiness without freedom, I have a *right to be free*.[24]

His language and tone prompted opponents to complain that his "Zeal for natural Rights, in this Instance, was carried to an intemperate Excess."[25] Immediately, however, the Sons of Liberty, citing his *Address*, followed his lead by adopting his language of rights.[26]

These invocations of *sacred* rights, as Dickinson frequently referred to them, were not unintentional. He repeated this alarming assertion about the origins of rights frequently. Writing as the Centinel in 1768, he declared: "I have heard it advanced by Men, who ought to know better, that the People derive their Rights and Liberties from the Charters granted by the Crown. Nothing can be more groundless than this. A People derive their Liberty from God, the

---

[24] A North-American [JD], *An Address to the Committee of Correspondence in Barbados. Occasioned by a late letter from them to their Agent in London* (Philadelphia: W. Bradford, 1766) 4–5.

[25] A Native of Barbados, *Candid Observation on Two Pamphlets Lately Published* (Barbados: George Esmand, 1766) 13.

[26] See the Sons of Liberty, "The Sons of Liberty in the County of Sussex, on Delaware, to the Sons of Liberty Residing in the Northern and Southern Colonies," *Pennsylvania Gazette*, April 3, 1766.

Author of their Being."[27] He reiterated the assertion again in 1774 when writing for Congress.[28]

Although Dickinson's language sounds familiar, it was not merely an early or extreme expression of the usual Whig rhetoric. When we consider the Quaker culture within which he thought and the exceptional stances he took on rights during his career, we see that the difference between Dickinson's conception and that of other Founders thinking in the Whig-republican tradition was not just one of degree, it was one of kind. Whig-republicans and Quakers conceptualized rights in significantly different ways.[29] After agreeing that rights were given by God and should be protected by a constitutional government, they departed in most other aspects, including the epistemology of rights, the ends of rights, who exercised them, and when and how they should be asserted. Given the restrictions of space, the following paragraphs enumerate only the most basic points of the differences between Whig-republican and Quaker thinking on the subject of rights.[30]

First, as noted, Whig-republican and Quaker thinking looked quite similar in that they agreed that God bestowed rights upon mankind in general. Second, Whig-republicans believed that men knew their rights through their powers of reason. Quakers believed that God's will was revealed directly in the human conscience through his Light. Quaker theology held that all individuals of all races, socio-

---

[27] A. B. [JD], "The Centinel. No. VII." *The Pennsylvania Journal; and the Weekly Advertiser*, May 5, 1768.

[28] De Bolla identifies the First Continental Congress as the moment when the intellectual shift from rights of Britons to rights of man took place. Interestingly, he proves his case using documents that Dickinson took the lead on drafting. *Architecture of Concepts*, 178–202.

[29] There has been no systematic, scholarly analysis of the Quaker conception(s) of rights. The only treatment seems to be *Nonsense Upon Stilts? A Quaker View of Human Rights*, ed. Nigel Dower, et al. (York, England: published for the authors by William Sessions Ltd., 2008).

[30] There is a vast literature, both primary and secondary, on the subject of the Whig-republican conception of rights. The most basic tenets enumerated here can be found in John Locke's *Second Treatise* (London, 1690).

economic statuses, and genders were capable of knowing God in their consciences through the Light within. Access to the Light was universal, but individuals must prepare their souls to receive it. They could not undertake this preparation if they were oppressed by the government, other men, or degrading circumstances such as poverty and ignorance. Thus, in order that individuals be able to fulfill their obligations to God, they must be free from such oppression. The universality of the Light thus equated to universality of rights of persons. These rights included the usual British rights, but also other undocumented rights, such as possession of basic physical necessities and education. As Dickinson put it, "Rights may exist before they are acknowl[edge]d by Laws."[31]

Third, for Whig-republicans, rights pertained mainly to worldly things: life, liberty, and property or the pursuit of happiness.[32] For Quakers, rights were primarily for an otherworldly purpose, namely the individual achieving salvation by following God's law. These differing ends of rights are why Quakers privileged the right of liberty of conscience above all others; Whigs recognized this crucial right only slowly and grudgingly.[33] Fourth, both Quakers and Whig-republicans

---

[31] JD, Set Two of Notes for An Essay on the Constitutional Power of Great Britain, [1774]. R.R. Logan Collection, Historical Society of Pennsylvania (hereafter RRL/HSP).

[32] Certainly there has been much discussion about what Jefferson meant by the phrase "pursuit of happiness." Although in the eighteenth century the term "happiness" could have connotations beyond materialism to the cultivation of mind and possibly the contentment of the soul, few Enlightenment thinkers equated it with the hereafter. Moreover, Jefferson might have meant it as a more abstract social good, as in the public weal. Either way, happiness was a this-worldly condition. Dickinson, by contrast, described happiness as something else: "[T]o *imitate* and *co-operate* with his Maker in a determined Extent, as a *Minister* sensible of *Trust* and *Dependence*, is the DISTINCTION of Man. It is *his* PRIVILEGE, *to be good.*—It is his DUTY, *to be happy.*" Further, he explained, "[I]n Truth, [Man] is to be rewarded with Happiness hereafter, *by consenting to observe the best Rules for promoting his Happiness here.*" John Dickinson, *A Fragment* (Philadelphia: Dobson, 1796) 11, 36.

[33] A. Gregg Roeber provides a succinct summary of the Founders' understanding of religious rights that challenges common conceptions that either paint

believed that rights should be protected by a constitutional government, although they differed on some specifics of how that government should function. Fifth, and significantly, Whig-republicans defined their rights within and against the state; the Quaker conception of right transcended states. Sixth, whose rights were protected was also a key difference: although in Whig-republicanism the term "man" or "mankind" theoretically meant humankind, in practice only certain humans—or set of humans—were seen as being fully capable of exercising those rights: white, propertied, Protestant men. Rights also applied collectively, not individually. Quakers, by contrast, believed more in what we would today call individual "human rights," namely that rights ought to be protected for the individual regardless of that person's race, social status, gender, religion, or nationality.

Seventh, Whig-republicans and Quakers also differed on the matter of the biggest threat to rights. Whig-republicans thought in terms of the king against the people collectively; until after the American Revolution they could not conceive of individuals needing their rights protected against the public as a whole, against democratic despotism.[34] Quakers, by contrast, routinely had their rights violated by everyone from the king to colonial assemblies to thugs on the street, all of whom targeted them because of their faith. Moreover, Quakers sought to free the individual from any worldly oppression that interfered with finding the Light within, including government policies of religious persecution but also material and social circumstances such as poverty or lack of education. The two groups thus resisted oppression and defended rights in different ways.

Eighth, Whig-republicans and Quakers both believed in beginning the assertion of rights with petitioning the government. When

---

them as hostile to religion or as possessing a modern, individualistic stance. See "The Limited Horizons of Whig Religious Rights," in Shain, *The Nature of Rights*, 189-199. Yet he cites only Madison as having a concern for true liberty of conscience; Dickinson, who began asserting religious liberty in the 1760s, is nowhere to be found. See Calvert, *Quaker Constitutionalism*, 198-201.

[34] Gordon Wood, "The History of Rights in Early America," in Shain, *The Nature of Rights*, 233-57.

Whig-republicans considered further defending their rights against an encroaching government, they believed that the violations must be severe and ongoing, at which point the people's representatives could overthrow the government, using violence if necessary, and establish a new one in its place. In short, they believed in revolution.[35] Quakers, on the other hand, believed that rights must be asserted at the first sign of injustice by individuals, with the support of the community. Individuals asserted their rights by ignoring the unjust laws, and publicly and peacefully breaking them with the intent to educate the public about the injustice. They accepted the punishments they received, thereby bringing more publicity to their cause. Eventually, ideally, public pressure would cause the government to change the laws. In short, they believed in civil disobedience.[36] Whig-republicans delayed assertion of rights because of the great disruption it caused to the polity. Quakers, by contrast, compelled to assure the individual's salvation, asserted rights when God led them, which meant immediately or at the earliest opportunity. As William Penn stated a century earlier, "Where Right or Religion is in question, then is the fittest time to assert it." Whoever hears the call and ignores it is "a Coward or a Hypocrite."[37] Some disruption of the public tranquility was acceptable because they were motivated by duty to God, love of their fellow man, and reverence for the fundamental constitution.

Modern Americans are confused by Jefferson's apparent hypocrisy because we think in terms of human rights. But Jefferson, thinking as a Whig-republican, could believe simultaneously that all men are created equal, that blacks possessed natural rights, and also that black people's natural right to liberty did not equate to their civil liberty. Their rights did not outweigh the safety of the public at large, which would be fundamentally jeopardized by an influx of people

---

[35] See Quentin Skinner, "Calvinism and the Theory of Revolution," in *The Foundations of Modern Political Thought: Volume 2: The Age of Reformation* (Cambridge: University of Cambridge Press, 1978) 189–348.

[36] Calvert, *Quaker Constitutionalism*, chapter 2, *passim*.

[37] William Penn, *Some Fruits of Solitude* (London: Thomas Northcott, 1693) 104.

unfit for liberty.[38] Moreover, their liberty, being mainly a worldly concern, was not an urgent matter, provided they were treated well. Jefferson and other inveterate slave-owners could console themselves about the inherent injustice of their bondage with the idea that one day it would be safe to liberate or export them abroad.[39] As Patrick Henry explained, "let us treat the unhappy victims with lenity, it is [th]e furthest advance we can make toward Justice."[40] In a sense, the white master was the slaves' representative, and they believed the "long train of abuses" was not enough to justify overthrowing the established order.

Quakers not only read the Declaration more (though not entirely) as we do today, as applying literally to all men and women, but they also felt compelled to act on their understanding. Quakers, wrote abolitionist Robert Pleasants to Patrick Henry, "have been induced to embrace the present favourable juncture, when the Representatives of the people have nobly declared *all men equally free*, to manumit divers of our Negroes; and propose, to invest more with the same inestimable priviledge." "Indeed," he continued, "very few, are now so insensible of the injustice of holding our fellow men in Bondage, as to undertake to vindicate it; nor can it be done, in my apprehension, without condemning the present measures in America."[41] Likewise, in 1783, New Jersey Quaker David Cooper wrote, "Now is the time to demonstrate to Europe, to the whole world, that America was in earnest, and meant what she said, when, with peculiar energy, and unan-

[38] See Thomas Jefferson, "Query XIV," *Notes on the State of Virginia* (Philadelphia: Prichard and Hall, 1788) 138–59.

[39] Thomas Jefferson to Edward Coles, August 25, 1814. *Founders Online*, National Archives (http://founders.archives.gov/documents/Jefferson/03-07-02-0439).

[40] Patrick Henry to Robert Pleasants, January 18, 1773. Allinson Family Papers, The Quaker Collection, Haverford College.

[41] Robert Pleasants to Patrick Henry, March 28, 1777. American Friends' Letters, The Quaker Collection, Haverford College. Henry's response to an earlier plea from Pleasants is telling. He could not free his slaves because he was "drawn along by [th]e general inconvenience of living without them." Henry to Pleasants, January 18, 1773.

swerable reasoning, she plead the cause of human nature, and with undaunted firmness insisted, that *all mankind* came from the hand of their Creator *equally free*."[42] Consciously following Dickinson's lead, he made this call under the penname "A Farmer."[43]

Over the course of his life, Dickinson reached the same conclusion as his Quaker friends and family. Far from fearing change, as numerous scholars have claimed, Dickinson put forth suggestions that many of his contemporaries considered too extreme for consideration. His earliest thoughts are evident when he was still young, studying law in the Middle Temple at London's Inns of Court. At the age of twenty-two, he was humbled by his sense of insignificance in the metropolis, which prompted him to reflect on his peers in America. "What a Nest of Vices shall We find in the Education of a Gentleman's Son in America?" he began.

> The little mortal can no sooner talk than he is exercising his Commands over the black Children about him; no sooner walks, but he is beating them for executing his Orders, too slowly or wrong. What Passions spring up from hence? What Crops of Pride, Selfishness, Peevishness, Violence, Anger, Meaness, Revenge & Cruelty? By governing Slaves from his Infancy, he becomes a Slave himself: From amongst them, he is out of his Element: He dreads the Sight of an Equal; He is Cowardly & Sheepish before Persons of any Fashion; barb'rous & tyrannical amongst Inferiors. What a poor Creature is this to come into the world? And yet this in a great Measure is the Case in the Colonies: By conversing constantly with Slaves, they acquire a mean groveling way of thinking with the utmost Pride & Conceit.[44]

---

[42] David Cooper, *A Serious Address to the Rulers of America on the Inconsistency of their Conduct Respecting Slavery, forming a Contrast between the Encroachments of England on American Liberty and American Injustice in Tolerating Slavery* (Trenton, NJ: Isaac Collins, 1783) 4.

[43] JD's *Letters from a Farmer in Pennsylvania to the Inhabitants of the British Colonies* (1767–68) was the widest-selling publication before Paine's *Common Sense* (1776).

[44] JD to Samuel Dickinson, August 15, 1754. John Dickinson Family Papers, Library Company of Philadelphia (hereafter JDFP/LCP).

The argument that slavery is worse for the master than the slave is a familiar one among even those who lifted not a finger to end slavery. But Dickinson's thinking on slavery, and his actions towards black people, expanded beyond this narrow, self-serving objection to consider the obvious detriments to the slaves themselves.

Before independence, he was among those who spoke passionately about Americans' potential enslavement to Britain. It was a trope he employed in many of his writings, usually in passing. In 1771, however, he articulated in more detail the stark difference leaders of his age recognized between freedom and bondage. "Slaves," he wrote, "who have nothing but a miserable Life to lose and whose Minds must be infected by their Condition, are influenced only by their feelings. Freemen, possest of the Blessing, that gives a Value to Life, ever attentive to its Preservation, believe they have a Right to consider their Situation, [&] the Dangers that threaten them."[45] Here is an assessment of the harsh condition of the enslaved, more nuanced, and untinged with the romanticism of the battle cry "liberty or death": without freedom, life has no value, and the individual's degraded position does not even allow him to think. He may only suffer.

Soon Dickinson had more opportunity for commentary, not just on white Americans' potential enslavement to Britain, but also on Americans' enslavement of Africans. Little evidence has surfaced thus far on his opinion of *Somerset v. Stewart* (1772), the case in Britain whereby chattel slavery was ruled to be incompatible with the English common law. But his brief mention of the case in a 1774 pamphlet, published to promote the efforts of the First Continental Congress, gives hints not just of his approval of the British ruling, but also of his condemnation of the illegality of white Americans' enslavement of blacks—and not black *Africans*, but black *Americans*: "Even those unhappy persons," he wrote of blacks, "who have had the misfortune of being born under the yoke of bondage, imposed by the cruel laws, if

[45] JD, Draft Petition to the King, February 12, 1771. JDFP/LCP. Authorial edits have been removed for the purposes of this essay.

they may be called laws, of the land, *where they received their birth* [emphasis added], no sooner breathe the air of *England*, though they touch her shore only by accident," and here he footnoted Somerset's case, "than they instantly become freemen." It was, he observed, a "Strange contradiction," that "[t]he *same* kingdom at the *same* time, [was both] the *asylum* and the *bane* of liberty."[46] He must have sensed he was talking about America as well. Evidence from Dickinson's legal practice suggests that, in addition to following Quaker principles, he had an understanding of British law that would have inclined him to favor the *Somerset* verdict. With *Somerset*, the British constitution at home was simply codifying what was already apparent in the Admiralty Court. He believed that "[t]he Adm[iral]ty is establishd on the generous Principles of Humanity & Publick Good," and because of this, "[i]t reg[ar]ds the barbarous Inhabit[ant]s of Africk & the polite people of Europe—with an Equal Eye."[47] One might well speculate that, with this view of the British constitution and laws, Dickinson's reasons for opposing independence were clear—there was a better hope for protection of rights under the British constitution than under as yet undecided America law.

Far from using the language of slavery "unselfconsciously," as one historian has put it, it is clear that the absurdity of comparing white Americans' position under the Tea Act and other British measures with that of chattel slavery resonated for Dickinson.[48] His own rhetoric seems to have made the most obvious impression upon him—that Americans could not in good faith bemoan their own potential slavery while actually holding men and women in bondage. At

---

[46] JD, *An Essay on the Constitutional Power of Great-Britain over the Colonies in America; with the Resolves of the Committee for the Province of Pennsylvania, and their Instructions to their Representatives in Assembly* (Philadelphia: William and Thomas Bradford, 1774) 51–52.

[47] JD, Notes on a Libel in the Admiralty on behalf of some Danish Sailors, [1759]. JDFP/LCP.

[48] Patricia Bradley, *Slavery, Propaganda, and the American Revolution* (Jackson, MS: University Press of Mississippi, 1998) 4. Bradley also wrongly refers to Dickinson as a "conservative Whig" (78).

one time, Dickinson was one of the largest slave owners in the Delaware Valley, holding at least 59 men, women, and children, most of whom he inherited from his father. He had long evinced a concern at the very least for the good treatment of his bondspeople. In a 1764 advertisement for the lease of Poplar Hall, the family plantation in Dover, Delaware, Dickinson specified that because the slaves to be let with the plantation "are remarkably honest and well behaved, Care will be taken, that they are not put under the Command of any one, but a good natured humane Man."[49] Likewise, in his business dealings, if his slaves were part of a lease of a tenant property, he stipulated in the contract that they "shall be treated with Tenderness and Care, both in Sickness and Health, well fed and warmly and properly cloathed."[50] Beyond this even, on several occasions, he took steps to prevent slaves he no longer owned from being sold into objectionable circumstances. In 1772, two female slaves who had been sold out of the family requested that Dickinson buy them back. He explained, "at [Dinah's] Request I bought her & her Child, to prevent their being sold against her Inclination to a person in Maryland."[51] Another, Nanny, requested Dickinson purchase her and her four children to prevent them from being "sold to disagreeable Masters," which he did.[52] An indication that life with the Dickinsons could be preferable to the alternatives was that when Tory raiders looted his property in 1781 and invited any slaves to escape with them, only one, Isaac, opted to go.[53]

Yet, as he grew older and adhered more closely to Quaker beliefs, Dickinson came to realize that kind treatment was not enough;

---

[49] JD, "To Be Lett, for a Term of Years," *Pennsylvania Gazette*, January 5, 1764.

[50] Rebecca J. Siders and Pamela C. Edwards, "The Changing Landscape of the St. Jones Neck Under the Influence of the Dickinson Family, 1680-1850: An Exhibit Script" (University of Delaware: Center for Historic Architecture and Public Policy, 1994) 16.

[51] Bill of Sale for Dinah, June 22, 1772. Logan/HSP.

[52] Bill of Sale for Nanny, November 13, 1772. 54/7, Rose Cottage, Dover, DE.

[53] William Molleston to JD, November 8, 1781. JDFP/ LCP.

he increasingly adopted Quaker abolitionism.[54] In 1776, the year after Philadelphia Quakers established their abolition society, he began to make his sentiments against slavery known more publicly. Among his many ideas for the Articles of Confederation rejected by his colleagues was an anti-slavery clause. On the committee draft he queried, "Should there not be an Article to prevent those who are hereafter brought into these Colonies, from being held in Slavery in these Colonies?"[55] With the *Somerset* case no doubt in mind, Southerners such as Edward Routledge hated his draft because it created a powerful central government that threatened their property by protecting the rights of "inhabitants" moving among the colonies.[56] The same year, 1776, Dickinson took a bolder stance for Pennsylvania, proposing a law be passed stating that "No person hereafter coming into, or born in this country, to be held in Slavery under any pretense whatever," and a law be repealed that discouraged manumission by requiring owners to provide "security" for young and healthy former slaves.[57] Pennsylvania, still strongly influenced by Quakers despite their pariah

[54] On Quaker abolitionism, see Gary B. Nash and Jean Soderlund, *Freedom by Degrees: Emancipation in Pennsylvania and its Aftermath* (New York: Oxford University Press, 1991); Brycchan Carey, *From Peace to Freedom: Quaker Rhetoric and the Birth of American Anti-slavery, 1657-1761* (New Haven, 2012).

[55] JD, "Committee Draft of the Articles of Confederation (1776)," Papers of the Continental Congress, RG 360, National Archives and Records Administration.

[56] Alfred W. Blumrosen and Ruth G. Blumrosen, *Slave Nation: How Slavery United the Colonies and Sparked the Revolution* (Naperville, IL: Sourcebooks, Inc., 2005) 147-150.

[57] JD, *An Essay of a Frame of Government for Pennsylvania* (Philadelphia: James Humphries, Jr., 1776) 16. This language is similar to that in Article 26 of the 1776 Delaware constitution: "No person hereafter imported into this State from Africa ought to be held in slavery under any presence whatever; and no negro, Indian, or mulatto slave ought to be brought into this State, for sale, from any part of the world." JD was with his battalion in New Jersey at the time of the Delaware convention, so he could not have been present. But his influence seems likely. His close friends George Read and Thomas McKean were its leading authors, neither one of them known to be abolitionists.

status during the Revolution, passed one of the earliest laws against slavery in the new states in 1780.

By the time the Pennsylvania abolition law was in effect, in 1780, Dickinson had already begun the process of freeing his own slaves. His motives, however, were actually different from those of some leading Quaker abolitionists. Warner Mifflin, for example, made it clear where his priorities lay and hoped Dickinson shared them. "I heard," wrote Mifflin to Dickinson, "that thou had recorded a manumission for thy Blacks, more on thy account than theirs." He continued, "for however People may think I favour black People, I think I am more in the white Interest, than the others when Labouring to have them freed from Oppression, which if rightfully done is Certainly in my view of more advantage to the Master than Slave."[58] But Mifflin had heard wrong. Dickinson explained to a friend that he "became uneasy in his mind" about holding slaves. At first he tried to reconcile the matter by ameliorating their conditions, "to render a State of Slavery easy to them." But still he "found his mind disturbed *on their acc[ount]t*."[59] His first manumission deed, written in 1777, conditionally freed thirty-seven individuals. According to the terms laid out, they would remain in bondage for another twenty-one years. Children born during that period would be considered free unless Dickinson maintained and educated them, in which case they would be held for as long as the mother remained in service. A note on the deed written by his daughter, Sally, explains, "My Father afterwards set all these Slaves Free— I do not recollect the date of this transaction, but well remember his saying, this his conviction of duty, on this subject, was so strong, that it seemed to Him, 'The recording Angel {stood} ready to make {Record} against Him in Heaven, had he neglected it.'"[60] Sally could have had two instances in mind. In 1781 Dickinson freed a few slaves unconditionally, and in 1786 he freed

---

[58] Warner Mifflin to JD, August 11, 1786. RRL/HSP.

[59] James Bringhurst to Elizabeth Coggeshall, October 8, 1799. Emphasis added.

[60] JD, Manumission Deed, 1777, RRL/HSP.

the rest unconditionally.[61] He estimated his financial loss to be between £8,000 and £10,000, but he gained "a peacefull easy mind."[62]

After freeing his own slaves, Dickinson then turned his attention to Delaware, his home state before and after the Revolution. A ban on the importation of slaves to that state had been debated since the late 1760s and finally made law in the new 1776 state constitution. But it was not enforced.[63] As president of Delaware in 1782, he urged the Assembly to follow the lead of Pennsylvania by "pass[ing] laws for alleviating the afflictions of this helpless, and too often abused part of their fellow creatures." He also implored that families not be "cruelly separated from one another, and the remainder of their lives extremely embittered."[64] Dickinson knew what he was asking. As he wrote those lines, he himself was in the process of purchasing Abigail, the pregnant wife and four children of one of his slaves, Nathan (all of whom, along with two more of their children, he would soon manumit unconditionally), to keep them from being sold away to Maryland.[65] But his plea had no effect.

In 1786, Quakers turned increasingly to Dickinson to advocate their cause. Upon the death of renowned abolitionist Anthony Benezet, James Pemberton wrote to Dickinson about some of his pamphlets to be published posthumously. Because "it gives me Satisfaction to perceive thy mind turned to promote his laudable views," explained Pemberton, he would send a number of pamphlets for Dickinson "to distribute in such way, as thou may judge most condu-

---

[61] JD, Manumission Deed, 1781. RRL/HSP; JD, Manumission Deed, 1786. Kent County Delaware Deed Book y-1, p. 217, Delaware Public Archives.

[62] James Bringhurst to Elizabeth Coggeshall, October 8, 1799. The sum was a significant amount, although it is unclear if JD was assessing the market value of his slaves accurately.

[63] William H. Williams, *Slavery and Freedom in Delaware, 1693–1865* (Wilmington, DE: Scholarly Resources Inc. Imprint, 1996) 171-72.

[64] JD, "Message from the President of the State of Delaware to the General Assembly," *Pennsylvania Packet*, November 7, 1782.

[65] See Hugh Durborow to JD, July 19, 1782. Logan/HSP; Indenture for the Purchase of Abigail (wife of Nathan), Joshua (8), Nancy (6), Curtis (4), Reuben (2), and Sally (7 mos.). January 14, 1783. Logan/HSP.

cive to the pious intention of our endeared deceased friend."[66] Later that year, "at the Request of some Friends," Dickinson again called for abolition legislation for Delaware. "I took some Pains in directing the Draft," he later explained, "to make all the proper provisions, adverting to precedents in other places."[67] A scrap of notes suggests that Dickinson had no part in writing the Pennsylvania law but used it as a model for Delaware's. Cognizant of a less receptive audience in Delaware, he first prescribed "A new Preamble—short—& free from every Expression that can possibly be construed to reflect on persons of different sentiments."[68] Whether Dickinson was aware of it or not, his approach was exactly like that of Quaker abolitionist John Woolman, who successfully and gently persuaded Quaker slave-owners to give up their slaves.[69] He then proceeded to correct the wording of the law, explaining that "for want of these Words great Contests have arisen in Pennsylvania," and he added citations to cases in A. J. Dallas.[70] He went as far as to write new sections and provisos, noting of the sixth section on the financial liability for freed slaves: "much Confusion having arisen in Pennsylvania, from the odd Manner of its being worded."[71] The bill was then "taken to Dover when the Assembly was sitting, but nothing effectual was done." He tried again at a later date to "bring the Affair forward" but "the Legislature were in such a temper, that it would be in vain then to renew the Attempt. I then recall'd the Bill, and have kept it by Me, waiting for an Opportunity when it might appear with a better Prospect of Success."[72] The most Delawareans were willing to pass were laws prohibiting selling slaves

[66] James Pemberton to JD, March 10, 1786. JDFP/LCP.

[67] JD to [James] Pemberton. July 21, 1792. Gratz, Old Congress Collection, HSP.

[68] JD, Notes for the Delaware abolition bill [1786], RRL/HSP.

[69] John Woolman, *Some Considerations on the Keeping of Negroes. Recommended to the Professors of Christianity of Every Denomination* (Philadelphia: James Chattin, 1754).

[70] JD, notes on the Pennsylvania Act for Abolishing Slavery, [n.d.]. RRL/HSP.

[71] Ibid.

[72] JD to [James] Pemberton. June 21, 1792.

out of the state.[73] It appears that Dickinson tried again in 1793, but the bill "die[d] in embrio."[74]

It was not long before Dickinson took his concern to the national stage. In the 1787 Constitutional Convention, he was one of the few delegates to object to the slave trade on moral grounds and moved to have it prohibited in the Constitution.[75] As Madison reported, "Mr. Dickenson considered it as inadmissible on every principle of honor & safety that the importation of slaves should be authorized to the States by the Constitution." Certain states could not be counted on to consider the best interest of the Union. He continued, "The true question was whether the national happiness would be promoted or impeded by the importation, and this question ought to be left to the National Govt. not to the States particularly interested. If Engd. & France permit slavery, slaves are at the same time excluded from both those Kingdoms. Greece and Rome were made unhappy by their slaves."[76]

In his notes from the Convention, Dickinson probed the matter more deeply, revealing that, as in Delaware, his reservation was not merely about the importation of slaves but the incompatibility of slavery with republicanism and America's international reputation. Believing that the Convention was "Acting before the World," he asked his colleagues, "What will be said of this new gov[ernmen]t, of found[in]g a Right to govern Freemen on a power derived from

---

[73] Williams, *Slavery and Freedom*, 172.

[74] Warner Mifflin to John Parrish, January 21, 1793. Cox Parrish Wharton Papers, HSP.

[75] The significant role JD played at the Convention means that scholars cannot omit him from their discussions. But most mention him only in passing, and there has never been a sustained study on every aspect of his contribution. One of the most recent works is typical: In Michael J. Klarman's hefty volume, *The Framers' Coup: The Making of the United States Constitution* (New York: Oxford University Press, 2016), on the matter of slavery, JD is noted only once, when he objected to the omission of the word (265).

[76] Obviously, this is an oblique reference to *Somerset*. Max Farrand, *Records of the Federal Convention of 1787* (New Haven: Yale University Press, 1911) 2: 372–73, 416.

Slaves,...themselves incapable of gov[ernin]g—yet giving to others what they have not." Americans' hypocrisy would be clear when the Constitution was published. "The omit[in]g the Word will be regarded as an Endeavour to conceal a princ[iple] of wh[ich] We are ashamed." A main concern was similar to one he may have had when he drafted the Articles of Confederation—the power of the individual states: that "[e]very Import[ati]on of Slaves will encrease the power of the State over others—This princ[iple] I wish to avoid."[77] On the record, he therefore "wished the [non-importation] clause to be confined to the States which had not themselves prohibited the importation of slaves, and for that purpose moved to amend the clause so as to read 'The importation of slaves into such of the States as shall permit the same shall not be prohibited by the Legislature of the U— S— until the year 1808'—which was agreed to nem: cont:."[78] This motion, emended to omit the word "slave," became Article 1, Section 9 of the Constitution.[79]

[77] JD, "Acting before the World" [1787]. JDFP/LCP.

[78] Farrand, *Records*, 2:416.

[79] There is evidence, albeit circumstantial, that Dickinson had a hand in limiting the legality of slavery in the Constitution. He was on the committee to review the fugitive slave clause (Art. IV, Sect. 2) and was probably the person who objected to the language proposed by James Madison and James Wilson stating "no person *legally* held to service or labour in one state escaping into another" (emphasis added). Madison's notes explain, "the term 'legally' was struck out; and the words 'under the laws thereof,' inserted after the word 'State,' in compliance with the wish of some who thought the term *legal* equivocal, and favoring the idea that slavery was legal in a moral view." Dickinson, having already spoken out in the Convention against slavery on moral grounds, is the only logical person to have registered the objection. The other delegates from Virginia, Pennsylvania, New Jersey, and Delaware were either following the lead of their more vocal members and satisfied with the existing language, hostile to the Constitution as a whole, or absent during the discussion. By process of elimination, despite the fact Dickinson's last day in the Convention was September 14, the day before the actual change, he remains as the major player who might have voiced dissent over this subtle but important matter. I am grateful to Gordon Lloyd for bringing this issue to my attention and providing the explanation. For Madison's notes from September 15, 1787, see Gordon Lloyd, "The Constitu-

Dickinson's actions with regard to slavery during the Convention received mixed reviews at the time. Writing as "A Countryman," Anti-Federalist New Yorker Hugh Hughes launched a full-throated condemnation of him for allegedly not living up to the Farmer's (i.e., his own) rhetoric. Over two letters in the *New-York Journal* in November, he complained that Dickinson not only did not work against slavery but was actually instrumental in "opening a Trade which is a Disgrace to Humanity!"[80] Quoting the Farmer's first letter in which he opines that "Benevolence towards Mankind excites Wishes for their Welfare, and such Wishes endear the Means of fulfilling them," Hughes hit him hard: "What gracious Sentiments and how sweetly expressed!" he exclaimed sarcastically. "But what are Sentiments, or the tenderest Expressions, when not accompanied by corresponding Actions? They certainly render the Author a greater Object of our Pity, if not of Contempt." Then Hughes attacked Dickinson for his biggest anti-slavery achievement in the Convention—the prohibition of the slave trade. Considering it rather a failure, Hughes demanded, "How is it possible, to reconcile the first Clause of the 9th Section, in the first Article of the new Constitution, with such universal Benevolence to all Mankind?" Not content to question Dickinson's efforts, he effectively charges him with racism. "Will this Gentleman say," he queried, "that the Africans do not come within the Discription of 'Mankind?' If he should, will he be believed?" Hughes went on to malign Dickinson's character, claiming, "he was early instituted in Virtue, which, now, in advanced Life, he seems either to have forgotten or stifled[.]"[81] Hughes was mistaken about Dickinson's role in the Convention, and it is unclear why Hughes assumed he was in favor of

---

tional Convention," in TeachingAmericanHistory.org (http://teachingamericanhistory.org/convention/debates/0915-2/).

[80] A Countryman [Hugh Hughes], "Letters from a Gentleman in Dutchess County to his Friend in New York. No. I," *The New York Journal*, November 21, 1787.

[81] A Countryman [Hugh Hughes], "Letters from a Gentleman in Dutchess County to his Friend in New York. No. II," *The New York Journal*, November 23, 1787.

slavery or did not work against it. But, given this assumption, that he would attack Dickinson particularly makes sense.[82] As the Farmer, Dickinson became an icon for liberty, and his countrymen continued to look to him to advance the cause.

On the other side, some commentary was closer to the truth. After the Convention, the news that Dickinson had manumitted all his slaves made the newspapers. In "An Anecdote," a friend of Dickinson's allegedly asked, incredulous, whether the rumor was true. "Yes," replied Dickinson, "it is; and I *now* feel myself qualified to deliberate upon a form of government, for the preservation of liberty. For no man's understanding (added he) is *perfectly erect* on the subjects of liberty or govornment [*sic*], while he keeps a single slave." To this the commentator exclaimed, "May the same conduct be adopted by, and the same spirit pervade all those citizens who should be called to share in the power and offices of the United States!"[83]

Although Dickinson's slaves were now free, he did not consider his obligation to them fulfilled. Nor did they feel the need to distance themselves from him. Once free, some former slaves remained on his property as tenant farmers, some indentured themselves to him, and many continued to work for him for pay.[84] For his part, Dickinson continued to provide material aid for those who could not work and education for those who wanted to better themselves. For example, Dinah, who long served in the Dickinson household, was manumitted in 1786. After her manumission, Dickinson purchased goods for her, including salt, sugar, molasses, and cloth for the remainder of his life, even after she married one of his tenants.[85] In other cases, he

[82] He also attacked Benjamin Franklin, but not as vociferously.

[83] "An Anecdote," *Federal Gazette and Pennsylvania Evening Post*, January 7, 1789.

[84] See Siders and Edwards, "Changing Landscape," 25. Also, for example, see the Indenture of James Millar, June 4, 1791; Land Indenture between JD and Tobey Stout, January 15, 1807. Logan/HSP.

[85] See, for example, Receipts to JD from Smith & Stevenson, October 8, 1790 and March-May 1791. RRL/HSP; Receipt to JD from King Dougal, November 15, 1792. RRL/HSP; Receipt to JD from Ephraim Stevenson, June-September 1793. RRL/HSP.

stipulated in land indentures detailed privileges former slaves still living on his property would hold under the contract. To one tenant, Thomas Emory, he specified,

> that the Black folks…shall not be disturbed or molested—that they shall have the priviledge of getting dead wood for firing, or live wood if cut by them in the Branch…also of keeping three horses, six Cows & six Calves on the Premises with Pasturage in the Marsh & Woods in Common with the said Thomas Emory's stock—also of cutting Hay in the Marsh for their Stock & securing the same—and also of keeping six Sows and their Pigs & Range for them, & of keeping Poultry, except Turkies—& of fishing on the Premises.[86]

If these dwellers paid rent, it was probably minimal. A later black tenant paid the nominal sum of one dollar per year.[87] Other poor dwellers paid nothing.[88] These low rents are especially noteworthy because Dickinson had a reputation for charging unusually high rents to his white tenants.[89] Further, to ensure the wellbeing of elderly former slaves in Kent County long after he had freed them and moved to Wilmington, Dickinson sent friends and associates to check on them. Thirteen years after he manumitted them, he was especially concerned about the widows.[90] When medical emergencies occurred, he paid for surgery.[91] He provided tuition for a number of former slaves and had plans for "grant[in]g 10 Acres…for establishing a Minister to instruct negros in Jones's Neck 12 times a Year."[92] Dickinson continued this care for the remainder of his life.

Dickinson got into trouble with the Quakers when he seemed to be a less ardent advocate than they wanted for black interests in the

---

86 Land Indenture between JD and Thomas Emory, November 10, 1790. Logan/HSP.

87 Land Indenture between JD and Tobey Stout.

88 Siders and Edwards, "Changing Landscape," 27.

89 Ibid., 29-30.

90 Nathaniel Luff to JD, June 26, 1798. Logan/HSP.

91 Receipt to JD from Dr. James Sykes, June 9, 1790. RRL/HSP.

92 See the receipt from Henry Pepper to JD for tuition paid for three servants, including James Miller (son of Dinah), March 20, 1793. RRL/HSP; JD, undated notes, RRL/HSP.

1792 Delaware constitutional convention. Although, he made clear, "It is and has been for some Time past my earnest Concern, that Slavery may be gradually and totally abolished," he found his colleagues intractable on the issue. In a letter to one of the Pemberton brothers, a "kinsman," he explained how the debate unfolded in the convention. His preference was "to declare all persons born after the establishing the Constitution, free, leaving to the Legislature to make Regulations concerning the Maintenance and Education of such as would otherwise have been deemed Slaves." He described how this measure was proposed in the first session to a poor reception, then the Friends' memorial against slavery was offered with the same result. At that juncture, the constitutional dilemma became clear: "Some of Us thought," explained Dickinson, "that any Prunings of this Tree of bitter fruits, would only strengthen it and make it last the longer. Alleviations of Slavery by the Convention, would have been constitutional Sanctions of it." The discussion then turned to enforcing the existing laws that prohibited the importation of slaves.[93]

The problem, as Dickinson saw it, was that the citizens of Delaware were not fully conscious of the problem. "Information concerning the Injustice and Impolicy of Slavery is wanting," he explained. But there was reason for optimism. The signs of its inhumanity "are growing more and more obvious, and, I believe, will be in a few Years very generally acknowledged." But it would happen "much the sooner, if those who are convinced of its Unlawfullness continue frequently and firmly to bear their Testimony against it, and to communicate Instruction for promoting the Influence of Truth and Benevolence." There was a risk to the cause and to black people themselves if the issue were forced. "Unless the Minds of Men in some parts of this State, become more softened than they appear at present to be," he explained, "it is much to be feared, that any Measures by which they might be irritated, would really add to the Distresses of those whom the humane desire to relieve." Dickinson then expressed his willingness to work for the cause. He enclosed the bill he had put forward in

[93] JD to [James] Pemberton, July 21, 1792.

1786 and requested the Quakers' help in improving it. When they returned it, he assured them, "it shall be my diligent Endeavour, as much as I am able, to promote its being pass'd into a Law."[94]

Some Quakers did not accept Dickinson's explanation of the political situation. Warner Mifflin, who had earlier praised him for manumitting his slaves, now accused him of making a half-hearted effort and claimed he was part of the problem. He cited in particular his suspicion, which turned out to be correct, that Dickinson had moved in the convention to prohibit blacks from owning property in Delaware.[95] Those who "came nearest to the truth and were not in it, and profess it, were its greatest enemies," inveighed Mifflin.[96] Other Quakers did not give up on Dickinson so easily. In 1799, James Bringhurst, a fervent abolitionist, considered Dickinson's "superior abilitys & eminent Qualifications for allmost every service with thy pen," and thought this "would ensure thy Influence with some Effect over thy Cotemporarys, & with our late beloved President G. Washington and some in exhalted stations respecting the Abolition of Slavery in their own family." He encouraged Dickinson, "[I]f thou should feel it right to take up the subject and more especially since thou hast wisely sett the example to the furtherance of thy own peace."[97] Dickinson's response was not exactly what Bringhurst hoped, but not entirely disappointing either. Now sixty-six years old and deeply engrossed in the study of theology, he wrote passionately about the ability of God's Light to penetrate "mental foggs," and also marveled at the "intellectual darkness" of someone such as Washington who would, despite being "a person of large understanding and many good qualities," nevertheless continue "holding members of his fellow men,

---

[94] Ibid.

[95] *Proceedings of the House of Assembly of the Delaware State, 1781–1792, and of the Constitutional Convention of 1792*, ed. Claudia L. Bushman, *et al.* (Newark, DE: University of Delaware Press, 1988) 879, 881-82.

[96] Warner Mifflin to Henry Drinker, June 27, 1792, in *Life and Ancestry of Warner Mifflin: Friend—Philanthropist—Patriot*, Compiled by Hilda Justice (Philadelphia: Ferris & Leach, 1905) 104–107, 104.

[97] James Bringhurst to JD, July 9, 1799.

at this time in severe Bondage." Yet, he demurred. "I fear," he lamented, "that thy Opinion is too favorable of me, in imagining that any Efforts of mine could be of use on that occasion. I know by experience the horrid Infatuation" of owning slaves. He also knew Washington's stubborn personality and was probably aware that earlier efforts by Quaker Robert Pleasants had failed.[98]

Perhaps Dickinson also had an earlier failure of his own in mind. Not only had he been an infatuated slave owner himself, he had also tried unsuccessfully in 1793 to convince his brother, Philemon, to free his slaves. Unfortunately, Dickinson's letter is not extant, but his brother's curt response suggests the content. Dickinson clearly appealed to him on the basis of American and Quaker principles, both for the sake of the slaves themselves and for the welfare of his brother's immortal soul. "I endeavor to regulate my Conduct," Philemon replied, "by the Principles of justice, & humanity, & I am strongly inclined to believe, you are not particularly acquainted with my conduct towards those persons who you deem so unhappy." He then preceded to enumerate the "facts" that proved his slaves' contentment in his possession. Ultimately, Philemon was not a Quaker. "Not being influenced by the same motives that you are," he concluded, "& my situation not permitting me to make so great a sacrifice as you request, I hope, I shall stand excused, even in your mind—I am greatly obliged, by your fraternal wishes for my future happiness, which, I am under no apprehensions will be endanger'd, by my holding that species of property, you so much reprobate."[99] Philemon's response was a sound rebuke to his older brother not to meddle. Thus Dickinson declined Bringhurst's request to appeal to Washington but gave his permission for his words to be used if they "might be an encouragement to [slave owners] to sett theirs free."[100]

From our vantage point, that some Quakers were disappointed in Dickinson is understandable. No record has yet been found to in-

[98] Joseph Ellis, *His Excellency: George Washington* (Knopf, 2004) 160–61.
[99] Philemon Dickinson to JD, February 16, 1793. JDFP/LCP.
[100] James Bringhurst to Elizabeth Coggeshall, October 8, 1799.

dicate Dickinson's rationale for attempting to deny blacks property ownership. One scholar suggests that those in favor of the motion were following the lead of a 1790 Virginia petition seeking to deprive blacks of property and drive them out of the state.[101] Although that explanation does not comport entirely with Dickinson's demonstrated concern for the betterment of blacks' situations—to educate them, keep families together, and ensure their well-being upon emancipation—he might have shared an impulse similar to some Quakers of urging blacks to become Quakers but not allowing them to join white meetings.[102] Such Friends wished them well and removed the biggest obstacles to that end, but then considered their job done and preferred them at a distance. It was not specifically about restricting the vote, because the property requirement for white men was abolished, while at the same time a requirement that voters be white and male was added.[103] These are, at best, imperfect and unsatisfying explanations. Interestingly, however, the possibility of blacks owning property and voting was something that Dickinson had pondered. During his tenure as president of Pennsylvania (1782–85), he wrote a note to himself about issues that needed consideration. One striking point was the "[Pro]priety of making Blacks freeh[olde]rs & giving them Votes."[104] Perhaps we must assume he ultimately decided that abolition and the security of basic needs—food, shelter, and education—was the furthest he would go.

On the matter of black freedom, however, Dickinson did not reveal himself to be a lukewarm abolitionist or of insufficiently fiery temperament but rather an astute and realistic politician. In 1803 he derided "the direful traffic in human flesh" and urged Britain to do as America decreed it would do in 1808 and "for ever abolish the *African* slave trade, that enormous sin, which, persevered in by national au-

[101] Williams, *Slavery and Freedom*, 94.

[102] Nash and Soderlund, *Freedom by Degrees*, 29.

[103] John A. Munroe, *History of Delaware* (Newark, DE: University of Delaware Press, 2006) 83.

[104] JD, "Memorandums of public Business in Pennsylvania" [n.d.]. JDFP/LCP.

thority, against conviction of its abominations, and in defiance of the clearest light that ever shone upon a people, menaces to sink her into perdition."[105] In notes for an as yet undiscovered essay, he wrote, "Slavery to be gradually abolished—treat this fully!"[106] He was an idealist, but also a pragmatist, bound to disappoint one side if he did not anger the other. Dickinson knew two things from his political experience: first, slave owners in Delaware would never agree to immediate emancipation; second, gradual emancipation was working in other states. There was every reason to think that a gradual plan might succeed, but that a decree from the highest levels of government would neither pass nor be enforceable. Subsequent history proved Dickinson right in the worst way. So stubborn was Delaware on the matter of slavery that it did not ratify the Thirteenth Amendment until 1901.

Although Dickinson was certainly passionate about abolition, he was not consistent over the years. For him, time and place mattered more than it did for Quakers. And black freedom was not his priority in every instance. Two issues in 1805 illustrate the matter. On the one hand, he was very much concerned with halting the slave trade. In correspondence with his cousin by marriage, Pennsylvania Senator George Logan, he conveyed news of the meeting of the Abolition Society in Philadelphia along with concerns that slave traffickers were engaged in "Fraudulent Management" of the penalty system, whereby a member of the company "turns Informer, gets all the forfeited Property, and then divides with his Accomplices." He suggested that giving half the forfeitures to the U.S. government "would be a considerable discouragement to these— What shall I call them?"[107] Clearly Dickinson had nothing but disgust for the traffickers.

On the other hand, in his later years, Dickinson's major concern seems to have shifted away from the injustice done to individuals by slavery to the existential danger the institution of slavery posed to the young republic—or, at least, this is what the very limited historical

[105] JD, *The Past, Present, and Eventual Relations of United States with France* (New York: T. and J. Swords, 1803) 9, 19.

[106] JD, religious notes, RRL/HSP.

[107] JD to George Logan, January 21, 1805. RRL/HSP.

record suggests. He took more of what we might anachronistically consider to be a Lincolnian approach to slavery: slavery should be abolished, but the first thing to consider is the welfare of the Union. In Dickinson's case, he also prioritized preserving relationships with foreign allies over black freedom, which meant that he could not see his way clear to support the slave revolt in Haiti.

Writing again to Logan in 1805, he seemed to express a theoretical support of a slave revolt. "If the Blacks of Jamaica or any other Island," he wrote, "should renounce obedience to the Government of the Island, and seize strong grounds would not the citizens of these States be as Justifiable in supplying them with arms, ammunition &c. as in supplying the Revolters against France with these Articles? To be sure." But, apparently for Dickinson, the blacks of Haiti lacked the "strong grounds" necessary to justify their actions. He thus concluded that "[t]he trade [with Haiti] ought...to be utterly prohibited under heavy Penalties, to any part of the Island held by the Blacks who have revolted from France." Thinking as a Democratic Republican who felt strong ties to France, he continued, "Our measures seem to be calculated for rendering Us detestable to the French, and despicable to other Nations."[108] Further, he suspected the motives of Americans who advocated trading with "the revolted Blacks." Rather than thinking they were truly interested in abolition of slavery, he said, "Considering the Title of France to the Island, our past and present Relations to her, and a Variety of other highly important Circumstances, this Assertion seems to Me to be dictated by the Eagerness of a commercial Spirit degenerated into an all-confounding Rapacity."[109]

In the first years of the nineteenth century, the revolution in Haiti weighed on Dickinson's mind and colored his perception of developments in his own country. For Americans who owned slaves, black violence in Haiti put a mortal fear in their hearts towards their own slaves. For Dickinson, the fear was not for himself personally,

---

[108] JD to George Logan, February 11, 1805. Maria Dickinson Logan Papers, HSP.

[109] JD to George Logan, February 18, 1805. Logan Papers, HSP.

but for his country. Although at the Founding of the nation he had seemed optimistic that slavery would gradually die out, that hope might have faded with the purchase of the Louisiana territory and the possibility that slavery might be allowed there. To Logan he wrote, "As Congress is now to legislate for our extensive Territory lately acquired, I pray to Heaven, that they may build up the system of the Government, on the broad and sacred Principles of Freedom. Curse not the Inhabitants of those Regions," he continued, "with a permission to introduce Bondage." And then he seemed to circle back around to the sentiments of his youth. "Slaves," he proclaimed, "are deeply, deeply injurious to the Morals of the Masters and their Families." But now it was more than just an individual injury; now it was a danger to the nation in more than one way. First, he noted, slaves "are internal Enemies allways to be watched and guarded against." A population of slaves, he explained, was no different from the threat of standing armies. But more than this, even, the presence of slaves prevented Americans from being true republicans, in so far as that meant planting and defending their own soil. "The Labor of Slaves," he wrote, "must in a certain proportion exclude the Cultivation of the Earth by Freemen, and thereby diminish our internal safety and external Security." This position is unsurprising, coming from the Pennsylvania Farmer, himself an avid improver of the soil, and written to Senator Logan, a leader in the democratic agrarian movement. He ended with a patriotic plea against slavery: "Let the pernicious project, the detestable precedent, never be sanctioned by Votes of the Sons of Liberty."[110]

As modern observers, we are disappointed by Dickinson's apparent retreat from the cause of freedom for the sake of black people, and his failure to embrace fully the Quaker commitment to abolition and black welfare. But we should not overlook the significance of the stance he did take—stronger than any other leading figure—when he freed his own slaves, worked for abolition, and provided for the material wellbeing and education of former slaves. On the matter of rights

[110] JD to George Logan, January 30, 1804. Logan Papers, HSP.

advocacy, not only have scholars' estimations of Dickinson as a timid conservative missed the mark, they have also misread the other Founders. They usually assume that it was the men who wanted independence who were the most radical espousers of rights, but Dickinson proves them wrong, and we see clearly that the other leading Founders, by comparison, were either interested in preserving the status quo or looking too far forward to a utopian future that might only exist, if ever, beyond their lifetime. That they refused to accord basic rights to substantial portions of the population was indeed a reflection of the dominant political and legal theory of the day. Although it is certainly true that we cannot hold historical figures to modern standards of rights, we might well hold them to Dickinson's and wonder why they fell short.

The ultimate significance of Dickinson's actions, however, lies not in his personal successes or failures relative to his peers. He was merely a celebrity spokesperson for a much larger movement slowly underway. The reason Dickinson failed may well be the same reason the human rights scholars have had such trouble discerning the origins of human rights—they are not paying sufficient attention to the Quakers.

PART II

1776 ABROAD

3

AN APOLOGY FOR ADAM SMITH, FRIEND OF DAVID HUME: THE *DIALOGUES* CONTROVERSY[1]

Dennis C. Rasmussen

When the ailing David Hume drew up his will in January 1776 he named Adam Smith, his best friend for more than a quarter of a century, as his literary executor.[2] One of the duties that Hume sought to bestow upon his friend was that of overseeing the posthumous publication of his *Dialogues Concerning Natural Religion*, but Smith resolutely refused to carry out this request. It is often claimed that this episode significantly tarnished their friendship and caused Hume great pain during his final months, and Smith's behavior is generally seen as unnecessarily cautious, utterly inexplicable, or even an act of betrayal—a denial of his best friend's dying wish. Such views are common even among scholars who are ordinarily highly sympathetic to Smith. Nicholas Phillipson comments that "Smith's behaviour in the last weeks of his closest friend's life is not easy to fathom" and that his refusal to agree to publish the *Dialogues* "cast a shadow over their relationship in the last weeks of Hume's life."[3] Ian Simpson

---

[1] This essay draws on chapter 10 of Dennis C. Rasmussen, *The Infidel and the Professor: David Hume, Adam Smith, and the Friendship That Shaped Modern Thought* (Princeton: Princeton University Press, 2017). I would like to thank Princeton University Press for permission to reuse this material.

[2] Smith had asked Hume to serve in the same role for him three years earlier, before heading off to London to complete *The Wealth of Nations*: see Adam Smith to David Hume, 16 April 1773, in *Correspondence of Adam Smith*, ed. Ernest Campbell Mossner and Ian Simpson Ross (Indianapolis: Liberty Fund, 1987) (hereafter CAS) 168.

[3] Nicholas Phillipson, *Adam Smith: An Enlightened Life* (New Haven: Yale

Ross agrees that Smith's actions "must have troubled Hume on his deathbed" and that Smith "erred on the side of prudence ... at the expense of benevolence towards Hume."[4] Ryan Hanley too maintains that Hume and Smith's "otherwise unblemished friendship ... was marred by [this] incident."[5] Gavin Kennedy, for his part, insists that "Smith behaved less than loyally to Hume" and that the whole episode "leaves a bad taste."[6]

Let us review the evidence before assessing these claims.

Hume wrote the first draft of the *Dialogues Concerning Natural Religion* in the early 1750s, in the midst of an extraordinarily productive couple of years in which he also composed the *Enquiry Concerning the Principles of Morals* (i.e. the *Second Enquiry*), the *Political Discourses*, and perhaps *The Natural History of Religion*. He returned to the work several times in subsequent years, revising it just after *The Natural History of Religion* appeared in print in 1757, making some more changes in the early 1760s, and finally adding a few polishing touches in 1776.[7] We do not know when Smith first read the work. It is possible that Hume shared it with him in the early 1750s, when he sent the first few sections to Gilbert Elliot, though it seems more likely that Smith did not see it until the early 1760s, when Hume discussed the revised manuscript with Elliot again and with Hugh

University Press, 2010) 244, 242.

[4] Ian Simpson Ross, *The Life of Adam Smith*, second edition (Oxford: Oxford University Press, 2010) 319, 445; see also 359-60.

[5] Ryan Patrick Hanley, "Skepticism and Imagination: Smith's Response to Hume's *Dialogues*," in *New Essays on Adam Smith's Moral Philosophy*, ed. Wade L. Robison and David B. Suits (Rochester: Rochester Institute of Technology Press, 2012) 173.

[6] Gavin Kennedy, *Adam Smith's Lost Legacy* (New York: Palgrave Macmillan, 2005) 9-10.

[7] See M. A. Stewart, "The Dating of Hume's Manuscripts," in *The Scottish Enlightenment: Essays in Reinterpretation*, ed. Paul Wood (Rochester: University of Rochester Press, 2000), especially 291, 300-3.

Blair.[8] At all events, Smith was familiar with the *Dialogues* well before 1776—long enough before to have potentially "forgotten" it by that point.[9]

The *Dialogues* resists easy summary, but roughly speaking the interlocutors address four main topics. The first is the argument from design, or the idea that the order of the world implies a supremely wise, powerful, and benevolent designer—namely, God. This is in fact the primary subject of the work: after some introductory discussion in Part 1, Parts 2 to 8 all focus on this argument. In Part 9 the interlocutors turn to the first cause argument, according to which everything in the world has a cause and if we trace the string of causes back to the very beginning we will necessarily arrive at an initial cause, a creator of the world—namely, God. Parts 10 and 11 then delve into the problem of evil, or the question of how the presence of evil in the world can be reconciled with the idea of a supremely wise, powerful, and benevolent God. Finally, Part 12 considers the effects of religious belief and devotion on morality and politics. Though the book's conclusion is highly ambiguous, over the course of the dialogue Hume makes the weaknesses of the argument from design and the first cause argument—the two leading philosophical cases for God's existence in his day, and probably ours as well—readily apparent. Likewise, he shows the problem of evil to be extraordinarily difficult to resolve satisfactorily, and he casts grave doubt on religion's moral and political benefits.

All of this was exceedingly controversial, of course, but in fact none of the broad arguments or inquiries of the *Dialogues* were wholly new. Hume had already intimated that the argument from design is a dubious and useless hypothesis in section 11 of the *Enquiry Concern-*

---

[8] See David Hume to Gilbert Elliot of Minto, 10 March 1751, in *The Letters of David Hume*, ed. J. Y. T. Greig, vol. 1 (Oxford: Clarendon Press, 1932) (hereafter HL I) 153-7; David Hume to Gilbert Elliot of Minto, 12 March 1763, in *New Letters of David Hume*, ed. Raymond Klibansky and Ernest C. Mossner (Oxford: Clarendon Press, 1954) (hereafter NHL) 71; and David Hume to Hugh Blair, 6 October 1763, in NHL, 72.

[9] See David Hume to Adam Smith, 15 August 1776, in CAS, 205.

ing Human Understanding (i.e. the *First Enquiry*). The shortcomings of the first cause argument were implicit in the discussion of causation in the *Treatise of Human Nature* and were made more explicit in Hume's recasting of that discussion in the *First Enquiry*.[10] While the problem of evil is addressed at greater length in the *Dialogues* than in any of Hume's other writings, it too had been taken up in the *First Enquiry*.[11] And the moral and political ills of religion were a prominent theme throughout Hume's *Essays*, the *Second Enquiry*, *The History of England*, and especially *The Natural History of Religion*. What *is* new in the *Dialogues* is the combination of all of these issues into a single devastating—and entertaining—package. While nearly everything Hume wrote bears on religion in one way or another, usually to its detriment, in his published writings he had always refrained from marshalling all of his skeptical challenges at once, thereby appearing to leave some kind of refuge for the devout. In his most trenchant examination of the leading arguments for God's existence, the *First Enquiry*, he avoided any detailed discussion of religion's moral and political effects. Conversely, in his most unsparing discussion of religion's moral and political effects, *The Natural History of Religion*, he appeared to leave the door open to something like the argument from design.[12] The uniqueness of the *Dialogues* lies in its comprehensiveness, which leaves the pious reader no way out, no safe haven.

---

[10] See especially David Hume, *An Enquiry Concerning Human Understanding*, ed. Tom L. Beauchamp (Oxford: Clarendon Press, [1748] 2000) 12.28-9, 122. For an argument that the shortcomings of the first cause argument were implicit in the *Treatise*, see Paul Russell, *The Riddle of Hume's Treatise: Skepticism, Naturalism, and Irreligion* (Oxford: Oxford University Press, 2008) chapter 10.

[11] See especially Hume, *An Enquiry Concerning Human Understanding*, 8.36, 77-8; and 11.17, 104-5.

[12] See Hume's opening statement that "the whole frame of nature bespeaks an intelligent author; and no rational enquirer can, after serious reflection, suspend his belief a moment with regard to the primary principles of genuine Theism and Religion"—a statement that some scholars have, rather inexplicably, taken at face value. David Hume, *The Natural History of Religion*, in *A Dissertation on the Passions and The Natural History of Religion*, ed. Tom L. Beauchamp (Oxford: Clarendon Press, [1757] 2007) intro.1, 34.

The stage was set for the exchange between Hume and Smith regarding the fate of the *Dialogues* when Hume, realizing that he would not recover from his illness, drew up a new will on January 4, 1776. He bequeathed most of his possessions to his brother and sister, though he also included his servants and a few other friends and relatives. To Smith he left "all my manuscripts without exception, desiring him to publish my Dialogues concerning Natural Religion … but to publish no other papers which he suspects not to have been written within these five years, but to destroy them all at his leisure." For Smith to carry out this duty, Hume continues, "though I can trust to that intimate and sincere friendship, which has ever subsisted between us … yet, as a small recompense of his pains in correcting and publishing this work, I leave him two hundred pounds, to be paid immediately after the publication of it."[13]

Smith was in London at the time, seeing *The Wealth of Nations* through the press—it would appear just three months later—and it is unclear when exactly he became aware of this combination of bequest and request. Hume wrote letters to Smith on February 8 and April 1, but they focused on Smith's new book and did not mention Hume's will at all. In late April, Hume set out for London in order to consult the doctors there about his health, and around the same time Smith and their mutual friend John Home, not knowing of Hume's plans, headed north toward Edinburgh in order to see him. Fortuitously, on April 23, while Hume was resting at an inn in Morpeth, on the road between the two capitals, his valet was standing at the gate when the carriage bearing Smith and Home drew up.[14] This meeting was probably the first Smith heard of Hume's will. In any event, at Morpeth Smith seems to have expressed reservations about overseeing the pub-

---

[13] See *The Letters of David Hume*, ed. J. Y. T. Greig, vol. 2 (Oxford: Clarendon Press, 1932) (hereafter HL II) 317 n. 1.

[14] See John Home, "Diary of a Journey with Hume from Morpeth to Bath," in James Fieser, ed., *Early Responses to Hume*, second edition, vol. 9 (Bristol, UK: Thoemmes Continuum, 2005) 279.

lication of the *Dialogues*, for soon after arriving in London Hume wrote him two letters on the matter. The first of these letters (addressed to "My dear Friend") contains updates on Hume's health and other matters in his usual, casual tone, while the second is a more formal message (addressed "My dear Sir") absolving Smith of any obligation with regard to the *Dialogues*. In the latter message Hume declares that "after reflecting more maturely" on his request that Smith publish the *Dialogues* he had "become sensible, that, both on account of the Nature of the Work, and of your Situation, it may be improper to hurry on that Publication." Exactly what Hume meant by Smith's "situation" is not entirely clear; it may be a reference to the fact that he had published *The Wealth of Nations* less than two months earlier and did not want the book's reception to be impaired by involvement with a controversial work. In any case, Hume amends his "friendly Request" that Smith publish the *Dialogues*, now resting content to "leave it entirely to your Discretion at what time you will publish that Piece, or whether you will publish it at all."[15]

Hume's more informal letter, however, reveals that he had not given up hope of convincing Smith to publish the *Dialogues*, his formal promise of "entire discretion" notwithstanding. Hume opens by noting that he was enclosing the letter of absolution "conformably to your Desire," but he immediately continues: "I think, however, your Scruples groundless." Hume compares Smith's situation to that of David Mallet, who had published some controversial works of Lord Bolingbroke back in 1752, immediately after Bolingbroke's death, and who seemed to suffer no ill consequences as a result. Indeed, Hume notes that Mallet later received an office from King George III and Lord Bute, "the most prudish Man in the World," and that Mallet "always justify'd himself by his sacred Regard to the Will of a dead Friend" (as, presumably, Smith would be able to do for the *Dialogues*).[16] Hume may have underestimated the damage done to Mal-

[15] David Hume to Adam Smith, 3 May 1776, in HL II, 317-18, and CAS, 195-6.

[16] David Hume to Adam Smith, 3 May 1776, in HL II, 316, and CAS, 194-5.

let's reputation in this instance, however. Witness Samuel Johnson's indictment of Bolingbroke, and of Mallet as his accomplice: "he [i.e. Bolingbroke] was a scoundrel, and a coward: a scoundrel, for charging a blunderbuss against religion and morality; a coward, because he had not resolution to fire it off himself, but left half a crown to a beggarly Scotchman [i.e. Mallet], to draw the trigger after his death!"[17] If Smith was aware of this comment he may have been dissuaded rather than encouraged by Hume's analogy.

Hume goes on, in his more informal letter, to tell Smith that if he were to live a few more years he would publish the *Dialogues* himself, but at all events he wanted to ensure that the work would be preserved for posterity. Thus he requests that "if, upon my Death, you determine never to publish these papers, you shoud leave them, seal'd up with my Brother and Family, with some Inscription, that you reserve to Yourself the Power of reclaiming them, whenever you think proper." Hume's concluding remark, however, hints that he knew what a potential burden he was seeking to place on Smith's shoulders: "I consider an Observation of Rochefoucault, that a Wind, though it extinguishes a Candle, blows up a fire."[18] Precisely what kind of a fire, and how big, Smith surely wanted to know, would he be facing if he carried out Hume's request? Smith's response—which may or may not have ever reached Hume—thanks Hume for "the unlimited confidence which you repose in me" and assures him that "if I should have the misfortune to survive you, you may depend on my taking every possible measure which may prevent anything from being lost which you wish to be preserved."[19] Smith pointedly does not, however, show any sign of changing his mind on the question of publication.

---

[17] James Boswell, *The Life of Samuel Johnson*, ed. David Womersley (New York: Penguin, [1791] 2008) 145.

[18] David Hume to Adam Smith, 3 May 1776, in HL II, 316, and CAS, 195.

[19] Adam Smith to David Hume, 16 June 1776, in CAS, 201-2. On whether this letter reached Hume, see Adam Smith to William Strahan, 6 July 1776, in CAS, 202.

Apparently this arrangement did not sit well with Hume, as a month later he wrote to William Strahan, who was the principal publisher for both Hume and Smith, to tell him about the *Dialogues* and to ask him to take on the responsibility of seeing it through the press. Hume instructs him that "it is not necessary you shoud prefix your Name to the Title Page," but he insists that since Strahan had publicly acknowledged publishing the *First Enquiry* "I know no Reason why you shoud have the least Scruple with regard to these Dialogues. They will be much less obnoxious to the Law, and not more exposed to popular Clamour."[20] Strahan agreed, so Hume changed his will to leave the property of the *Dialogues* to him rather than Smith. He further stipulated that if, for whatever reason, Strahan did not publish the work within two and a half years of Hume's death then "the Property shall return to my Nephew, David, whose Duty, in publishing them as the last Request of his Uncle, must be approved of by all the World."[21] In a note thanking Strahan for taking on this charge, Hume remarks that "it is an idle thing in us to be concerned about any thing that shall happen after our Death; yet this is natural to all Men, and I often regretted that a Piece, for which I had a particular Partiality, should run any hazard of being suppressed after my Decease."[22]

Even after amending his will Hume remained anxious about the fate of the *Dialogues*, so in mid-August he wrote to Smith to ask if he would accept a copy for safe keeping. "It will bind you to nothing, but will serve as a Security," Hume assures him. Yet he could not resist intimating once again that Smith's reservations were overblown: "On revising them (which I have not done these 15 Years) I find that nothing can be more cautiously and more artfully written. You had certainly forgotten them." Then, almost immediately after assuring Smith that he was not seeking to bind him to anything, he backtracks and suggests yet another change to his will: "Will you permit me to

---

[20] See David Hume to William Strahan, 8 June 1776, in HL II, 323-4.

[21] See HL II, 453.

[22] David Hume to William Strahan, 12 June 1776, in HL II, 325-6.

leave you the Property of the Copy, in case they shoud not be published in five Years after my Decease?"[23] Smith responded with his assurances that he would be "very happy" to receive a copy of the *Dialogues* and that "if I should happen to die before they are published, I shall take care that my copy shall be as carefully preserved as if I was to live a hundred years." He also tells Hume that "you may do as you think proper" with regard to leaving him the property of the work after five years, though he does not promise to see the work through the press himself. In addition, he warns Hume not to "menace Strahan with the loss of anything in case he does not publish your work within a certain time. There is no probability of his delaying it, and if anything could make him delay it, it would be a clause of this kind, which would give him an honourable pretence for doing so."[24] Hume's final response to Smith on the matter, in the last letter he ever wrote, expresses his confidence in Strahan and informs Smith that he had decided to leave the current version of his will intact.[25] Their dispute, such as it was, was finally at an end, and Smith was excluded altogether from the publishing arrangements, suitable to his desires. Yet the matter had not been settled entirely.

A couple of weeks after Hume's death, Smith wrote to Strahan to confer about the *Dialogues*. The work, he says, "tho' finely written I could have wished had remained in Manuscript to be communicated only to a few people. When you read the work you will see my reasons without my giving you the trouble of reading them in a letter. But he [i.e. Hume] has ordered it otherwise." If it were entirely up to him, Smith continues, "the manuscript should have been most carefully preserved and upon my decease restored to [Hume's] family; but

[23] David Hume to Adam Smith, 15 August 1776, in HL II, 334, and CAS, 205.

[24] Adam Smith to David Hume, 22 August 1776, in CAS, 206.

[25] See David Hume to Adam Smith, 23 August 1776, in HL II, 335-6, and CAS, 208.

it should never have been published in my lifetime." Smith instructs Strahan that, whatever he may decide on the matter, under no circumstances should the *Dialogues* be published together with the account he planned to write of Hume's final illness—what became the *Letter from Adam Smith, LL.D. to William Strahan, Esq.*—"as I am resolved, for many reasons, to have no concern in the publication of those dialogues."[26] Though Smith does not spell out these "many reasons" here, in a pair of draft letters that he wrote a few weeks later (but never actually sent to Strahan) he remarks that he is "still uneasy about the clamour which I foresee [the *Dialogues*] will excite," a clamor that could be expected to affect both his own "quiet" and the sales of the new edition of Hume's collected writings.[27]

Strahan responded to promise that "I shall do nothing precipitately, and without the Advice of my Friends, to whose Opinion, and particularly to yours, I shall pay great Regard." He looks forward to giving the *Dialogues* "a very attentive Perusal" in order to form his own opinion, but he expresses surprise at the depth of Smith's reservations: "I own I did not expect to hear they were so very exceptionable, as in one of his [i.e. Hume's] late Letters to me he tells me *there is nothing in them worse than what I have already published*, or Words to that Effect." Especially given Hume's "extreme Solicitude" that the work be published, Strahan says, "if it is at all judged proper to let them see the Light, I should wish to execute his Intentions."[28] In the end, however, Strahan seems to have judged it improper to let the *Dialogues* see the light, at least under his auspices: after wavering for around six months he decided that the work "might be published with more propriety" by Hume's nephew "*in obedience to the last request of his Uncle*, as ... Hume himself expressed it."[29]

---

[26] Adam Smith to William Strahan, 5 September 1776, in CAS, 211.

[27] Adam Smith to William Strahan, October 1776, in CAS 216; and Adam Smith to William Strahan, October 1776, in CAS, 216-17.

[28] William Strahan to Adam Smith, 16 September 1776, in CAS, 212.

[29] William Strahan to John Home of Ninewells, 3 March 1777, in *Letters of David Hume to William Strahan*, ed. G. Birkbeck Hill (Oxford: Clarendon, 1888) 362.

Hume's nephew duly saw the *Dialogues* through the press in 1779, three years after Hume's death. Recent scholarship has been almost unanimous in maintaining that the work's publication brought none of the expected outcry,[30] but an inspection of the periodicals of the time suggests otherwise. In the first major review of the work, in September 1779, the *Critical Review* commented that if Hume's "pernicious" principles were allowed to prevail they "would throw a gloom over the whole creation, and really terminate in the blind amazement, the diffidence and melancholy of mankind."[31] That same month the *London Magazine* declared baldly that Hume's outlook "terminates in Atheism" and lamented that "he left no sincere friend behind him, who had so much regard for his character as to bury [the *Dialogues*] with him." The anonymous reviewer went on to advise those readers "who do not wish to disturb their reason and endanger their peace of mind" to forego reading the work.[32] The *Monthly Review*, for its part, insisted that Hume had done little more than "throw the most exceptionable parts of his philosophical works into a new form." According to this reviewer, Hume sought to establish principles whereby "the wicked are set free from every restraint but that of the laws; the virtuous are robbed of their most substantial comforts; every generous ardor of the human mind is damped; the world we live in is a fatherless world; we are chained down to a life full of wretchedness and misery; and we have no hope beyond the grave." The work must "shock the sense and virtue" of all good citi-

[30] See, for example, Ross, *The Life of Adam Smith*, 423; Phillipson, *Adam Smith: An Enlightened Life*, 246; and James A. Harris, *Hume: An Intellectual Biography* (Cambridge: Cambridge University Press, 2015) 445. These scholars appear to base this claim almost entirely on a single letter from Hugh Blair, written just months after the book's release, in which he expresses surprise that the *Dialogues* had "made so little noise." See Hugh Blair to William Strahan, 3 August 1779, in HL II, 454.

[31] *Critical Review*, vol. 48 (September 1779), in James Fieser, ed., *Early Responses to Hume*, second edition, vol. 6 (Bristol, UK: Thoemmes Continuum, 2005) (hereafter Fieser VI) 204.

[32] *London Magazine*, vol. 48 (September 1779), in Fieser VI, 206.

zens.[33] The *London Review*, the sole periodical to issue a reasonably favorable review, came under attack from its readers for doing so.[34] As far afield as Germany, the *Göttingischen gelehrten Anzeigen* regretted that Hume had "flung such stains on the otherwise so beautiful canvas of his character" and warned "young men not yet practiced in thinking against a precipitate reading of this book."[35] Ultimately, then, it seems that James Boswell's reaction to the *Dialogues* was more the rule than the exception: while he liked Hume's nephew personally, he said, he was "offended by his publishing his uncles posthumous poison."[36]

What are we to make of this episode? To begin with, there is little evidence to support the common claim that the disagreement between Hume and Smith over the *Dialogues* was particularly acrimonious. Hume was clearly partial to the work and anxious to see it published, but the idea that Smith's refusal to take on this responsibility caused Hume great pain and significantly tarnished their friendship seems decidedly exaggerated. Indeed, Hume's feelings of affection toward Smith do not seem to have diminished in the slightest. The first letter that we have from Hume on the subject—the one in which he tells Smith that his scruples are "groundless"—concludes with a characteristic plea for Smith to write more often, along with an equally characteristic expression of regret at not being together in person: "If you write to me, hem! hem! I say, if you write to me, send your Letters under Cover to Mr Strahan, who will have my Direction. I regret much, in leaving Edinburgh, that I shall lose much of your

[33] *Monthly Review*, vol. 61 (November 1779), in Fieser VI, 209, 221.

[34] See Fieser VI, 230.

[35] *Zugabe zu den Göttingischen gelehrten Anzeigen*, vol. 48 (27 November 1779), in Fieser VI, 229.

[36] James Boswell, *Boswell: Laird of Auchinleck, 1778-1782*, ed. Joseph W. Reed and Frederick A. Pottle (New York: McGraw Hill, 1977) 173.

Company, which I shoud have enjoy'd this Summer."[37] Soon afterward Hume invited Smith to stay at his house for over a month, from the time of his return to Edinburgh on July 3 through mid-August, just a couple of weeks before his death.[38] When Smith requested permission to add an account of Hume's final illness to his recently completed autobiography, *My Own Life*—again, what became the *Letter to Strahan*—Hume readily gave him complete discretion on this score: "You are too good in thinking any trifles that concern me are so much worth your attention, but I give you entire liberty to make what Additions you please to the account of my Life."[39] While Hume's tone here is cheerfully complaisant, this was no small proposition that he was accepting. *My Own Life* was, after all, Hume's final message to his readers, the one that would serve as the preface to future editions of his collected works. His immediate willingness to grant Smith "entire liberty" regarding such a central ingredient of his posthumous legacy reveals an extraordinarily high degree of trust and confidence. His last letter to Smith both opens and closes by calling him "My Dearest Friend."[40] None of this suggests a serious falling out or deep-seated feelings of resentment.

The main question confounding most scholars, though, is *why* Smith was so adamant in his refusal to publish the *Dialogues*. The difficulty of comprehending Smith's behavior has been heightened by two factors. First, Smith himself emphasizes the sanctity of deathbed wishes in his jurisprudence lectures, remarking that "we naturally find a pleasure in remembering the last words of a friend and in executing his last injunctions," in part because we realize "how much we would

---

[37] David Hume to Adam Smith, 3 May 1776, in HL II, 317, and CAS, 195.

[38] See David Hume to John Home of Ninewells, 25 July 1776, in Sadao Ikeda, *David Hume and the Eighteenth Century British Thought: An Annotated Catalogue* (Tokyo: Chuo University Library, 1986) 219.

[39] David Hume to Adam Smith, 23 August 1776, in HL II, 336, and CAS, 208. For Smith's request to add to *My Own Life*, see Adam Smith to David Hume, 22 August 1776, in CAS, 206.

[40] David Hume to Adam Smith, 23 August 1776, in HL II, 335-6, and CAS, 208.

be distressed to see our last injunctions not performed."[41] Why, then, many have wondered, would Smith refuse a request that his best friend made, if not on his deathbed then at least in his will, during his final illness? Adding to the mystery is the extremely high esteem in which Hume's *Dialogues* is now held. Leading scholars have called it "one of the glories of the Scottish, and indeed the European, Enlightenment"; "beyond any question the greatest work on philosophy of religion in the English language"; "perhaps the most remarkable treatise upon this subject ever composed"; Hume's "philosophical testament"; and "the epitome of his life's work."[42] How could Smith have refused to publish a work of such obvious greatness?

One surprisingly common answer to these questions has been that Smith objected to the contents of the *Dialogues*—that he was disturbed or even scandalized by the work, or saw it as deeply incompatible with his own philosophy, or was personally unable to come to grips with Hume's barrage of skepticism.[43] This answer raises an ex-

[41] Adam Smith, *Lectures on Jurisprudence*, ed. R. L. Meek, D. D. Raphael, and P. G. Stein (Indianapolis: Liberty Fund, [1762-4] 1982) 466-7; see also 63-4.

[42] Alexander Broadie, *The Scottish Enlightenment: The Historical Age of the Historical Nation* (Edinburgh: Birlinn, 2001) 128; Terence Penelhum, *Hume* (London: Macmillan, 1975) 171; Isaiah Berlin, *The Age of Enlightenment: The 18th Century Philosophers* (New York: George Braziller, 1956) 163; Ernest C. Mossner, "Hume and the Legacy of the *Dialogues*," in *David Hume: Bicentenary Papers*, ed. G. P. Morice (Austin: University of Texas Press, 1977) 3; and Peter Gay, *The Enlightenment: An Interpretation*, vol. 1: *The Rise of Modern Paganism* (New York: W. W. Norton, 1966) 414.

[43] See, for instance, T. D. Campbell and Ian Ross, "The Theory and Practice of the Wise and Virtuous Man: Reflections on Adam Smith's Response to Hume's Deathbed Wish" *Studies in Eighteenth-Century Culture,* 11 (1982) 70-2; Karl Graf Ballestrem, "David Hume und Adam Smith: Zur philosophischen Dimension einer Freundschaft," in *Adam Smith als Moralphilosoph*, ed. Christel Fricke and Hans-Peter Schütt (Berlin: Walter de Gruyter, 2005) 344-5; Brendan Long, "Adam Smith's Theism," in *The Elgar Companion to Adam Smith*, ed. Jeffrey T. Young (Cheltenham, UK: Edward Elgar, 2009) 81-2; Annette C. Baier, *The Pursuits of Philosophy: An Introduction to the Life and Thought of David Hume* (Cambridge, MA: Harvard University Press, 2011) 121; and Hanley, "Skepticism and Imagination."

tremely thorny question of its own, one that I cannot do full justice to here, namely that of Smith's religious views. Smith generally went to great lengths, in both his writings and his personal life, to avoid revealing his religious beliefs (or perhaps lack thereof), and as a result there is little consensus as to his views on this score. The conjectures range from sincere Christian belief to closet atheism, though the majority of scholars come down somewhere in the middle, reading Smith as a deist of some kind.[44] My own view is that Smith was in fact fairly skeptical of most forms of religious belief and devotion; if forced to apply a label to his views, I would describe him as a skeptical deist (as opposed to an outright skeptic like Hume).[45] Though substantiating this view fully would lead the present essay too far astray, one key piece of evidence cannot be ignored: the *Letter to Strahan*. Only a few months after his exchange with Hume over the *Dialogues*, Smith went on to publicly describe his unbelieving friend as a paragon of wisdom and virtue, writing that Hume approached "as nearly to the idea of a perfectly wise and virtuous man, as perhaps the nature of human frailty will permit."[46] In a private letter written during Hume's

[44] Among the works that go furthest in reading Smith as a *Christian* believer (as opposed to a deist) are Long, "Adam Smith's Theism," and several of the essays collected in Paul Oslington, ed., *Adam Smith as Theologian* (New York: Routledge, 2011). The most detailed reading of Smith as a closet atheist, at least later in his life, can be found in Peter Minowitz, *Profits, Priests, and Princes: Adam Smith's Emancipation of Economics from Politics and Religion* (Stanford: Stanford University Press, 1993) especially chapters 6-10.

[45] I have tried to substantiate this reading throughout Dennis C. Rasmussen, *The Infidel and the Professor: David Hume, Adam Smith, and the Friendship That Shaped Modern Thought* (Princeton: Princeton University Press, 2017). For similarly skeptical readings, see Emma Rothschild, *Economic Sentiments: Adam Smith, Condorcet, and the Enlightenment* (Cambridge, MA: Harvard University Press, 2001) 129-34; Gavin Kennedy, "The Hidden Adam Smith in His Alleged Theology" *Journal of the History of Economic Thought* 33.3 (September 2011): 385-402; and Colin Heydt, "The Problem of Natural Religion in Smith's Moral Thought" *Journal of the History of Ideas*, 78.1 (January 2017): 73-94.

[46] Adam Smith, *Letter from Adam Smith, LL.D. to William Strahan, Esq.*, in David Hume, *Essays, Moral, Political, and Literary*, ed. Eugene F. Miller (Indianapolis: Liberty Fund, [1777] 1987) xlix.

final days he had put the point even more harshly, writing that "Poor David Hume is dying very fast, but with great chearfulness and good humour and with more real resignation to the necessary course of things, than any Whining Christian ever dyed with pretended resignation to the will of God."[47] Such statements seem difficult to square with the idea that Smith was overly troubled by Hume's skepticism.

This general reading of Smith's stance toward religion, and toward Hume's skepticism, is corroborated by some of his statements and actions related to the *Dialogues* itself. Recall that Smith promised time and again that he would be "very happy" to take "every possible measure" to ensure that the work would be "most carefully preserved," and he also deemed it "finely written"—he just wished that it "had remained in Manuscript to be communicated only to a few people."[48] In other words, while Smith seems to have thought that such bold criticisms of religion are best kept away from the public eye, he had no problem with the idea of circulating the work among friends. In fact, Smith appears to have actively disseminated the work himself—how widely we do not know—as we have a letter from the duc de La Rochefoucauld (the moralist's great-grandson) thanking Smith for sending a copy of the *Dialogues* to him in France almost immediately after it was released.[49]

The likeliest explanation for Smith's refusal to publish the *Dialogues* is also the simplest: as he himself indicated in his draft letters to Strahan, he was wary of the public "clamor" that the book would provoke and the effects that this clamor would have on his own "quiet" and Hume's posthumous reputation. Smith may have also had the interests of the public in mind. In *The Theory of Moral Sentiments* he had suggested that religion often helps to buttress morality by rein-

---

[47] Adam Smith to Alexander Wedderburn, 14 August 1776, in CAS, 203.

[48] Adam Smith to David Hume, 16 June 1776, in CAS, 201-2; Adam Smith to David Hume, 22 August 1776, in CAS, 206; Adam Smith to William Strahan, 5 September 1776, in CAS, 211.

[49] See the duc de La Rochefoucauld to Adam Smith, 6 August 1779, in CAS, 238.

forcing people's adherence to moral norms[50]; perhaps he worried that a work like the *Dialogues* might weaken this buttress. We have a letter from Anne Keith, whose family was close to Hume, reporting that Smith "remonstrated against publishing" the *Dialogues* on the grounds that the work was "of a nature prejudicial to Society."[51] (She also notes that Hume "is in general condemned for rejecting Mr Smith's advice.") Indeed, Smith's refusal to publish the *Dialogues* may have been, at least in part, a matter of simple politeness: his mother, the majority of his friends, and indeed almost everyone he knew would have been offended by the work, and by his involvement with it. At any rate, the bottom line is that Smith was always far more wary of public controversy than Hume was, and it is thoroughly unsurprising that he would exercise greater caution with respect to a work like the *Dialogues*.

Was this, then, an instance of excessive caution, or even cowardice, as is often suggested? If it was, then it was a failing that was not unique to Smith: every one of Hume's friends who knew about the *Dialogues* urged him not to publish it, at least if the surviving record is anything to go by. We know that Gilbert Elliot opposed publication, as we have a letter from Hume to Elliot in which he complains: "Is it not hard & tyrannical in you, more tyrannical than any Act of the Stuarts, not to allow me to publish my Dialogues? Pray, do you not think that a proper Dedication may atone for what is exceptional in them?"[52] Hugh Blair likewise admonished Hume, "for Gods sake let that be a posthumous work, if ever it shall see the light: Tho' I really think it had better not."[53] (In reply Hume told Blair that "I have no present thoughts of publishing the work you mention," but then teasingly added: "when I do, I hope you have no objection of my dedicat-

[50] See, for instance, Adam Smith, *The Theory of Moral Sentiments*, ed. D. D. Raphael and A. L. Macfie (Indianapolis: Liberty Fund, [1759-90] 1982) III.5.3, 163.

[51] Anne Keith to Sir Robert Murray Keith, 6 November 1776, Public Record Office of Northern Ireland, Belfast, D2433/D/1/25.

[52] David Hume to Gilbert Elliot of Minto, 12 March 1763, in NHL, 71.

[53] Hugh Blair to David Hume, 29 September 1763, in NHL, 73 n. 4.

ing it to you.")[54] We have a report that Adam Ferguson too "remonstrated" against publishing the work.[55] And of course Strahan, who was close to Hume personally as well as professionally, ultimately declined to publish the *Dialogues*—and this after he had, unlike Smith, promised Hume that he would do so.

If the unanimous counsel of some of Hume's closest friends is not enough to exonerate Smith from charges of cowardice, then Hume's own words and actions should be. Despite Hume's greater willingness to court controversy and despite his obvious fondness for the *Dialogues*, he himself had refrained from publishing the work for *two and a half decades*. Indeed, he did not even mention the manuscript's existence to his publisher until just a couple of months before his death. He did ponder the possibility of publication from time to time, as the letter to Elliot quoted above suggests, but he realized that it would be an audacious move, even for him—hence his acknowledgment, in that letter, that there is something "exceptionable" about the work that would require a proper dedication to "atone for." Even more striking is Hume's explanation, in his letter to Strahan of June 1776 asking him to take on responsibility for the *Dialogues*, of why he had not published long ago: "I have hitherto forborne to publish it, because I was of late desirous to live quietly, and keep remote from all Clamour: For though it be not more exceptionable than some things I had formerly published; yet you know some of these were thought very exceptionable; and in prudence, perhaps, I ought to have suppressed them. I there introduce a Sceptic [i.e. the character Philo], who is indeed refuted, and at last gives up the Argument ... yet before he is silenced, he advances several Topics, which will give Umbrage, and will be deemed very bold and free."[56] In other words, up until his final illness Hume had refrained from publishing the *Dialogues* for the exact same reason that Smith refused to do so: because

[54] David Hume to Hugh Blair, 6 October 1763, in NHL, 72.

[55] See Anne Keith to Sir Robert Murray Keith, 6 November 1776, Public Record Office of Northern Ireland, Belfast, D2433/D/1/25.

[56] David Hume to William Strahan, 8 June 1776, in HL II, 323.

it would create a "clamor" that would prevent him from living "quietly." Even the wording of their explanations is nearly identical.

The more perplexing question, in a way, is not why Smith refused to publish the *Dialogues* but rather why Hume was suddenly so adamant about publication after holding the work back for twenty-five years, and even more why he sought to foist this obligation on Smith. Hume may have reckoned that he had little left to lose at that point, with one foot almost in the grave, but obviously Smith was not in the same position. Moreover, Hume knew full well that Smith was always anxious to preserve his privacy and tranquility—his "quiet." It would not have taken a great feat of sympathy to realize that Smith would be averse to the public "clamor" that Hume himself foresaw would be provoked by the *Dialogues*. Nor should it be forgotten that Hume asked Smith to bear this burden only a month and a half after *The Wealth of Nations* was published. Given the many years of painstaking effort that Smith had poured into the book, the great anticipation that surrounded its release, and Smith's high hopes that its arguments would prove influential in both thought and practice, this was among the worst possible times for him to become mired in public controversy. All things considered, then, Hume's part in this exchange is more difficult to account for than Smith's.

4

HUME'S "OF SUICIDE" AND ITS FRENCH RECEPTION: NECESSITY AND NATIVE LIBERTY

Adam Potkay

David Hume, who died on August 25, 1776, was a pragmatic defender of American secession, a friend of Benjamin Franklin, and a lifelong friend of liberty, which he set just below authority in importance to the state. This essay concerns Hume's effort to extend the sphere of liberty to include, under certain circumstances, the freedom to end one's own life. Hume's essay "Of Suicide"—written circa 1755 and posthumously published in 1777—is among the most important defenses of suicide from any period.[1] I will first provide a brief overview of what Hume explicitly sets out to do in his essay: namely, to show that, contrary to the beliefs of his day, suicide is not an immoral act. Second, I argue that Hume's implicit aim is to challenge the very notion of suicide as a "free" act in one sense of that term, that is, free from determining causes. "Of Suicide" premises, as several recent commentators have noted, a deterministic view of the universe, whereby chains of causes and effects set in motion by God (or nature) undercut any notion of duty to God, since whatever happens does so by his mediated design.[2] I follow Hume's determinism to its logical

---

[1] "Of Suicide" appears in Hume, *Essays: Moral, Political and Literary*, ed. Eugene F. Miller (Indianapolis: Liberty Fund, 1985) 577-89. Further citations appear in parentheses in the body of my essay. Michael MacDonald and Terence R. Murphy call Hume's essay "the most influential argument for the legitimacy of suicide, and indeed it is the only contribution to the [eighteenth-century] debate that philosophers still read" (*Sleepless Souls: Suicide in Early Modern England* [Oxford: Clarendon Press, 1990] 161).

[2] Thomas Holden, "Religion and Moral Prohibition in Hume's 'Of Suicide,'" *Hume Studies* 31:2 (2005): 189-210; Max Grober, "Concepts of God in

conclusion, arguing that for Hume suicide is not and cannot be entirely elective, that is, a choice made independently of antecedent conditions. Suicide appears, rather, as the necessary outcome of causes that are variously physical and moral. In the absence of constraint, the act of suicide may be called a free one, but it is not free from the causes that necessarily lead to it; for Hume, as we shall see, the primary cause of suicide is pain or, more capaciously, "misery."

Suicide is the blameless remedy to an insufferable existence, a remedy for which Hume seeks social tolerance. Hume argues that suicide is not a criminal act, in a United Kingdom that would prove very slow to heed his words: religious penalties for suicide persisted until 1823, civil penalties until 1870, and decriminalization was not enacted until 1961.[3] But while Hume considers suicide as blameless, and concedes that in certain situations it may be courageous, he does not, on balance, depict it as praiseworthy, or still less as heroic. For Hume, suicide is an event far removed from its depiction, in classical and German idealist philosophy, as the assertion of rational autonomy over external causes and the vagaries of *fortuna*. In Hume's account, as in later accounts, discussed below, by the French materialists indebted to him, suicide is not a violation of one's duty to God, community, or self, but neither is it a transcendence of circumstances. Suicide is a natural result of the antecedent events and circumstances that would lead to it more readily, with less inner conflict, in the absence of false religious and ethical beliefs.

The implicit determinism of "Of Suicide" is rendered explicit in the writings on suicide by Hume's French acquaintances, Baron d'Holbach and Denis Diderot. Yet a moral weakness of Hume's defense of suicide—its blindness to the bad reasons that might tempt

---

Hume's Essay 'Of Suicide,'" delivered at the International Hume Society Conference, Antwerp, July 2010 (unpublished); Jonathan Kramnick, *Actions and Objects from Hobbes to Richardson* (Stanford: Stanford University Press, 2010) 219-30.

[3] Georges Minois, *History of Suicide: Voluntary Death in Western Culture*, trans. Lydia G. Cochrane (Baltimore: Johns Hopkins University Press, 1999) 297. Minois notes that of Western European and North American states, England was "the last to decriminalize suicide" (294).

young people to it, especially disappointment in love—is revealed in the writings of another of Hume's one-time French friends, Jean-Jacques Rousseau.

Before teasing out the implications of Hume's "Of Suicide," let me summarize its explicit argument. Developing the defense of suicide sketched in Montesquieu's *Persian Letters* (no. 76, 1721),[4] Hume marshals a moral and theological defense of suicide that responds point by point to Thomas Aquinas's three-pronged argument why it is unlawful to kill oneself. Suicide, Aquinas argued, is contrary to the natural law and to charity; it injures the community; and it is a sin against God (*Summa Theologica* Part 2, Question 24, A5).[5] To elaborate on these one by one: Aquinas writes, first, "suicide is contrary to the inclination of nature, and to charity whereby every man should love himself." Second, "every man is part of the community, and so, as such, belongs to the community. Hence by killing himself he injures the community." Third, "because life is God's gift to man, and is subject to His power...whoever takes his own life, sins against God... For it belongs to God alone to pronounce sentence on life and death."

Hume, in inverse order, argues that suicide is "a transgression of our duty" neither "to God, our neighbor, or ourselves" (580). Hume's central concern is to refute theological arguments against suicide: three quarters of his essay is occupied by his counter-arguments that suicide cannot be a violation of our duty to God. As Thomas Holden has argued, Hume implies that no human action can ever violate a

---

[4] Hume's point-by-point debt to Montesquieu's argument, as well as his verbal echoes of Montesquieu's prose, are traced in Grober, "Concepts of God in Hume's Essay 'Of Suicide.'"

[5] On Hume's essay as a refutation of Aquinas, see T. L. Beauchamp, "An Analysis of Hume's 'Of Suicide'," *Review of Metaphysics,* 30 (1976-7): 92-5. Aquinas's arguments against suicide as a violation of our duties to self, neighbor and God persist in the "practical ethics" tradition Colin Heydt traces in the writings of Hutcheson, Beattie, Reid, Stewart and Paley: see Heydt, "Practical Ethics," in James A. Harris, ed., *The Oxford Handbook of Eighteenth-Century British Philosophy* (Oxford: Oxford University Press, 2013) 369-89. My quotations from Aquinas are from the excerpt of *Summa Theologica* in John Donnelly, ed., *Suicide: Right or Wrong?* (Buffalo: Prometheus, 1990) 33-36.

duty towards God, or invade his prerogatives: "since our actions are fixed and predetermined by God [or the causes that he sets in motion], it makes no sense...to speak of those actions as moral offenses against him."[6] Hume assumes, against Christian doctrine, that there is no "particular providence,"[7] but rather that God operates through the inviolable laws of nature that He sets in motion, a tenet of ancient Stoicism and modern deism. "Shall we assert," Hume asks, "that the Almighty has reserved to himself, in any peculiar manner, the disposal of the lives of men, and has not submitted that event, in common with others, to the general laws, by which the universe is governed?" "This," he concludes, "is plainly false" (582): as indeed it is, as long as one discounts Christian theology.

In defending suicide against the charge of impiety, Hume's principal object is to allow misery, unimpeded by false constraints that only prolong it, to lead naturally to the "refuge" of suicide. Of the "superstitious man," Hume writes, "tho' death alone can put a full period to his misery, he dares not fly to this refuge, but still prolongs a miserable existence, from a vain fear, lest he offend his maker, by using the power, with which that beneficent being has endowed him" (579). After concluding his detailed rebuttal of theological sanctions against suicide, Hume shows in more summary fashion that it violates no duty towards community or oneself. With regard to community he sketches several arguments that appear implicitly liberal or contract-

---

[6] Holden, "Religion and Moral Prohibition in Hume's 'Of Suicide'," 195. Hume's essay blurs scientific and theological determinisms, presumably with the rhetorical purpose of not entirely precluding theism.

[7] "Particular providence" is a phrase Hume uses in the title of section 11 of *An Enquiry concerning Human Understanding* (*Enquiries concerning Human Understanding and concerning the Principles of Morals*, 3rd edition, ed. L. A. Selby-Bigge, rev. Peter H. Nidditch [Oxford: Clarendon Press, 1975] 95; further references to the *Enquiries* are to this edition.). "Particular providence" refers to God's oversight of particular individuals and His potential intervention in their lives (to illumine, reward, or punish); Hume disallows this type of providence (crucial to Christian belief and practice), admitting for argument's sake only "general providence," or the chain of causes and effects set in motion by the Deity and regulated by the inviolable laws of nature.

based: for example, "all our obligations to do good to society seem to imply something reciprocal...when I withdraw myself altogether from society, can I be bound any longer?" (586).[8] Hume refers briefly to the possible civic *virtue* of suicide, alluding to the Stoic and more generally ancient doctrine that taking one's life may in certain cases contribute to the good of the community and thus to one's own happiness or flourishing, understood objectively. Thus: "A man is engaged in a conspiracy for the public interest; is seized upon suspicion; is threatened with the rack; and knows, from his own weakness, that the secret will be extorted from him: Could such a one consult the public interest better than by putting a quick period to a miserable life?" (587). Yet even here Hume's emphasis is not on the patriotism, heroism, or happiness of a life offered up for the common good; it is, rather, on the desirability of quickly ending "a miserable life."

Misery is the key theme of Hume's paragraph on suicide in relation to the self, which begins: "That Suicide may often be consistent with interest and duty to *ourselves*, no one can question, who allows, that age, sickness, or misfortune may render life a burthen, and make it even worse than annihilation. I believe that no man ever threw away life, while it was worth keeping. For such is our natural horror of death, that small motives will never be able to reconcile us to it" (588). It takes a strong motive to gainsay "our natural horror of death," and the motive that Hume consistently supplies is aversion to a pain that is or appears intolerable and incapable of being assuaged: throughout the essay he speaks of "misery" and "miseries" (579, 586, 588), "a miserable existence" (579, 586), "a miserable life" (587), a "life...which, were it to continue, would render me miserable" (583), "pain and sorrow" (579, 585), "pain and sickness" (584), "the horror of pain" (584), and "incurable depravity or gloominess of temper" (588). The plangent last word of "Of Suicide" is "misery": the unen-

[8] Cf. Montesquieu, *Persian Letters*, no. 76: "Society is founded on mutual advantage; but when that society becomes onerous to me, who is to prevent my renouncing it?" (*The Persian Letters*, trans. George R. Healy [Indianapolis: Bobbs-Merrill,1964] 130).

cumbered availability of suicide "would effectively free" us "from all danger of misery" (588).

Aversion towards acute or chronic pain or misery serves, in Hume's system, as the trigger for suicide—or, at least, a trigger that *would* work automatically *were* humanity freed from "superstition and false religion" (577). Hume's essay would expand the conditions under which those who would benefit from suicide are undeterred from committing suicide by the artificial constraints of Christian theology. Hume seeks in his essay to "restore men to their native liberty" (580)—a liberty that derives, paradoxically, from our purely natural determination, in the absence of theological or counter-natural determination.[9] The Christian (and confessional state's) prohibition of suicide, an artificial constraint, serves as an external cause that can only aggravate the suffering of those whom, without it, "might their own quietus make."[10]

Without Christian and legal disincentives, our natural inclination to avoid severe and (at least seemingly) hopeless pain would be an all-but-sufficient motive to suicide, although Hume also thrice invokes in his essay the supplement of "human prudence" (twice on p.583), concluding "If it be no crime, both prudence and courage should engage us to rid ourselves at once of existence, when it becomes a burthen" (588). "Courage" appears as icing on the cake; what's really at stake is "prudence," a term which Hume seems to use in the sense of minimally-reflective self-interest. Prudence seems to

---

[9] Earlier, in the "Dialogue" that concludes *An Enquiry concerning the Principles of Morals*, Hume assailed the "*artificial* lives and manners" that, deriving from "extravagant philosophy" (such as Diogenes' Cynicism) and "modern religion" (i.e., Christianity), deviate from nature and "the universal standard of morals" (341-43). "When men depart from the maxims of common reason, and affect these *artificial lives*..., no one can answer for what will please or displease them" (343).

[10] I quote here from Hamlet's famous soliloquy, in which fear of an afterlife and divine punishment deter him from his suicidal intentions: without these, he asks, "who would bear the whips and scorns of time, / Th'oppressor's wrong, the proud man's contumely," "When he himself might his quietus make / With a bare bodkin?" (Shakespeare, *Hamlet*, 3.1.71-77).

work in "Of Suicide" in the same way that "the least reflection" works in Hume's analysis of justice in *A Treatise Human Nature* (3.2.2). In the *Treatise*, avidity (the desire for property) finds, by means of "the least reflection," success in its own restraint[11]; in "Of Suicide," aversion from pain achieves its aim, prudentially, in self-extinction.

Suicide ought to be available to as many who naturally seek it as a remedy from intense pain or misery—this remedy, for Hume, belongs to the native liberty of mankind. Suicide is not culpable: it breaches no moral duty, and no moral blame can justly accrue to it. On the contrary, Hume makes suicide seem at least quasi-virtuous: it can be an act of prudence and even courage. But how can these tentative virtues square with suicide as the instinctive evasion of misery? Some critics of determinism have alleged that no person can be held morally responsible for his or her actions if those actions do not proceed from liberty or free will.[12] But Hume, in his *Treatise of Human Nature* (2.3.1-2) and later in his essay "Of Liberty and Necessity," argued that determinism was not only compatible with a (weak) sense of liberty, but also requisite to a (robust) sense of moral responsibility. For Hume, determinism admits liberty, of a sort; following Hobbes, Hume simply defines the type of liberty that agents have as the absence of external constraint. "By liberty," writes Hume, "we can only mean *a power of acting or not acting, according to the determinations of the will*; that is, if we choose to remain at rest, we may; if we choose to move, we also may. Now this hypothetical liberty is universally allowed to belong to everyone who is not a prisoner and in chains" ("Of Liberty and Necessity," *Enquiry concerning Human Understanding*, 95).[13] Hume maintains, in other words, that we often do what we

[11] *A Treatise of Human Nature*, ed. David Fate Norton and Mary J. Norton, 2 vols. (Oxford: Clarendon Press, 2007) 1:316.

[12] See, for example, the arguments of the Anglican theologians John Bramhall and Samuel Clarke against Hobbes and Anthony Collins, summarized in Kramnick, 27-48.

[13] Historians of philosophy generally concur that Hume's argument in "Of Liberty and Necessity" recapitulates the essential points of Hobbes, *Of Libertie and Necessity* (1654); for a dissenting voice that emphasizes Hume's distinctive,

want to do (we have, in a technical sense, "liberty of spontaneity"), but this is not evidence that we could do otherwise than in fact we do (we don't have "liberty of indifference").[14] Hume then affirms that both necessity and liberty "are not only consistent with morality, but are absolutely essential to its support" (97). The doctrine of necessity links actions, as effects, with the causes of an individual's "internal character, passions, and affections" (99), and this link is the basis for all the praise and blame, reward and punishment, accruing to an individual. The liberty of spontaneity, conversely, allows for the voluntary nature of our actions—without which our actions could be neither meritorious nor blameworthy. Taking one's life, even if it is the natural response to sustained misery, may nevertheless display a meritorious prudence, in assessing one's overall self-interest, and courage, in overcoming one's equally natural fear of death.

However, in "Of Suicide" Hume primarily shows that suicide is not blameworthy. It might sometimes be meritorious, but for Hume it is at least, and more fundamentally, morally neutral, nature's escape route from a pain that seems unbearable. But—and here's the rub—perhaps the pain that a particular suicide would avert only *seems* unbearable. As Max Grober has argued, eighteenth-century critics of suicide worried that self-murder might be *untimely*: that is, that the pain it would avoid might after all subside; the threat it would deflect might come to nothing.[15] The hope it forecloses might have proved redemptive, despite the odds: it is for hastily abandoning such a hope that Addison, for example, implicitly criticizes Cato's suicide at the

---

non-metaphysical conception of necessity, see James A. Harris, *Of Liberty and Necessity: The Free-Will Debate in Eighteenth-Century British Philosophy* (Oxford: Clarendon Press, 2005) 4-12, 64-87.

[14] *A Treatise of Human Nature*, 262.

[15] Max Grober shows that "in many literary narratives of suicide in the eighteenth century…suicide is most likely the hasty choice of a mind clouded by passion, and…that it reflects premature despair of possible future good, either for the suicide or others." See "'A Steady Contempt of Life': Suicide Narratives in Hume and Others," *The Journal of Scottish Philosophy*, 10:1 [2012]: 51-68) quotation from p.56.

end of his much-admired drama, *Cato: A Tragedy* (1713).[16] Likewise, a 1756 essay in the periodical *The World* drolly recounts an anecdote of an unpleasant great lord, "turned of sixty-seven, and...devoured by the stone [kidney or bladder stones] and gout," who had determined to shoot himself; "However the fit abated, and the neighborhood is still waiting with great impatience to be *surprized* with an account of his lordship's having shot himself."[17] This story, or another like it, became mixed up in the mind of certain literati with Hume's "Of Suicide"; thus Sir John Hawkins reports of Samuel Johnson: "He would never hear Hume mentioned with any temper:--'A man,' said he, 'who endeavoured to persuade his friend who had the stone to shoot himself.'"[18] The uncertain persistence of pain may suggest the fallibility of any prudential calculation about suicide.

Another problem with suicide was identified by Hume's friend Adam Smith: for Europe's elites, suicide appears glamorous in the light of ancient Roman history, but that history is a false model for modern Europe. The Roman practice of suicide, Smith argued, went against nature—it was itself (as Hume criticized the Christian prohibition against suicide for being) an artificial "refinement of philosophy," as well as the product of specific historical conditions under the late Roman republic and early empire: specifically, civic discord and the loss of political liberty.[19]

---

[16] "There are numerous, broad hints in Addison's text," Grober writes ("A Steady Contempt of Life," 55-56), "that Cato's suicide is not, in fact, the consequence of due philosophical reflection... Addison drives the point home...by bringing news from Spain, just at the moment of Cato's final thrust, that Pompey's son 'rouses the whole nation up to arms. / Were Cato at their head, once more might Rome / Assert her rights, and claim her liberty' (*Cato* 5.4.57-9)."

[17] *The World*, number CXCV [195], Thursday, September 23, 1756, p. 1171. *The World* was published by Robert Dodsley, and included anonymous contributions by Horace Walpole and Lord Chesterfield.

[18] *Johnsonian Miscellanies*, ed. George Birkbeck Hill, 2 vols. (Oxford: Clarendon Press, 1897) 2:10.

[19] *The Theory of Moral Sentiments* (Part 7, Section 2, Chapter 1), ed. D. D. Raphael and A. L. Macfie (Oxford: Oxford University Press, 1979) 279-88.

In "Of Suicide" Hume has nothing to say about Roman decadence, but he does seem to share Smith's negative view of suicide as a philosophical "principle" in the ancient world.[20] The particular cast of Hume's determinism, according to which suicide is reduced to a more or less inevitable reflex to a certain degree of pain, puts him at odds with the heroic claims made on behalf of suicide by its apologists in antiquity. For the ancients, suicide could be the ultimate act of moral autonomy, an act by which the individual might always transcend determination by external circumstances. Hume flirts with this view in "Of Suicide," footnoting from Seneca's twelfth *Epistle*, on old age, a tag that reads, in English, "And let us thank God that no man can be kept in life" (583). (D'Holbach, following Hume, quotes at somewhat greater length from this same Senecan epistle in his own defense of suicide.[21]) But if Hume (or d'Holbach) fully endorsed the ancient Stoic and Epicurean view of suicide, he might have quoted or adapted Seneca's exhortation, in another epistle, to "praise and imitate the man whom it does not irk to die, though he takes pleasure in living." Such a man cannot be "thrust out" from life, because when the proper time to die comes, he goes away willingly: "He escapes necessity, because he wills to do what necessity is about to force upon him."[22] Or again: "the wise man will live as long as he ought, not as long as he can… As soon as there are many events in his life that give him trouble and disturb his peace of mind, he sets himself free. And this privilege is his, not only when the crisis is upon him, but as soon as Fortune seems to be playing him false…. [D]ying well means escape from the danger of living ill."[23] Seneca's praise of suicide is fully moral

[20] Smith writes: "The principle of suicide, the principle which would teach us, upon some occasions, to consider that violent action as an object of applause and approbation, seems to be altogether a refinement of philosophy" (287).

[21] Paul Henri Thiry, Baron d'Holbach, *Systême de la Nature, ou des Loix du Monde Physique et du Monde Morale* (London [i.e., Amsterdam]: 1777) Chapter 14, 227-43; Seneca is quoted, in a Latin footnote, on 239.

[22] Epistle 54, in *The Epistles of Seneca*, 3 vols., trans. Richard M. Gummere (Cambridge Harvard University Press/Loeb Classical Library, 1917) 1:365.

[23] Epistle 70, 2:59.

in a way that Hume's is not: for Seneca, suicide is important only insofar as it helps the wise man to fashion a happy or flourishing life. This moral strain is still clearer in Cicero's *De Finibus*, Book 3:

> [I]t is on occasion appropriate [*officium*] for the Wise Man [*sapiens*] to quit life although he is happy, and also of the foolish man [*stultus*] to remain in life although he is miserable.... For the virtuous man is not necessarily retained in life by virtue, and also those who are devoid of virtue need not necessarily seek death. And very often it is appropriate for the wise man to abandon life at a moment when he is enjoying supreme happiness, if an opportunity offers for making a timely exit. For the Stoic view is that happiness...is a matter of seizing the right moment.[24]

Eighteen centuries later, echoing these Stoic sentiments on the far side of the Kantian revolution, Friedrich Schiller writes:

> Cases can occur in which fate surmounts all the ramparts upon which man founds his security and nothing else remains but for him to flee into the sacred freedom of the spirit—cases in which there is no other recourse in order to placate the lust for life than to will that fate—and no other means of withstanding the power of nature than to anticipate her, and by a free renunciation of all sensuous interest to kill himself morally before some physical force does it.[25]

Hume offers no such hope of moral freedom in "Of Suicide." Despite his nod, in a concluding footnote, to the "heroic" suicides of Cato and Brutus, Arria and Portia (589), in the body of his essay

---

[24] Cicero, *De Finibus Bonorum et Malorum*, with a translation by H. Rackham, Loeb Classical Library (Cambridge, MA: Harvard University Press, 2nd ed., 1931) 279-81; from the character Cato's exposition of Stoic ethics, Book III, sections 60-61.

[25] Schiller, "On the Sublime," in *Naïve and Sentimental Poetry and On the Sublime*, trans. Julius A. Elias (New York: Frederick Ungar, 1966) 208. Similarly, for Friedrich Schelling, the sublime of the tragic hero is suicidal: by voluntarily atoning for what is thrust upon him, his "freedom transfigure[s] itself into the highest identity with necessity" (quoted, with explicative commentary, by Julian Young, *The Philosophy of Tragedy: From Plato to Žižek* [Cambridge: Cambridge University Press, 2013] 90-92).

Hume reflects upon the seemingly heroic suicide only once, and that fleetingly, in his example of the person who kills himself rather than betray his patriotic conspiracy—and even here his emphasis is not on the conspirator's evasion of fortune, but rather on his natural reaction to "a miserable life." No one escapes necessity in Hume's essay, or in his broader philosophy. Thus while Hume allows the Roman defense of suicide to embroider the edges of his essay (Seneca, Cicero, and Pliny are all noted), the heart of his argument for why suicide is natural and blameless is, in its rejection of the undetermined will, opposed to the aspirations of classical (as later, of Kantian and post-Kantian) philosophy. "The essay 'Of Suicide' begins and ends with courage and freedom," writes one Hume scholar; "In advocating suicide," it "evokes the examples of Cato, Brutus, and other heroes of ancient Rome."[26] I would counter that "Of Suicide" begins with a salvo against the "superstition" that "prolongs a miserable existence" (579), and ends with the evasion of that misery. The liberty Hume endorses in his essay is, in Isaiah Berlin's well-known terms, a negative, not a positive one.

In his understanding of suicide, Hume is close in spirit to his Parisian acquaintances, Baron d'Holbach and Diderot. These writers, in my estimation, make explicit the implicit materialism and determinism of Hume's "Of Suicide"—an essay that d'Holbach, for one, knew well. Along with Hume's sometime friend Rousseau, d'Holbach and Diderot address suicide in writings to which I turn in the order of their publication: Rousseau's *Julie, ou La Nouvelle Héloïse* (1761), d'Holbach's *Systême de la Nature* (1770), and Diderot's *Jacques le Fataliste* (composed by 1778; serially and partially published, 1778-80; published in complete form, 1796).

Rousseau includes what amounts to a Ciceronian dialogue on suicide in two letters of his epistolary novel *Julie* (Part 3, letters 21 and 22). Julie's former tutor and disappointed lover, St. Preux, pens a broad defense of suicide, in which moral well-being (*bien-être*) counts for more than life; he receives a spirited rejoinder from his philosoph-

[26] Max Grober, "'A Steady Contempt of Life,'" 54.

ical English friend, Milord Edouard Bomston, who disapproves of suicide except in the case of age and incurable physical illness—that is, those cases that Hume, for his part, seems to have chiefly in mind in his own defense of suicide. A point on which St. Preux agrees with Hume is that, as Hume puts it, "age, sickness, or misfortune may render life a burthen, and make it even worse than annihilation. I believe that no man ever threw away life, while it was worth keeping. For such is our natural horror of death, that small motives will never be able to reconcile us to it" (588). St. Preux, in his letter, makes a similar point in roughly the same terms: "we have received from nature a very great horror at death....but when once the vexation of living (*l'ennui de vivre*) takes away the horror of dying, then life is evidently a great evil (*un grand mal*), and one cannot deliver oneself from it too soon."[27] In reply to St. Preux, Bomston wisely distinguishes, as Hume does not, valid and invalid reasons for suicide: old age and the loss of one's mental faculties may in certain cases be valid reasons, he concedes, but an invalid reason, he counsels his young friend, is erotic disappointment in one's youth (a motive for suicide which the temperate Hume seems not to have considered).

Hume's point about our natural horror of death being overcome by no trivial motive is reprised by the Baron d'Holbach in his *Systême de la Nature*. D'Holbach, closely associated with Hume during the latter's Paris years (1763-66), came into possession of Hume's essay "Of Suicide" at some point in the 1760s, and is generally thought to be the person who translated it, along with "Of the Immortality of the Soul," for their unauthorized 1770 publication in French.[28] Chapter 14 of *Systême de la Nature*, also published in 1770, concludes with a section "Of Suicide," in which d'Holbach maintains: "Life being for man commonly the greatest of all goods, it is to be supposed that the one who gets rid of himself is swept away (*entraîné*) by an invincible

[27] *Julie, ou la Nouvelle Héloïse*, ed. Michel Launay (Paris: Garnier-Flammarion, 1967) 281, my translation.

[28] E. C. Mossner, *The Life of David Hume*, 2nd ed. (Oxford: Clarendon, 1980) 330 (d'Holbach's role in the French publication of Hume's essays); 475-6 (Hume's association with d'Holbach in Paris).

force. It is excess of misfortune [*malheur*], despair, the derangement of the machine caused by melancholy that lead a man to kill himself... if man is not free in any instant of his life, he is still less free in the act that terminates it."[29]

What Hume implies in "Of Suicide" through his rhetorical emphasis on the misery that, as it were, pulls the trigger, d'Holbach here states plainly: suicide has circumstantial and material causes that function as "an invincible force"; it results from the disordering of the human "machine." To some extent d'Holbach borrows his man-machine metaphor from Montesquieu's *The Spirit of the Laws* (1748), which assigns English (as distinct from ancient Roman) suicide to physical, and more narrowly climatological, causes: "among the English, it [suicide] is the effect of an illness [explained as 'an illness of climate']; it comes from the physical state of the machine."[30] In a footnote to his passage, d'Holbach nods to Montesquieu's climatological theory, and to the more general French assumption that suicide is the characteristically English disease.[31] However, for d'Holbach, as for Hume, the necessity that accounts for suicide admits moral as well as physical causes, "misfortune" as well as malfunction, and these causes are not restricted to English soil. With Hume, d'Holbach acknowledges that injustice, indigence and shame extricate the unfortunate individual from any social obligation or bond: "he is restored to liberty" (*il est remise en liberté*),[32] which Hume calls "native liberty." This liberty must be understood, however, as freedom from physical constraint, not freedom from antecedent determination. D'Holbach

[29] D'Holbach, 242; translations from d'Holbach are my own.

[30] *The Spirit of the Laws,* Part 3, Chapters 12-13, ed. and trans. Anne M. Cohler *et al.* (Cambridge: Cambridge University Press, 1989) 242. Mossner calls Montesquieu "the first distinguished thinker to recognize the genius of Hume," and addresses their correspondence, including Hume's detailed criticism of *Esprit des Loix,* 229.

[31] On French perceptions of English melancholy and its connection to English liberty, see Eric Gidal, "Civic Melancholy: English Gloom and French Enlightenment," *Eighteenth-Century Studies,* 37:1 (2003): 23-45.

[32] D'Holbach, 238.

emphasizes the necessity of all actions, a necessity that becomes particularly visible in the act of suicide:

> [T]he actions of men, these weak playthings in the hand of necessity, are inevitable and dependent on a cause that moves them without their knowledge... If the same force that compels all intelligent beings to cherish their existence, makes that of a man so painful and so cruel, that he finds it odious and insupportable, he leaves his kind [*il sort de son espece*], order is destroyed for him, and in depriving himself of life, he accomplishes an end [*arrêt*] of nature, which wants him no longer to exist.[33]

Conversely, one cannot commit suicide by an unmotivated act of volition: the point is made by Diderot in an episode of his novel, *Jacques the Fatalist.* Hume and Diderot met regularly at the baron d'Holbach's Parisian salon, and their extant correspondence bespeaks, as Mossner puts it, "deep intimacy and complete understanding."[34] Hume's impress—as well, perhaps, as d'Holbach's—is found, in Diderot's novel, in the title character Jacques, a confirmed determinist (a former solider, he was taught the doctrine of necessity by his captain), as well as the clever servant of his less reflective master. Against his master's appeal to free will, Jacques offers a thought experiment concerning, in effect, attempted suicide (throwing oneself off one's horse), to prove that the will is never causally undetermined:

> MASTER: But it seems to me that I can sense within me that I am free in the same way that I think.
> JACQUES: My Captain used to say: 'That may be true at this moment when you do not want to do anything, but what if you wanted to throw yourself off your horse?'
> MASTER: I'd throw myself off.
> JACQUES: Happily, without repugnance, without effort, as when you dismount at the door of an inn?

---

[33] D'Holbach, 238.

[34] Mossner, *The Life of David Hume*, 478.

> MASTER: Not exactly, but what does it matter so long as I throw myself off, and prove that I am free?
> JACQUES: My Captain used to say: 'What! Can you not see that were it not for my contradiction you would never have taken it into your head to break your neck. It is therefore me who takes you by the foot and throws you out of your saddle. If your fall proves something it is not that you are free but that you are mad...' My Captain also used to say that the enjoyment of freedom which could be exercised without any motivation would be the real hallmark of a maniac.

Developing the implications of Hume's "Of Suicide," Jacques argues that suicide—breaking one's neck—isn't something one can simply will to do contra-causally, in order to prove one's autonomy. The very attempt to prove one's freedom from causal determination is a type not of philosophy but of insanity. As long as we are sane, we are, as Jacques informs his master, "nothing but...living and thinking machines."[35]

Hume made the same point in the *Treatise*: the desire to flaunt one's liberty may become one's motive, but "we can never free ourselves from the bonds of necessity."[36] Thus no one can commit suicide without being causally determined to do so, and in "Of Suicide" Hume allots a minimal role to the causes of will and reflection, certainly in relation to the philosophic defenses of suicide found in ancient and German philosophy. D'Holbach, in his essay on suicide, diminishes the role of volition (*la volonté*) still further, finding little more of it in one's "voluntary" death than in one's involuntary birth.[37] Yet while d'Holbach and Diderot's Jacques may be "harder" determinists than Hume, they nonetheless bring to the fore Hume's rhetorical emphases in "Of Suicide," in which suicide appears less chosen than reflexive, linked to antecedent conditions. We fine-tune our un-

---

[35] Diderot, *Jacques the Fatalist and His Master*, trans. Michael Henry (Harmondsworth: Penguin, 1986) 235-36.

[36] *A Treatise of Human Nature,* (2.3.2), 262.

[37] D'Holbach, 238.

derstanding of Hume's essay in revisiting it through the lenses of the *philosophes* he inspired.

However, an important difference between Hume's "Of Suicide" and d'Holbach's is that the latter appears written as if, or for an audience for whom, religion no longer matters, and thus for whom "superstitious" belief cannot serve as a countervailing cause impeding the natural course of suicide. Hume's essay, with its weighted argument for why suicide is not a breach of divine duty, remains a more consoling and liberating work wherever theological discourses of free will and divine displeasure have not given way to the doctrine of necessity.

5

LAWFUL RETURN VS. WILL TO TRANSFORMATION: FRIEDRICH VON GENTZ ON THE AMERICAN AND FRENCH REVOLUTIONS

Scott Philip Segrest

The American and French Revolutions each provoked intense reactions across the Western World, but the reactions outside America, Britain, and France are not well known to educated Americans today, if they ever were. Among these outside responses, those in Germany are especially notable, and one of the most brilliant comparisons of the two revolutions ever made was penned by a German observer: the journalist, political counselor, and diplomat Friedrich von Gentz.[1] Now mostly forgotten, Gentz was a well-known figure in Europe in his day. Greatly admired for his insight into international affairs, his independent assessments of European developments were sought by foreign ministers not only in his adopted home state of Austria,[2] but also in Britain, Russia, and even in the Ottoman Empire. In the great European congresses in the aftermath of the Napoleonic wars he became effectively the "Secretary of Europe," advising the various delegations to find mutually acceptable language and writing the treaty documents.[3] The respect given to his judgment and insight by the great powers of Europe was truly extraordinary.

---

[1] For a thorough overview of German elite reactions, see G. P. Gooch, *Germany and the French Revolution* (New York: Russell & Russell, Inc., 1966). Gooch addresses Gentz's response in Chapter 4.

[2] Gentz grew up and started his career in Prussia.

[3] The designation "Secretary of Europe" is Gentz biographer Golo Mann's. On why Gentz deserves the moniker, see Golo Mann, *Secretary of Europe: The Life of Friedrich Gentz, Enemy of Napoleon*, trans. William H. Woglom (New

Gentz wrote his essay on the American and French revolutions early in his career in the pages of the *Historisches Journal*, his own publication, through which he first made a name for himself.[4] We have the article in English thanks to a young John Quincy Adams, who made the translation during a long fact-finding mission in Prussia.[5] Adams titled the piece *The Origin and Principles of the American Revolution Compared With the Origin and Principles of the French Revolution*, and he recommended it as "highly interesting" to his fellow Americans, "First, because it contains the clearest account of the rise and progress of the revolution which established [Americans'] independence, that has ever appeared within so small a compass; and secondly, because it rescues that revolution from the disgraceful imputation of having proceeded from the same principles as that of France."[6]

Like many young intellectuals in Europe and America, Gentz was initially enthusiastic about the French Revolution. He had studied under Kant at Königsberg, had joined a regular student discussion group Kant hosted in his home, and had embraced the great philosopher's liberal assumptions. In 1790 Gentz wrote exuberantly that, "The spirit of the age stirs strongly and vigorously in me; it is high time for mankind to awaken from its long sleep. I am young, and the universal striving after freedom, which breaks forth on all sides, inspires in me sympathy and warmth." Then, late in that year: "I should consider the collapse of [the French] revolution one of the greatest misfortunes that the human race ever met with. It is the first practical

Haven: Yale University Press, 1946) 210-11. The context of the passage is Gentz's role at the Congress of Vienna.

[4] Gentz wrote the entire content of the journal. It was in effect a public record of his reflections on Prussian and international affairs.

[5] For details on Adams' engagement with Gentz's writings, see Kirsten Belgum, "Accidental Encounter: Why John Quincy Adams Translated German Culture for Americans," *Early American Studies*, 13:1 (2015): 227-31. As far as I have been able to discover, Adams never met Gentz face to face.

[6] Preface to Friedrich von Gentz, *The Origin and Principles of the American Revolution Compared With the Origin and Principles of the French Revolution*, trans. John Quincy Adams (Indianapolis: Liberty Fund, Inc., 2010) 3. Cited hereafter internally by number in parentheses.

triumph of philosophy, the first example of a constitution based on definite principles and embodying a consistent system of ideas; it is our hope and comfort in the face of the multitude of hoary evils under which mankind sighs."[7] Gentz even wrote an essay in defense of the French Revolution as his first published work.[8]

But like so many others, Gentz grew disillusioned as events in France turned increasingly ugly.[9] His initial change of perspective came in the course of reading and translating Burke's *Reflections on the Revolution in France*. Gentz's translation, to which he added his own introduction, interpretive essays, and extensive footnotes, would become the primary source of Burke's influence on German opinion of the Revolution.[10] Gentz was always somewhat more rationalistic than Burke. Later in life he quoted an unnamed author as describing the "quintessence of my [Gentz's] philosophy": "A rationalistic training, when too biased, and pushed beyond its proper limits, requires its traditional complement as much as a traditional training, conversely, requires rationalistic vitalizing when it has grown rigid and foreign to

[7] Paul R. Sweet, *Friedrich Von Gentz: Defender of the Old Order* (Madison: University of Wisconsin Press, 1941) 16.

[8] Golo Mann, 19-20.

[9] For the details of Gentz's change of heart, see M. A. Bond, "The Political Conversion of Friedrich von Gentz," *European History Quarterly*, vol. 3, no. 1 (1973): 1-12; Sweet, 20-23; and Mann, 20-23.

[10] See Jonathan Allen Green, "Friedrich Gentz's Translation of Burke's *Reflections*," *The Historical Journal*, 57:3 (2014): 639-59, and John Whiton, "Friedrich Gentz and the Reception of Edmund Burke in Post-Revolutionary Germany," *German Life and Letters* 46:4 (1993): 311–18. Gentz's analytical supplements for the translation are of interest not only for how they helped shaped German perspectives but also for their philosophical development of Burke's intuitions. Gentz was implicitly critical of Burke's failure to define the principles he assumed in his argument, but he thought the rudiments of a principled philosophical account were implicit in the *Reflections*, and he endeavored in his appended footnotes and essays to make the principles explicit. Specifically, "Gentz provided an explicit defense of his Kantian philosophical commitments, and adumbrated their political implications... [Gentz's] interpretive footnotes carved out a new space for a priori right in the logic of the text." Green, 642, 646, 651.

the nature of mankind."[11] Gentz always aimed at balance in his analysis of events, oriented to justice but acutely aware that the means to achieve it must vary with the circumstances. Thus, for instance, while he greatly admired the British system, he recognized that it was not transplantable to Germany or other parts of the Continent. As close adviser to Metternich in Austria, he was rightly pegged as a conservative, but his conservatism was more akin to Burke's than to Maistre's, and he despised the tyranny of despotism as much as that of radical democracy.[12] In the post-Napoleonic period he expressed disgust at the rise of German nationalism, supporters of which he called "Germanomaniacs" and "Teutomagogues," and he opposed the counterrevolutionaries as "[equally] narrow, arrogant, and sarcastic" as the revolutionaries.[13]

John Quincy Adams's translation of Gentz's essay should be seen in the context of American and British pamphlet wars over the French Revolution, especially in response to Burke's *Reflections*, which was published in early September of 1790. That same year, Adams's famous father penned a lengthy critique of the French Revolution in *Discourses on Davila*, for which his political opponents labeled him a quasi-monarchist.[14] Burke's book provoked critical book-length responses by Mary Wollstonecraft, Catherine Macaulay, Joseph Priestley, James Mackintosh, and, most famously, by Thomas Paine in his *Rights of Man*.[15] In counter-response, Burke wrote his *Address from the*

---

[11] Mann, 280.

[12] For Maistre's own commentary on the French Revolution, see Joseph de Maistre, *Considerations on France*, trans. Richard A. Lebrun, with an introduction by Isaiah Berlin (Cambridge: Cambridge University Press, 1994).

[13] Mann, 215, 280.

[14] The *Discourses* can be found in *The Works of John Adams, Second President of the United States*, vol. 6, ed. Charles Francis Adams (Boston: Charles Little and James Brown, 1851).

[15] The full titles of these works, respectively: Mary Wollstonecraft, *A Vindication of the Rights of Men, In a Letter to the Right Honourable Edmund Burke, Occasioned by His Reflections on the Revolution in France*; Catherine Macaulay, *Observations on the Reflections of the Right. Hon. Edmund Burke on the Revolution in France, In a Letter to the Right Hon. Earl of Stanhope*; Joseph Priestley, *Letters to*

New to the Old Whigs.[16] John Quincy Adams himself, though critical of Burke's "severe and indiscriminating censure [in the *Reflections*] upon almost all [the French National Assembly's] transactions,"[17] found Paine's argument philosophically superficial and practically ill-considered, as of course did Gentz.[18] Accordingly, at the tender age of 23, John Quincy wrote a brilliant critique of Paine's book in eleven

---

the Right Honourable Edmund Burke, Occasioned by His Reflections on the Revolution in France, &c.; James Mackintosh, *Vindiciae Gallicae: Defence of the French Revolution and Its English Admirers, Against the Accusations of The Right Hon. Edmund Burke, Including Some Strictures on the Late Production of Mons. De Calonne*; and Thomas Paine, *Rights of Man: Being an Answer to Mr. Burke's Attack on the French Revolution*. All texts are available in full at the Online Library of Liberty (http://oll.libertyfund.org). Notably, Mackintosh later recanted his criticism of Burke, although Burke was skeptical of the "supposed conversion"; see R. B. McDowell and John A. Woods, eds., *The Correspondence of Edmund Burke*, 2 vols. (Cambridge: Cambridge University Press, 1970) 193-94, 204-205; and Patrick O'Leary, *Sir James Mackintosh: The Whig Cicero* (Aberdeen: Aberdeen University Press, 1989) 23.

[16] See Edmund Burke, *An Appeal from the New to the Old Whigs*, in *Further Reflections on the Revolution in France*, ed. Daniel E. Ritchie (Indianapolis: Liberty Fund, 1992).

[17] John Quincy Adams, *Publicola: Observations on Paine's* Rights of Man *in a Series of Letters* (Quincy, Massachusetts: Liberty's Lamp Books, 2014), Letter 1.

[18] Gentz briefly acknowledges in *Origin and Principles* Paine's influence on the American Revolution "among certain classes of people" through his "contemptible" *Common Sense*, but insists that "the spirit and principles of the American revolution" should not be judged by that influence, which "would be as unjust, as to confound the efficaciously active heads in the English revolution, of 1688, with the authors of some popular lampoon against the house of Stewart; or the opposition of lord Chatham, with that of Mr. Wilkes" (72-73). In a long footnote on the same pages, Gentz contrasts Paine's zealotry, as he saw it, to the moderation of "the great authorities of the American revolution, such as Dickinson, John Adams, Jay, Franklin, &c." In the footnote, Gentz also contrasts, as a rough parallel, the attitudes of Price and Burke in relation to the French Revolution. Gentz surely underestimates the significance of Paine's *Common Sense* in America, and the German was doubtless more elitist than the American leaders he praises, but there is no question that Americans largely soured on Paine after the latter's anti-Christian *Age of Reason*, no doubt leaving some of them wondering if Paine had been all along more radical than they realized.

letters ultimately published as *Publicola*.[19] Unsurprisingly, when the younger Adams discovered Gentz's favorable comparison of the American to the French Revolution, he was well pleased. As he wrote Gentz in 1800, "It cannot but afford a gratification to every American attached to the honor of his country to see its revolution so ably vindicated from the imputation of having originated, or been conducted upon the same principles as that of France, and I feel myself as an American citizen highly obliged to you for the consideration you have bestowed on the subject, as well as for the honorable manner in which you have borne testimony to the purity of principle upon which the revolution of my country was founded."[20]

In what follows I review Gentz's essay in some detail (since it will be unknown to most readers) and then evaluate its argument regarding justice, tradition and circumstance, and the character of the revolutions. I do so in light of Burke's similar treatment of Gentz's themes in the *Reflections*, Aristotle's also similar but ultimately (in my view) superior treatment of justice and prudence in his *Ethics* and *Politics*, and Alexis de Tocqueville's suggestions in his *Ancien Régime and the French Revolution* about the peculiar religious quality of the French movement, which in my view gets to the deepest heart of the difference between the revolutions. I conclude with a few thoughts on the continuing relevance of Gentz's essay for today.

* * *

---

[19] *Publicola* itself sparked considerable debate; see James R. Zink, "The *Publicola* Debate and the Role of the French Revolution in American Constitutional Thought," *American Political Thought*, 4:4 (2015): 557-87. On the larger American discussion of Burke's and Paine's arguments in which the *Publicola* debate took place, see Francis Canavan, S.J., "The Relevance of the Burke-Paine Controversy to American Political Thought," *The Review of Politics*, 49:2 (1987): 163-76.

[20] John Quincy Adams, "To Friedrich von Gentz, Berlin, June 16, 1800," in *The Writings of John Quincy Adams*, vol. 2, ed. Worthington Chauncey Ford (New York: The MacMillan Company, 1913) 463.

Gentz makes his comparison in *Origin and Principles* in terms of the revolutions' respective origins, progress, and ends. In the American case the origin was a shift in British policy from salutary neglect to intrusive innovation, specifically the imposition, for the first time in the colonies' history, of internal taxation. The reasons for this policy shift were varied. Immediately, the aim was alleviating the tax burden on the people of Great Britain after the Seven Years' War (the "most pardonable" motive), though achieving this through taxing the colonies was, Gentz says, "most improbable" (16). Ultimately, the causes were an imperious desire to assert British, and specifically British parliamentary, supremacy over the colonies combined with a foolish, erroneous "opinion that the victory over the colonies would be infallible and easy" (31).[21] On every point, the British innovations were irrational and passion-based. Achieving significant tax relief for Britons through taxing the colonies was, again, unrealistic (16). The growing quest for supremacy was rooted in "dangerous passions": "a destructive jealousy [for power]" (24) and "the deep exasperation [with colonial resistance], the inflexible pride, the false ambition, all the angry passions" (31). British ministers also harbored a "secret apprehension that America might grow weary of her fetters, [and this fear] misled them to the dangerous experiment of fastening still narrower chains upon her" (17).

The colonists' response, in contrast, was not merely emotional, but was rational and principled, based on a sound perception of their rights. These included their rights under "the British constitution," their rights under the colonial charters, and the right of revolution, properly understood. The scope of their rights under "the British constitution" had unfortunately never been clearly defined (38). But "the spirit of the English constitution" had been grounded in the right of consent to which the colonists so often appealed, including the principle they expressed as "no taxation without representation" (18). In

[21] It was from the doctrine of "the legal supremacy of parliament [that] the pretention to bind America by act of parliament, in all cases whatsoever [was] formally derived" (42); Gentz alludes to the Declaratory Act.

addition to these implicit British constitutional rights, the colonists had certain contractual rights indicated in the colonial charters (39).

Gentz's interpretation of the colonists' right of revolution is notable for its departure from the simple Lockean interpretation typically assumed today. It is based on a quasi-medieval, distinctly non-Enlightenment understanding of sovereignty. It is true that "the firmest foundation of all sovereignty ... is in the wants of the governed" and the general right of self-government (36-37, 39). But Americans, Gentz stresses, did not treat their principles abstractly but rather as rooted in "their constitution, [which] before the revolution was evidently a monarchy, more or less limited by the influence of their provincial assemblies" (46).[22] With regard to the right to revolution, Gentz makes a crucial "distinction between an insurrection in a *simple*, and one in a *complicated*, or *mixed constitution*."[23] In a simple constitution, he suggests, revolution is never or rarely ever justified; in a mixed constitution, it may sometimes be justified because each part of its constitution has its own "constitutional rights and prerogatives; and those of any one part, though in themselves more important, cannot be more sacred than those of any other. When either of them exceeds its legal bounds, and oppresses, or endeavours to destroy another, this latter, unless the constitution be an empty name, must have the right of resisting, [and] if the old balance cannot again be

---

[22] On this point, we might recall the curious line in the Declaration of Independence in which King George is accused of subjecting the colonists "to a jurisdiction foreign to our constitution." The "foreign jurisdiction," of course, is the British Parliament, but what is this "constitution" the Americans claimed to have? One could say the American constitution in the colonial period, in the complete sense, consisted of the colonial charters, the system to which Gentz refers of colonial legislatures working with the crown, and the unwritten constitution of English common law that the colonists as Englishmen had assumed as belonging to them as much as to any part of the British Empire.

[23] I do not know whether the frequent textual emphases of words or phrases were in the original or were added by John Quincy Adams. Unless otherwise noted, all emphases are in Adams's text, and may be Gentz's or Adams's. The possibility that Adams added them should be borne in mind as potentially coloring our interpretation of Gentz and revealing something of Adams's perspective.

restored, the contest must necessarily, and *legally* end with the dissolution of the constitution" (44). Thus, paradoxically, a revolution may be constitutional—and to be legitimate, *must* be constitutional—and this was the case with the American colonies: "the colonial assemblies had a constitutional right to resist [the king], when he violated their constitutional powers" (46-47).

In addition to this constitutional authority, colonial conduct leading up to the revolution had been exemplary. Part of their right to revolt was the fact that they conducted themselves in the right way. Specifically, they had peacefully petitioned, according to lawful means. "It was not until after the ministry had spurned at peace, rejected every proposal of conciliation, and finally required unconditional submission, that is, had *dissolved the constitution*, that the [continental] congress proceeded to the declaration, which substituted a new government, in the stead of that which was destroyed" (48).

The colonists, according to Gentz's reading, understood the right of revolution to be grounded not in some kind of abstract Rousseauian general will but in the concrete right of one part of a mixed government to resist encroachments from another part—in this case of the colonial legislatures to resist encroachments by the crown. In essence, Gentz does not recognize a right of revolution in the Lockean sense (meaning a movement by "the people" as a mass) at all, only resistance to tyranny on the part of the people's authorized representatives. This assumption will be important for Gentz's critique of the French revolutionaries. Technically, Gentz's reading implies that there really *had been no revolution* in the American case, but rather an effective dissolution of the constitution *by the British* when the ministry summarily rejected colonial proposals and demanded "unconditional submission" (48). The essence of British injustice was its destruction of the lawful order and the unconditionality of royal demands.

To put the whole matter in just war terms, the American Revolution had just cause, and the justness of the cause was, for Gentz, closely tied to the lawfulness of the justification. American actions were lawful (petitions), and even when extra-legal in the narrow sense of "legal" (as with the non-importation agreement, participation in which was voluntary), were "commensurate" to the threat (54), a strictly "necessary defence" (56), and in all cases peaceful (57). (Gentz means in all cases authorized by colonial representatives.) Unlike the French, Americans, as they said explicitly in one of their petitions to the British government, demanded "*no new rights*" (58), only the satisfaction of constitutional rights and elementary justice. In short, in all their collective actions, American leaders exhibited "moderation" (60), and they resorted to revolution only when it had become a "necessity" for the sake of securing a just order (62).[24]

At this point we should observe that Gentz does not think much of the statement of principles in the Declaration of Independence, which he calls an "empty pomp of words [that had] no visible influence upon their practical measures and resolves" (70). This may be a forced assessment from an obviously Burkean bias, but it does seem important to acknowledge that the abstract principles in the first part of the Declaration had been practically grounded in the institutions and practices catalogued in the middle part. Indeed, the statement of principles itself links principles and constitution in suggesting that a form of government is needed to uphold the abstract rights. In any case, Gentz appeals to natural right in his own way, and he seems to think the Americans had a true grasp of natural right, even if they unfortunately sometimes spoke of it too abstractly.

So much for Gentz on the origin of the American Revolution. As Gentz sees it, the origin of the French Revolution had been entirely different, with regard both to rights and conduct. To begin

---

[24] With respect to the point about Americans' demanding no new rights, consider Jefferson's suggestion of the same in his May 8, 1825 letter to Henry Lee: "[T]he object of the Declaration of Independence [was] not to find out new principles, or new arguments, never before thought of, not merely to say things which had never been said before; but to place before mankind the common sense of the subject, in terms so plain and firm as to command their assent." Thomas Jefferson, "To Henry Lee, May 8, 1825," in *The Works of Thomas Jefferson*, vol. 12, ed. Paul Leicester Ford (New York: G. P. Putnam's Sons, 1905) 409.

with, the interaction between the crown and the legislature was precisely the reverse of the American case: the French king had been a model of moderation, had in fact been conciliatory to a fault, and had acted in accord with constitutional forms and procedures. The French revolutionaries became immoderate in the extreme and from the outset flouted lawful process.[25] The outstanding fact of the French Revolution for Gentz was its dismissal of both constitutional and natural law in favor of "an imaginary right of the *nation*, to do whatever they, or their representatives should please" (49-50)—that is, whatever they pleased without regard to justice. The French Estates could have enacted major reforms constitutionally, he asserts, but a reckless rebellion made that impossible (50-51). It is here that Gentz first appeals directly to natural right, saying we should "judge" the actions of the French revolutionaries ultimately by "uncorrupted reason, and the eternal prescriptions of *real right*" (50). From their unlawful beginning, the revolutionaries before long "murdered justice herself, in the person of the most conscientious and upright monarch, who had ever adorned a throne" (53).

The French revolutionaries, as epitomized in their execution of the king, were no more like the Americans in their conduct than in their grasp of justice. Their conduct, like the British government's during the American conflict, was rooted in dangerous passions. But the French passions went beyond the usual complement of self-interest and pride manifest in the British case to become truly deranged and deranging, radically distorting reason and will. They used the "*right of the nation*, sometimes likewise called *right of man* [as] a sort of magic spell, with which all the ties of nations and of humanity were insensibly dissolved." They used "the chimerical principle of the sovereignty of the people [as a] talisman, [sparing] themselves and others the trouble of enquiring into the lawfulness of their proceedings; for in their system, all was right, which they resolved upon in

[25] For instance, members of the Third Estate moved unilaterally and without formal popular authorization to make the meeting of the Estates into a constitutional convention, and then dissolved the other Estates altogether.

the name of the *people*, or in the name of mankind" (50). The kind of unreal, magical thinking to which Gentz refers—figuratively casting "magic spells" and worshiping "talismans"—rendered the French Revolution not just ill-considered but downright abnormal, an aberration of nature.[26] Burke in the *Reflections* and later Tocqueville in his *Ancien Régime and the French Revolution* likewise remarked on the magical quality of French revolutionary thinking, and, as I argue below, this quality is the key to understanding the descent into extreme radicalism and terror.

As to the *progress* of the revolutions, Gentz's main point is that, "The American revolution was from beginning to end, on the part of the Americans, merely a *defensive revolution*; the French was from beginning to end, in the highest sense of the word, *an offensive revolution*" (53). Gentz's summary statement of the American case is worth quoting in full:

> Never, in the whole course of the American revolution, were the *rights of man*, appealed to, for the destruction of the *rights of a citizen*; never was the sovereignty of the people used as a pretext to undermine the respect, due to the laws, or the foundations of social security; no example was ever seen of an individual, or a whole class of individuals, or even the representatives of this, or that single state, who recurred to the declaration of rights, to escape from positive obligation, or to renounce obedience to the common sovereign; finally, never did it enter the head of any legislator, or statesman in America, to combat the lawfulness of foreign constitutions, and to set up the American revolution, as a new epocha in the general relations of civil society. (71)

The contrast with the French revolutionaries could not be more stark: "As the American revolution had exhibited a model of moderation in defence, so the French one displayed an unparalleled example

---

[26] Eric Voegelin suggested that this element of magic, or "sorcery" as he also called it, has been present in all the modern radical movements. See especially Voegelin's "Wisdom and the Magic of the Extreme: A Meditation," in *Published Essays, 1966-1985, The Collected Works of Eric Voegelin*, vol. 12, ed. Ellis Sandoz (Baton Rouge: Louisiana State University Press, 1990) 315-75.

of violence and inexorable fury in attack. As the former had always kept the vigour of its defensive measures in rigourous proportion to the exigency, so the latter, from the weakness of the resistance made against it, became more and more violent and terrible, the more cause it had to grow milder" (63). Eventually the "thirst for destruction had gone so far, that it was at a loss for an object. The well known saying, that Robespierre meant to reduce the population of France by one half, had its foundation in the lively sense of the impossibility of satisfying the hitherto insatiate revolution, with any thing less, than such a hecatomb." Not content to stop at internal destruction, "When there was nothing more left in the country to attack, the offensive frenzy turned itself against the neighbouring states, and finally declared war in solemn decrees against all civil society" (66). A "hostile demon" had been released, and its activity would bear "the most poisonous fruits" (78). In contrast to the American Revolution, "The French revolution, true to the character of a most violent offensive revolution, could not but proceed so long as there remained objects for it to attack, and it retained strength for the assault" (67).

The difference in the progress of the revolutions, Gentz suggests, resulted from the difference of the aims of the revolutions:

> As the American revolution was a defensive revolution, it was of course finished, at the moment, when it had overcome the attack, by which it had been occasioned... The American revolution, at every stage of its duration, had a fixed and definite object, and moved within definite limits, and by a definite direction towards this object. The French revolution never had a definite object; and, in a thousand various directions, continually crossing each other, ran through the unbounded space of a fantastic arbitrary will, and of a bottomless anarchy. (66-67)

The American aim specifically was "to preserve" an old order. The French were driven by "the deadly passion for making political experiments with abstract theories, and untried systems" (69). Note the suggestion again of magic in the above phrase, "a fantastic arbitrary will." Accordingly, the French Revolution was marked by "a perpetual mutability in the choice of the means and in the modification of principles" (78). The only clear object of the French Revolution was to destroy the old order, and this end justified any means (79).

One of the most valuable features of Gentz's analysis is his recognizing the spiritual qualities of the respective revolutions and his penetration to their ultimate conditions and causes. Consider these contrasts:

Substantive vs. empty: In the American case, the revolution was defined by concrete rights and traditions. In the French case, "The republic had been proclaimed; but this republic was a word without definite meaning, which every one believed he might explain, according to his inclinations, and according to the fantastic whims, which he called his principles" (82). (Note again: "fantastic"—magic.)

Lawful vs. raw power: In the American case, exercise of power was according to lawful forms and processes. In the French case, "Force alone could determine the issue of this horrible contest; and the victory must necessarily remain to the most resolute" (83).

Preservative vs. experimental: As just noted, in America the aim was "to preserve" pre-existing goods. "What [the 'ancient form'] contained of good and useful remained untouched; the revolution only removed that in which it had been oppressive" (86). The French, by contrast, were driven by a "deadly passion" to gamble on sweeping political change without regard for, or even recognition of, the hard won achievements of French civilization (69).

Limited vs. universal: In the American case, the aim was only to address concrete, local problems. In the French case, "the revolution was to be considered, not as a local transaction, but as one of those, which give a new form to civil society, and which must draw all mankind within its vortex. For the ambition, or for the enthusiasm of this insatiable party, the theatre, which France offered to their thirst for destruction, was too small; they wished to tear up the world from its poles, and commence a new era for the whole human race" (81).[27]

[27] Americans did speak of establishing a *novus ordo seclorum*, so perhaps Gentz's contrast here is too stark. It is significant, however, that American revolutionaries did not, like the French, seek to foment or carry out armed revolution abroad.

This will to remake the world indicates again the magical thinking Gentz keeps hinting at, for men are not gods that they can create something by fiat. The essence of magic is the will to remake reality, the effort to control or reshape or create reality by sheer force of will. The new order established by the American founding, Gentz might say, was like a scientific experiment to see whether a new arrangement of available materials would produce the desired result; the experimentation of the French Revolution was more like a crew of witches trying out new potions.

Just order vs. mass leveling: With respect to civil society, the French Revolution, unlike the American, attacked not just the political but even the social order: "it no longer spared any private right whatsoever, when it declared all political prerogatives to be usurpations," robbing and humiliating "the clergy" and the "holders of estates" and virtually abolishing private property (87).

Pragmatic vs. purist: In contrast to American efforts at negotiated settlement, the French revolutionaries "declared, that between their revolution and those who rejected it, no further intercourse could exist" (83). As with all total revolutions, the French version was driven by an urge for purification, and both attitude and action correspondingly became puritanical.

Merely political vs. "religious": The Americans, though sometimes appealing to Providence for support, tried to address straightforwardly political problems by old-fashioned political means. "The [French] revolution," by contrast, "prepared against Europe, and Europe against the revolution, a war, with which only the most dreadful religious wars, that ever scourged the world, can be compared" (84). The French revolutionary movement became a kind of political religion.[28]

---

[28] Eric Voegelin was a pioneer in developing the concept of "political religion"; see Voegelin, *The Political Religions*, in *Modernity Without Restraint*, ed. Manfred Henningsen, *The Collected Works of Eric Voegelin*, vol. 5 (Columbia, Missouri: University of Missouri Press, 2000). On the scholarly discussion and debate of the concept's analytical/interpretive usefulness, see Emilio Gentile, "Political Religion: A Concept and Its Critics – A Critical Survey," *Totalitarian Movements and Political Religions*, 6:1 (2005): 19–32; Hans Maier, "Political Re-

As one of Gentz's German contemporaries, Friedrich Schlegel, commented, "The few revolutionaries there were in the [French] Revolution were mystics, who made their doings a religion."[29]

Natural right vs. lust for power: "The Americans were wise enough to circumscribe themselves within the bounds, which right, on one side, and the nature of things, on the other, had drawn round them. The French in their giddiness no longer acknowledged the prescriptions of the clearest right, nor the prescriptions of nature. They were so proud as to think they could bend impossibility itself, under the arm of their violence, and so daring that they thought the clearest right must yield to the maxims of their arbitrary will" (88). "Bend impossibility"—break the bounds of nature itself—by violent, "arbitrary will": this is, again, magic.

Moderation vs. wrath and revenge: Whatever random excesses Americans may have committed in the conduct of their revolution, as their leadership generally took their bearings from law and natural justice, these were nothing in comparison to French violations. The French revolutionaries meted out unjust and unlimited punishment and, fleeing the pricks of conscience, descended into savage inhumanity: "fear of a just reaction drove the authors of these oppressions to measures of still deepening cruelty against the victims of their first crimes...treat[ing] as an offender deserving death, every man, who did not immediately and actively associate with them." The American Revolution "never involved itself in this horrible labyrinth, where voluntary iniquities can only be covered by necessary misdeeds, and where every earlier crime became the only justification for an hundred

---

ligion: A Concept and Its Limitations," *Totalitarian Movements and Political Religions*, 8:1 (2007): 5–16; and Stanley G. Payne, "On the Heuristic Value of the Concept of Political Religion and its Application," *Totalitarian Movements and Political Religions*, 6:2 (2005): 163–74.

[29] Gooch, *Germany and the French Revolution*, 234. Note Schlegel's implicit denial that the French was a truly popular revolution; it was rather, he hints, a case of a cadre of radicals who took the opportunity of general discontent to seize power and take a course for which it had no clear popular mandate. One is reminded of Lenin's "vanguard."

other ones" (89). If some Americans persecuted Loyalists or formed unruly mobs, these acts were sporadic and unauthorized by the governing authorities; French terror was official and "systematic" (90).

Reason vs. unreason: Americans, as observed, had recognized natural right and the nature of things. In France, "reason herself, abused, desecrated reason, ascend[ed] the theatre of misery, solemnly to justify, by cold blooded, criminal appeals to principles and duties, these revolutionary confusions" (91).[30]

Given such different origins and progressions of the revolutions, different *results* were inevitable. The American Revolution established a new order that preserved, extended, and secured old rights and privileges. The French Revolution culminated in the unprecedented formation of a "revolutionary state [which] brought into play what was called the system of terror" and then "an uninterrupted series of revolutions, and counter-revolutions" (83). To sum up the French case:

> The French revolution ... began by a violation of rights, every step of its progress was a violation of rights, and it was never easy, until it had succeeded to establish absolute wrong, as the supreme and acknowledged maxim of a state completely dissolved, and yet existing only in bloody ruins... For so soon as in a great undertaking, a step is taken wholly out of the boundaries of definite rights, and every thing is declared lawful, which imaginary necessity, or unbridled passion inspires, so soon is the immeasurable field of arbitrary will entered upon; and a revolution, which has no other principle than to attack the existing constitution, must necessarily proceed to the last extremities of imagination and of criminal guilt. (53, 79)

At the root of all, then, was "unbridled passion" and an unlimited, "arbitrary will" to destroy every vestige of the past.

Gentz's overall conclusion is that, contrary to common perception, the French "copied the Americans only in two points, of which

[30] Parisian revolutionaries famously made Notre Dame into a Temple of Reason, for just one of many similar examples of "desecration," and appeals to Reason with a capital "R" were almost as ubiquitous as the appeals to "the people."

one was the idlest, and the other the most objectionable of any throughout their revolution; in the declaration of the rights of man, and in paper-money" (footnote, 92). Beyond these points, they really had nothing in common. In short, the American was a lawful revolution that in fact (not just in theory) respected and secured rights; the French Revolution expressed a will to power that achieved rights only in theory (not in fact) and in fact was, in both form and substance, irreconcilable with real rights.

* * *

I have quoted Gentz extensively to let the reader feel the power of his writing and of his insight. His essay deserves to be much better known. But how should we assess its argument? I propose going back to 1776, to the Declaration of Independence, and considering the argument first in light of that document, which was after all the official statement of American purpose in the conflict with Britain. Gentz rests his case on the justice of Americans' claims and conduct and the injustice of their French counterparts'. He suggests that the American revolutionaries understood natural right better than the French and that this difference manifested itself in their contrasting actions. Yet at the same time he calls the Declaration's statement of principles an "empty pomp of words," which he suggests were unnecessary to the success of the American cause and in fact potentially dangerous, as evident in the way the French used similar abstractions to justify injustice.

I take these points one at a time. As to the practical efficacy of the abstract principles, Gentz seems to be mistaken. First, the universal appeal of the abstract principles (presented from "a decent respect to the opinions of mankind") may have been a factor in winning France's crucial support in the war against Britain; it certainly was intended to do so. Second, to whatever extent the Declaration was itself an immediate source of fighting inspiration, the allegedly empty abstractions seem to have bolstered Americans' convictions and resolve in promoting their claims, as evidenced by frequent appeals to the principles before, during, and after the war—in condemning British injustices, in firing up the townsfolk, and in grounding state constitutions and bills or declarations of rights.[31]

On the second point, about the potential danger of beautiful abstractions ("glittering generalities" as one of Lincoln's critics put it),[32] Gentz seems to be correct. Such abstractions—in the French case, *liberté, egalité, fraternité*—can become an "empty pomp of words," and worse, the emptiness can be filled with "hostile demons," like the man in the parable whose soul was an unoccupied house.[33] What prevented the abstractions from becoming dangerous in the American case was that they were grounded, as Gentz tries to show, in substantive justice and anchored in practice in long-standing institutions like elected legislatures that held government accountable to the governed and like trial by jury and the common law courts that protected individual rights. And the British government really *had* mistreated the American colonists, as detailed in the Declaration's very concrete list of grievances. The French government, at the time of the French Revolution, had been quite conciliatory. King Louis XVI was widely

---

[31] On appeals to natural rights related to the conflict with Britain, see, for example, Samuel Adams, "The Rights of the Colonists: The Report of the Committee of Correspondence to the Boston Town Meeting, Nov. 20, 1772," in *Old South Leaflets*, no. 173 (Boston: Directors of the Old South Work, 1906) 7: 417-428; and Steven M. Dworetz's account of the frequent appeals by founding era clergy in *The Unvarnished Doctrine: Locke, Liberalism, and the American Revolution* (Durham: Duke University Press Books, 1994). Founding-era state constitutions explicitly invoked natural rights or some variation of the term in Massachusetts, Virginia, Pennsylvania, New Hampshire, Vermont, and Maryland. See also Philip Hamburger, "Natural Rights, Natural Law, and American Constitutions," *Yale Law Journal*, 102 (1993): 907-960. Hamburger's essay is pertinent also for showing founding Americans' restrained, practical approach to natural rights claims.

[32] See Lincoln's 1859 "Letter to H. L. Pierce and Others" in *The Language of Liberty: The Political Speeches and Writings of Abraham Lincoln*, Revised Bicentennial Edition, ed. Joseph R. Fornieri (Washington, D.C.: Regnery Publishing, Inc., 2009) 749. Lincoln famously grounded his whole political philosophy on those "glittering generalities."

[33] Matthew 12:43-45.

seen as a liberalizing monarch, as evidenced, notably, in the support he gave to the American Revolution and in his willingness to call up a meeting of the Estates General, the first time any monarch had done so in 175 years. Whatever mistakes Louis XVI made in the run-up to revolution owed more to weakness than to malice or any of the "angry passions" that Gentz said drove the British government; the angry passions were rather driving the revolutionaries. On the question of rights, part of the reason for French impatience with the king and with constitutional process was that they had made abstractions about rights into magic talismans, as if they could conjure them like a genie in a lamp to make their wishes instantly materialize.

What accounts for this? Gentz does not say explicitly. My own assessment is that the French revolutionaries, as Burke suggested, indeed lacked practical sense and also that (something Burke and Gentz also intimated) the emptiness of their abstractions was derived from a certain emptiness in themselves—their souls in too many cases *were* unoccupied houses. This personal emptiness specifically was a deficiency of character, what the American founders called "virtue," and this lack of moral substance directly related to the lack of prudence. As Aristotle suggested, prudence is a virtue, and only the morally virtuous—those in control of their passions—are capable of prudence. The French revolutionaries, including relative moderates like the Abbé Sieyès,[34] gave free vent to Gentz's "dangerous passions": "destructive jealousy," "exasperation," "pride," "ambition," and "all the angry passions." These passions became intense enough to derange reason and turned into the magic-making will to dominate reality that Gentz so brilliantly captured. All this was prepared by over two decades of intemperate attacks on French institutions in the writings of

---

[34] See Emmanuel Joseph Sieyès, *What Is the Third Estate?*, in *Political Writings: Including the Debate Between Sieyes and Tom Paine in 1791* (Indianapolis: Hackett Publishing Company, Inc., 2003). *What Is the Third Estate?* played a role in sparking the French Revolution akin to that of Thomas Paine's *Common Sense* in the American setting. Sieyès opposed the Terror and the radicalism of the Montagnards, but the language of his potent little book could not be called a model of cool restraint.

the *philosophes*, who stoked the passions and gave them form and direction through their ideas, supplying the magic talismans.

In contrast to his treatment of the American case, Gentz does not give much attention in his essay to the facts of the French case, despite his comprehensive knowledge of French developments.[35] He seems to assume his European readers to be much better acquainted with the details of the French than of the American Revolution. Without question, in his interpretation of French events he was greatly influenced by Burke, and his judgments on the French revolutionaries give a sense of being a commentary on Burke's reading, getting to the core of Burke's criticisms and indicating more sharply than Burke the underlying existential drivers. Gentz also is not explicit in what he means by "real right," but we can reasonably guess that he understood it much the way Burke did when Burke spoke of "real rights" in the *Reflections*. It would thus be helpful for getting to the heart of Gentz's understanding to take a quick look at the relevant points as Burke made them.

In many respects, Burke's analysis is markedly Aristotelian. He affirms the notion of human rights but insists that, to be meaningful,

---

[35] Gentz gathered extensive materials on the French Revolution with intent to write a book on the subject, which unfortunately never happened. In time his knowledge of the Revolution was probably at least as great as Burke's, whose mastery of relevant materials was extraordinary. One biographer avers that, "By 1798 Gentz was one of the best-informed men in the world on the French Revolution" (Sweet, 31). In my judgment, Gentz's assessment in *Origin and Principles* is entirely in keeping with the evidence. For a richly detailed modern account broadly supporting Gentz's view of the Revolution as a whole, see Simon Schama, *Citizens: A Chronical of the French Revolution* (New York: Alfred A. Knopf, 1989). To survey the wealth of evidence in relation to the Terror, see David Andress, *The Terror: The Merciless War for Freedom in Revolutionary France* (New York: Farrar, Straus and Giroux, 2005); Hugh Gough, *The Terror in the French Revolution*, 2nd ed. (New York: Palgrave MacMillan, 2010); and especially R. R. Palmer, *The Year of the Terror: Twelve Who Ruled France, 1793-1794* (Oxford: Basil Blackwell, 1989). Palmer's book follows the members of the Committee on Public Safety through the course of the Terror, in context of their personal biographies, treating them as fairly as possible while ultimately interpreting their words and actions much as Gentz did.

they have to be understood in concrete terms. The "*real* rights of men" (Burke's emphasis) include a right to the benefits of civil society once established, based indeed on a universal "right to justice," but Burke qualifies this by saying that though in the partnership of society "all men have equal rights," they do not have a right to "equal things"—people have a right to what they deserve, and some deserve better than others.[36] So far, this is perfectly Aristotelian.[37] Burke goes on to say that, "Government is not made in virtue of natural rights, which may and do exist in total independence of it; and exist in much greater clearness, and in a much greater degree of abstract perfection: but their abstract perfection is their practical defect."[38] So natural rights *do* exist, but treated abstractly they have little practical value. "The pretended rights of these [French] theorists are all extremes; and in proportion as they are metaphysically true, they are morally and politically false. The rights of man are in a sort of *middle*, incapable of definition, but not impossible to be discerned."[39] This is a clear allusion to Aristotle's Golden Mean. Burke concludes: "By these [French] theorists the right of the people is almost always sophistically confounded with their power [and] till power and right are the same, the [body of the community] has no right inconsistent with virtue, and the first of all virtues, prudence. Men have no right to what is not reasonable, and to what is not for their benefit."[40] In the *Reflections*, Burke outlines his view of the low quality of the men who composed the National Assembly,[41] and of course frequently hints at the moral vacuity or degradation of the atheistic French *philosophes* and the harassing French mobs. As to prudence, as Aristotle said,

---

[36] Burke, *Revolutionary Writings: Reflections on the Revolution in France* and the first *Letter on a Regicide Peace*, ed. Iain Hampsher-Monk (Cambridge: Cambridge University Press, 2014) 60.

[37] See Aristotle, *Nichomachean Ethics* V.3 and *Politics* III.9 1280a10-24 and V.1 1301b26-1302a15.

[38] Burke, *Revolutionary Writings*, 61.

[39] Ibid., 63.

[40] Ibid.

[41] Ibid., 42-53.

right is determined by reason, but not by what Burke calls "naked reason"—individual reason acting on its own, without the support of a moral imagination, and without regard to limiting circumstances; rather, it is reason informed by dispassionate reflection and discussion and drawing on the fund of wisdom embedded in "the general bank and capital of nations, and of ages."[42]

It is here, however, that we can detect a divergence from Aristotle. Certainly Aristotle suggests the value of the common sense latent in the community[43] and of tradition in the form of customary *nomoi* or mores[44]; he indicates, too, the value of what Burke calls the moral imagination in appreciating the educative power of nobly formed eloquence[45]; and of course Aristotle makes prudence, *phronesis*, the highest practical virtue. But Aristotle describes prudence as a matter of reason's connecting "universals" and "particulars," and universals (though, contra Plato, they do not exist independently of the particulars in aggregate) can only be expressed abstractly.[46] From an Aristotelian perspective, it is not problematic or inherently dangerous to articulate abstract universals; in fact, it may often be necessary for the sake of achieving clarity, and especially for helping others get clarity, on the patterns in the particulars and their larger significance, and for orienting mind and feelings properly in relation to the concrete facts. The American founders intuitively grasped these points and were perhaps more Aristotelian than they knew in how they handled their universal, abstract claims.[47] They were Burkean in their appreciation

---

[42] Ibid., 90.

[43] Aristotle, *Politics* III.11 1281a40-b9 and b15-22

[44] Aristotle, *Politics* III.16 1287b5 and *Rhetoric* I.14 1375a16

[45] See Aristotle's various oratorical strategies in the *Rhetoric*. Burke references the "moral imagination," *Revolutionary Writings*, 79—see the entire surrounding passage.

[46] See Aristotle, *Nichomachean Ethics* VI 7 1141b15-17 and VI 8 1142a13-14.

[47] In the 1825 letter to Henry Lee referenced earlier, Jefferson mentions among the inspirations for the Declaration "the elementary books of public right, as Aristotle, Cicero, Locke, Sidney, &c.," so the author of the Declaration in fact

of the value of traditions and more generally of "experience," to which they never tired of appealing, and in this respect they were nothing like the French revolutionaries. But they were essentially Aristotelian in their understanding of universals and in relating the universals to the particulars of history and circumstance. (Ironically, their orientation was really not much like that of their early hero Thomas Paine's, the deficiencies of whose *Rights of Man* John Quincy Adams attacks so effectively in *Publicola*.) Their statement of principles in the Declaration was not an "empty pomp of words" because they were not disconnected from experience, because Americans knew how to apply the abstract principles to the circumstances (as shown in the list of grievances), and because they had sufficient virtue not to let their passions cloud their judgment on the meaning of justice as it touched their conflict with Britain.[48]

One of the most remarkable parts of Gentz's argument for the Americans is his treatment of constitutional questions. His conception of the British crown's actions as constitutional violations, ultimately amounting to a destruction of the American constitution, is compelling. It effectively establishes that the American Revolution was an act of self-preservation, and makes the British crown a kind of

acknowledged Aristotle's influence, even if he did not have the Greek's understanding of prudence and first principles directly in mind.

[48] As John Witherspoon, Presbyterian minister and president of Princeton, put it, "though it would be a miracle if there were not many selfish persons among us, and discoveries now and then made of mean and insterested transactions, yet [in the controversy with Britain] they have been comparatively inconsiderable both in number and effect... There has been, by common consent, a much greater degree of order and public peace, than men of reflection and experience foretold or expected." Witherspoon concluded that Americans' "principles [were] pure...[that] your present opposition to the claims of the British ministery does not arise from a seditious and turbulent spirit, or a wonton contempt of legal authority; from a blind and factious attachment to particular persons or parties; or from a selfish rapacious disposition, and a desire to turn public confusion to private profit—but from a concern for the interest of your country, and the safety of yourselves and your posterity." John Witherspoon, *The Dominion of Providence Over the Passions of Men*, in *Political Sermons of the American Founding Era, 1730-1805*, ed. Ellis Sandoz (Indianapolis: Liberty Press, 1991) 551-52.

homicide. What could be more just than countering a homicide? Equally compelling is the implicit case for the value of a mixed constitution, which enables the various parts to hold the others accountable to the public good.

But still, Gentz's way of linking the right to revolution to the constitutional order leaves some important questions unanswered. What of peoples unlucky enough not to live under a mixed constitution? Are there no circumstances under which they may rightly revolt, no tyranny terrible enough to warrant a popular uprising in the absence of constitutional representatives?[49] And further, what is the basis of the justness of a constitution and of the obligation to respect the constitution? If Gentz responded to the second question by saying, as he in fact does, that government's purpose is to serve the common good, of what does this common good consist? Would it not have to be understood in abstract terms, even if the abstractions pointed to concrete potentialities? Is not, in fact, the principle of serving the public good an abstraction? And if the purpose of a mixed constitution is to hold governmental actors accountable to achieving, or at least aiming at, the common good, would not abstractly formulating this principle of accountability and its foundation help clarify the constitution's purpose? The statement of principles in the Declaration of Independence defines the common good as, in relation to government at least, protection of citizens' natural rights, and hints at the concrete meaning of natural rights by spelling out, in the middle section of the document, how those rights have been violated. The statement suggests the principle of accountability in its assertion that the "just powers" of government are derived from "the consent of the governed." If someone like Burke or Gentz complains that this implies the illegitimacy of all non-elective governments, this argument is

[49] In fairness to Gentz, France *did* have a mixed constitution in the form of the crown, the three Estates, and the *parlements*, and the people *did* have constitutional representation through the Third Estate, a representation not merely notional but concretely operational at the outset once the king called a meeting of the Estates. So in this particular case, his argument would hold, even if theoretically he fails to account for the case of simple despotism.

undermined by the explicit right to change the form of government if a different form seems more likely to achieve the common "safety and happiness"—i.e., any number of forms might do the trick, and whether a republican form should be adopted rather than some other is a prudential judgment each people has a right, in the last resort, to make for itself as a community. Clearly the Americans had concluded that monarchy was not a form of government likely to attain the goal and that a mixed government would work best, but the mixed government they had enjoyed before had included an unelected monarch, and they would later, after the failed experiment with the Articles of Confederation, bring back a monarchical component in the form of an indirectly elected, independent, single executive. The larger point is that the abstract principles of the Declaration were not *to Americans* an empty pomp of words; the words were for them grounded in experience and considered with an eye to practical means. Gentz does indeed imply that natural law is the ultimate standard for judging, but he does not make explicit the connecting links between natural law and the circumstances, something he really needs to do to clinch his ultimate case that the American Revolution was right and the French Revolution was wrong.[50]

In the end, however, the difference between the American and French revolutions comes down to something deeper than a divergence in thinking about rights and circumstance. It is not as if the French Revolution went the way it did merely from a failure to master some intellectual puzzle that the Americans managed to solve. The critical point is why the Americans and the French should have been *disposed* to thinking of rights as they did. On this question, per-

[50] Gentz *had* tried to adumbrate the "a priori" principles implicit in Burke's analysis in his translation of Burke's *Reflections* (see footnote 10, above), so his failure to articulate first principles in this essay was not a general failure of his political philosophy. In light of that, his dismissive attitude toward the Declaration's statement of principles is somewhat baffling.

haps no thinker has ever addressed the key factors with as much penetrating insight as Alexis de Tocqueville.[51]

Regarding the French case, Tocqueville says in his *Ancien Régime and the French Revolution* that the old regime would have died inevitably. The questions for him were why it collapsed so suddenly and why the collapse was followed by such a disaster. The basic reason for the sudden collapse, in Tocqueville's judgment, was that the monarchs preceding Louis XVI had systematically demolished all the old "intermediary powers" between the state and the people, in the process destroying old local liberties[52] and breaking the bonds that held classes, and individuals within the classes, together in a tolerable harmony.[53] At the same time, this removed all external supports that could have helped the government weather severe crises like the financial crisis and bread shortages immediately preceding the Revolution. The population was left abjectly dependent on the government, which now was the only means of getting anything done, and which made them feel that when problems arose in society the government alone was to blame and the government alone could provide a solution.[54] The final result was that, "Nothing was left that could obstruct the government, nor anything left that could hold it up."[55] When the storm came, and the government was unable to respond effectively, it quickly collapsed and was easily replaced by an equally absolute government, there being no external means to check the new, popular government either, especially after the new constitution was suspended in the name of a need for extraordinary emergency powers.

---

[51] A reading of Tocqueville's *Ancien Régime and the French Revolution* should be supplemented by François Furet's superb *Interpreting the French Revolution*, trans. Elborg Forster (Cambridge: Cambridge University Press, 1981). Furet takes Tocqueville's analysis of the Revolution as a primary inspiration for his interpretation.

[52] Alexis de Tocqueville, *The Ancien Regime and the French Revolution*, trans. Arthur Goldhammer (Cambridge: Cambridge University Press, 2011) 93-111.

[53] Ibid., 80-92.

[54] Ibid., 67-70.

[55] Ibid., 124.

The old regime's collapse was followed by disaster partly because the government had wrecked the people themselves by destroying their liberties and communities, and partly because their minds had been prepared for extreme action by the radical writings of the *philosophes*. These "false ideas, corrupt habits and wicked inclinations that [their] rulers had imparted to them or allowed them to acquire" rendered the people "incapable of governing themselves."[56] Underlying the various "systems" of the *philosophes* was "one very general notion ... a general notion that seems to have preexisted, and to be the common source of, all the other, more specific ideas," and that was the notion "that it was proper to replace the complex traditional customs that governed the society in which they lived with certain simple, elementary rules, which could be deduced from reason and natural law." Here we find Tocqueville at his most Burkean. The particular idea that took center stage for the *philosophes* was "the idea of a natural equality of conditions." This had been "compelled" rather naturally by "the sight of so many abusive and ridiculous privileges, whose oppressiveness was increasingly felt yet whose grounds were less and less apparent." Unfortunately, "The situation of these writers fostered in them a taste for abstract, general theories of government, theories which they trusted blindly. Living as they did almost totally removed from practical life, they had no experience that might have tempered their natural passions."[57]

It was especially the ideas of the *philosophes*, or rather the popular enthusiasm for those ideas, that gave the Revolution its magical quality. What the *philosophes* had produced was not really philosophy but "passion disguised...as philosophy," or what we today might call "ideology," and this ideological passion was in some sense the very "substance" of the Revolution.[58] The people, having been corrupted under

---

[56] Ibid.

[57] Ibid., 128-29.

[58] Ibid., 16. The term "ideology" was actually coined by a late eighteenth-, early nineteenth-century French philosopher, Destutt de Tracy. Ironically, Tracy meant the term to denote a science—a science of ideas. Thomas Jefferson was an admirer of Tracy's work and published in English an outline of his massive *Ele-*

the absolutism of the monarchs, allowed the perverting substance of ideological passion to fill the void of their lost virtue. The popularity of the ideology had been enabled, ironically, by the indulgence of the nobles, who played with the theories as "ingenious intellectual games," oblivious to how they were undermining their own social positions.[59] This "game" played by the intellectuals and the nobles was treated as much more than a game by the leaders of the Revolution. Voltaire's verbal raging against the Church (*ecrasez l'enfame!*) turned into the arbitrary arrest and murder of priests; Rousseau's incautious Platonic thought experiment in *The Social Contract* was taken (mistakenly, I think, but not altogether implausibly) to justify terror in the name of "the people."[60]

---

ments of Ideology for American readers. See Destutt Tracy, *A Treatise on Political Economy, to Which is Prefixed a Supplement to a Preceding Work on the Understanding, or Elements of Ideology*, trans. Thomas Jefferson (Georgetown, D. C.: Joseph Milligan, 1817).

[59] Ibid., 130-31. Eric Voegelin noticed a similar enabling phenomenon among German intellectuals preceding the rise of Hitler and called it *divertissement*, a term he borrowed from Pascal. See Voegelin, *Hitler and the Germans*, trans. Detlev Clemens and Brendan Purcell, in *The Collected Works of Eric Voegelin*, vol. 31 (Columbia: University of Missouri Press, 199) 242-51.

[60] Robespierre and his strongest supporter, Saint-Just (also on the Committee for Public Safety), were deeply enamored of Rousseau and took him as a guiding light. See Ruth Scurr, *Fatal Purity: Robespierre and the French Revolution* (New York: Henry Holt and Company, 2006) 231-32, and R.R. Palmer, *The Year of the Terror*, 74-77. Rousseau was a genuine philosopher—his thought was more than mere ideology—but as with Nietzsche in later days, some of his words were imminently serviceable for extreme ideological projects. Four points from *The Social Contract* lend themselves, for superficial readers, to potentially disastrous misunderstandings, all of which were adopted by the radical revolutionaries: (1) confusion of majority will for the general will, which really was Rousseau's conception of the common good; (2) the assertion that the general will cannot err; (3) the idea of a wise "lawgiver" who could recognize and interpret the general will for the people (Robespierre saw himself as uniquely capable of doing this); and (4) the idea that those who resisted the general will by pursuing a factional "particular will" would be "forced to be free," thereby eliminating factions. Jean-Jacques Rousseau, *The Major Political Writings of Jean-Jacques Rousseau: The Two Discourses and The Social Contract*, trans. John T. Scott (Chicago: University of Chicago Press, 2012) 185, 182, 190-94, 175, 182-83.

Ideological fervor—"passion disguised as philosophy"—was the essence of the Revolution's magic. As Burke had observed in the *Reflections*, the French revolutionaries acted from "a pious implicit faith in the dogmatism of philosophers," or rather, of "a cabal, calling itself philosophic," who offered in their system a "panacea" for everything that ailed France. At the instigation of these dogmatists, the revolutionaries "put [their national traditions] into the kettle of magicians, in hopes that by their poisonous weeds, and wild incantations, they may regenerate the paternal constitution, and renovate their father's life" (the life of the country that birthed and raised them).[61] Or, as Tocqueville put it,

> On top of the real society, whose constitution remained traditional, confused, and haphazard, and in which laws were still diverse and contradictory, ranks clearly defined, conditions fixed, and tax burdens unequal [Tocqueville was much more critical of the *ancien régime* than Burke was], an imaginary society was constructed piece by piece, in which everything seemed simple and coherent, uniform, equitable, and shaped by reason.
>
> Gradually, the imagination of the multitude deserted the former and retreated into the latter. People lost interest in what was in order to dream about what might be, and in their minds they lived in the ideal city that the writers had constructed.[62]

The dream became universalized; it was a dream not just for the French but for mankind. Their bold enterprise—for they meant to live out the dream—was driven by a kind of religious passion:

> Since it appeared to aim at the regeneration of the human race even more than at the reform of France, it kindled a passion that not

---

[61] Burke, *Revolutionary Writings*, 92, 100.

[62] Tocqueville, *Ancien Régime*, 133. Eric Voegelin calls the phenomenon Tocqueville describes here "second reality." (The precise equivalence of their separate descriptions is quite remarkable.) Voegelin spoke of fabricating and trying to live in second realities as "magic operations," and he thought understanding these was the key to understanding modern revolutionary activism. See *Hitler and the Germans*, 108, 239-256, 262-64.

> even the most violent political revolutions had ever aroused before. It inspired a proselytism and propaganda and therefore came to resemble a religious revolution, which was what contemporaries found so frightening about it. Or, rather, it itself became a new kind of religion.[63]

The central doctrine of the new religion was belief in "the perfectibility or power of man" and "in themselves," the French people, that it was their special mission to "transform society" and save the world.[64] They believed in the imaginary world and in a human power to make it suddenly appear because they badly wanted to believe it. They believed in their will to transform. They believed, in other words, in magic.

The American disposition concerning justice and its requirements had been shaped by factors quite different from those obtaining in the French case. In contrast to the situation in absolutist France, Americans enjoyed deep-rooted, long-standing traditions of liberty inherited from England and supplemented by more than 150 years of continuous local self-government. Their religious situation was also dramatically different. Tocqueville thought that the irreligion of the *philosophes* had played a role in "deranging minds" of the French revolutionaries, though he thought the long-term effects of the "antireligious efforts" were minimal, since Catholicism had after the Revolution been restored to an honorable place.[65] He thought that "it was much less as religious doctrine than as political institution that Christianity aroused [in France] such fanatical hatred."[66] In any case, it was certain that the Church in France had been a political

---

[63] Ibid., 21. "Religion" indeed is a more adequate term for what was happening than "ideology," which connotes ideas or concepts but not immediately the passions the ideas disguise or the mass movements driven by those passions. The ideas give form to the movement, but passion is what drives it and what gives the ideas their great power.

[64] Tocqueville, *Ancien Régime*, 142.

[65] I think Tocqueville was mistaken about the effects being short-lived. I am inclined to believe the irreligion permanently affected the French intellectual class, and that this did much in the long run to shape modern French culture.

[66] Ibid., 141, 16.

power and that this had contributed greatly to discredit it. In America, by contrast, while a number of colonies, and then states, had church establishments, special church privileges were minimal compared to the French case, religious public discourse was scrupulously non-sectarian, and there was never any movement toward a national (as opposed to regional) establishment. In *Democracy in America*, Tocqueville had in fact suggested that the root of American democracy was its combination of "the spirit of religion and the spirit of freedom,"[67] and by the time of the founding there was nowhere in America anything like the strict religiously controlled community of the old Massachusetts Bay Colony. Far from hating their churches, Americans universally praised them for their role in the moral education of citizens (even if there were some complaints about denominational intolerance).

There were, moreover, crucial differences between American religion and the "new religion" of the French Revolution. First, and most obviously, the Americans' religion was not new or cooked up by *avant-garde* intellectuals, but traditional (at least in relation to Protestantism) and deeply rooted in American mores. Second, while religion was a major motive force for fighters in the American Revolution,[68] the religion itself was not revolutionary but conservative. It was conservative in the dual sense of being thoroughly established and of discouraging radical thinking or behavior. As Tocqueville said, American religious beliefs imposed "habits of restraint" so that, despite their great political freedom, their "religion prevents them from conceiving everything and forbids them to dare everything." "Up to now," he said (meaning to the 1830s), "no one has been encountered in the United States who dared to advance the maxim that everything is permitted in the interest of society."[69] A Calvinistic pessimism about human nature prevented them from "believing in themselves" or "the

[67] Alexis de Tocqueville, *Democracy in America*, trans. Harvey C. Mansfield and Delba Winthrop (Chicago: University Press of Chicago, 2000) 43.

[68] See Alice M. Baldwin, *The New England Clergy and the American Revolution* (Durham, N.C.: Duke University Press, 1928).

[69] Tocqueville, *Democracy in America*, 279-80.

perfectibility" or transformative "power of man" the way the French did, and, regular churchgoers as they were, their ministers never let them forget that sin is always crouching at the door. Their impassioned belief in the justice of their revolutionary cause and faith in American progress was checked at every turn by remembrance of "the Supreme Judge of the world" and the awful mystery of "Providence" (to use the language of the Declaration of Independence), who would surely bless them if they kept his commands but curse them if they did not.[70] If this attitude was more typical of ordinary Americans than of the intellectual elite, it was sufficiently pervasive to compel the Continental Congress to order during the Revolution several national days of "fasting, humiliation, and prayer," or of "thanksgiving," as the occasion seemed to warrant.[71]

The intellectual context of the American Revolution was also quite different from the French context. The French *philosophes*, though read by some of the most educated Americans, were not a major source of revolutionary inspiration. The only French thinkers significant for American political thought were Montesquieu and natural law theorist Jean Barbeyrac. The primary inspirations relative to the American Revolution were English thinkers (especially Locke) and leading lights of the Scottish Enlightenment (especially Hume, Smith, and Thomas Reid). None of these thinkers were radical in relation to the American context, at least not concerning politics. (Whatever obviously radical elements were there, such as Hume's skepticism, were roundly rejected.)

---

[70] There *was* religious exuberance in the American Revolution. See, for example, Nathan O. Hatch, *The Sacred Cause of Liberty: Republican Thought and the Millennium in Revolutionary New England* (Yale: Yale University Press, 1977). But whatever apocalyptic fervor was involved, it was largely kept in check by sober clergymen and political leaders.

[71] For a comprehensive overview of the religious leanings of the Continental Congress, see Derek Davis, *Religion and the Continental Congress, 1774-1789: Contributions to Original Intent, 1774-1789* (Oxford: Oxford University Press, 2000). Days of religious observance are addressed in Chapter 5.

Friedrich von Gentz recognized that the situations in America and France on the eve of their revolutions were dramatically different, though he did not give much detailed attention to the factors just addressed, except in relation to the American political background. But he succeeded, I would argue, at getting down to the most decisive difference between the revolutions: the prudence and moderation of the American movement against the ideological passion of the French. He did not take note of American religiosity in *Origin and Principles*, and he only hinted at the religious quality of the French Revolution. But he brilliantly captured that quality in the French case under the heading of "magic," or more precisely "fantastic arbitrary will." As we have seen, Burke noticed this too, as did Tocqueville, but Gentz brought it into sharper focus than either of them, and unlike them, he offered a direct, extended comparison of the French and American revolutions by which those great events are mutually and glowingly illuminated.[72] For these achievements, Gentz's essay deserves the appellation of a minor classic, a worthy companion to Burke's and Tocqueville's masterworks.

Now, for a final word, the basic insights of these three writers are as applicable to revolutionary politics in the twentieth and twenty-first centuries as they were to those earth-shaking movements we have just examined. Virtually all the modern revolutions have followed the French model. Tocqueville was right when he said that the French Revolution produced "revolutionaries of a previously unknown species, who carried boldness to the point of folly, whom no innovation could surprise nor scruple slow, and who never shrank from executing any design." He ominously added that, "One must not think... that these new beings were the singular and ephemeral creations of a

---

[72] I have just indicated that viewing Tocqueville's *Democracy in America* and *Ancien Regime* together provide a kind of *indirect* comparison, and though Burke wrote on the American Revolution (largely favorably), he never treated it systematically nor made any significant comparative analysis with the French. Burke's view of the American Revolution can be gleaned from his "Thoughts on the Cause of the Present Discontents" and "The Two Speeches on America," in *Select Works of Edmund Burke*, vol. 1 (Indianapolis: Liberty Fund, Inc., 1999).

moment, destined to vanish when it did. They have since formed a race that has perpetuated itself and spread to all the civilized corners of the earth, a race that has everywhere retained the same appearance, the same passions, and the same character."[73] Marx celebrated the French revolutions of 1789, 1848, and especially the aftermath of 1870 (which resulted in the Paris Commune), as did Lenin after him.[74] Lenin made French-style terror a tool of the state, employed to maximum degree and devastating effect by Joseph Stalin, as did Mao Zedong in China and Pol Pot in Cambodia, all of them committed to total, transformative revolution. Around the late Stalinist era, jihadist ideologists like Sayyid Qutb began to adopt Leninist categories and methods that were themselves ultimately traceable to the original French Revolution—perceiving the world in terms of irreconcilably antagonistic systems, forming an enlightened vanguard to awaken and lead the people, proposing universal designs, propaganda campaigns, purges, and a drive to sweep away the existing world through total revolution—and jihadists continue to think and operate on these lines today.[75] Surely it would be too much to blame the carnage of all these movements on the French Revolution, and we have not the space here to consider positive outcomes of that event owing to its earlier, more moderate phase. But a close study of the French Revolution, in comparison with the American Revolution, would surely help us to understand later revolutionary movements more deeply and think through the possibilities for preventing, directing, or responding to revolutionary change. In such an effort, assistance from works like Gentz's might prove invaluable.

---

[73] Tocqueville, *Ancien Régime*, 142.

[74] See Marx's "The Class Struggles in France, 1848-1850"; *The Eighteenth Brumaire of Louis Bonaparte*; and "The Civil War in France," in Karl Marx and Friedrich Engels, *The Marx-Engels Reader*, 2nd ed., ed. Robert C. Tucker (New York: W. W. Norton & Company, 1978) 586-652. Lenin comments on the French revolutions and their significance in "Socialism and War" and *The State and Revolution*, in Vladimir Il'ich Lenin, *The Lenin Anthology*, ed. Robert C. Tucker (New York: W. W. Norton & Company, 1975) 184, 363-67.

[75] See Scott Philip Segrest, "ISIS's Will to Apocalypse," *Politics, Religion & Ideology*, 17:4 (2016): 361-363.

PART III

1776 IN AMERICAN MEMORY

6

"FAME IS A FORM OF INCOMPREHENSION": HOW WE READ 1776

Brian Steele

> "of all the ways of acquiring books, writing them oneself is regarded as the most praiseworthy method....
>
> Actually, inheritance is the soundest way of acquiring a collection.... and the most distinguished trait of a collection will always be its transmissibility."
>
> Walter Benjamin, "Unpacking My Library" (1931)

When historians are asked to wrestle with the question of legacies, as we have been in this volume, they face a conundrum of sorts, because the legacy—the continuing present significance—of any historical event or phenomenon, say of 1776, cannot be *quite* the same thing as 1776 itself (however obviously and intimately related the two may be). This point is in essence a description of the difference between history and the past: between everything that happened in 1776 and the narratives we tell about it, narratives that are not inherent in the events themselves.[1] It's also a description of the difference between intention or meaning on the one hand, and *significance*, on the other, a distinction well-described by the "Cambridge School" associated with Quentin Skinner and J.G.A. Pocock whose work has profoundly influenced my thinking even as I would like to say something a bit different than what their work over the years has insisted upon. I'd

---

[1] See Hayden White, "Historical Text as Literary Artifact," in *Tropics of Discourse: Essays in Cultural Criticism* (Baltimore: Johns Hopkins University Press, 1986) 81-100.

like to begin by noting straight away that the most *significant* thing that happened in 1776 was the founding of a nation, the inauguration of a tradition, the creation of a public, an interpretative community within which the opinions of the "fathers" of the revolutionary generation are heard, and within which their actions continue to have meaning.[2] I say this about 1776—and I am able to say it (it is thinkable, *sayable*, in other words)—only because it is retroactively made the case, and because we, 1776's "posterity," have continued in various ways to affirm what they did.

I also say it against an enormous and growing—and quite compelling—body of literature that emphasizes the contingency of nationhood and union in 1776 and into what we now call the "early republic."[3] Few historians would now say what I have said—that the most significant thing that happened in 1776 was the creation of a nation—without substantial qualification and without noting the teleological and anachronistic assumptions embedded in the statement. Philip Roth is not wrong to say that history, insofar as it is treated as a "science" often "hides" what was felt at the time as "the terror of the unforeseen," and transforms "disaster" or profound uncertainty "into an epic" almost impossible to read as anything but determined, inevitable.[4] But he might be wrong to imply that professional historians are not with him all the way in his insistence upon contingency. In fact, it is rather our national collective memory that tends to fuse significance and meaning, turning a fragile Union hanging on for dear life—whose collective work would have been remembered only by

---

[2] Hannah Arendt, *On Revolution* (New York: Viking Press, 1963); Arendt, *Between Past and Future* (New York: Viking Press, 1954) 153; Douglass Adair, "Fame and the Founding Fathers," in Trevor Colbourn, ed., *Fame and the Founding Fathers: Essays by Douglass Adair* (Indianapolis: Liberty Fund, 1998) 3-36.

[3] See, among others, David Hendrickson, *Peace Pact: The Lost World of the American Founding* (Lawrence: University of Kansas Press, 2003), and (even more germane to this essay), David Armitage, *The Declaration of Independence: A Global History* (Cambridge, MA: Harvard University Press, 2006).

[4] Roth, *The Plot Against America* (New York: Houghton Mifflin, 2004) 113-114.

historians of the British Empire had the Continental Army not won the war—into the natal story of a great Republic.

And so, if many historians would not say it at all, it is also worth remembering that my emphasis on nation-making in 1776 is not of necessity a normative and unqualifiedly celebratory statement. What, after all, would the creation of the nation mean? If 1776 was a constitutive moment—a radically equalizing moment—from the perspective of insiders, it was surely also a settler revolt to protect the corporate integrity and prerogatives of long-standing communities of British provincials in North America, prerogatives that included social supremacy vis-à-vis subordinated groups—including slaves—and the right to continental expansion and the dispossession of Indians unhindered by London. That is to say that the American Revolution was from one perspective a wrenching of imperial prerogative from London by settlers who saw dispossession of Indians and unencumbered domination of slaves as essential to the radically egalitarian project celebrated even today by the national mythology.[5] But I am making the claim here about the founding of a nation, and hope to defend it in spite of the fact that this literature is so compelling. And that takes us to my central preoccupation—or one of them. I'd originally planned to distinguish the ways that historians (I speak in general terms) read historical events like 1776 (and the texts that emerge from them) from what political theorists, generally speaking, tend to do with the same. And I'd planned to argue that we need both ways of approaching these questions if we're really going to make sense of the founding and understand its legacy. Some of this will come out in the essay that follows, but I hope to get at these questions in a more

[5] See Aziz Rana, *The Two Faces of American Freedom* (Cambridge, MA: Harvard University Press, 2011); Jack P. Greene, *Peripheries and Center* (W.W. Norton, 1990); Jack P. Greene, ed., *Exclusionary Empire: English Liberty Overseas, 1600-1900* (Cambridge: Cambridge University Press, 2009); Craig Yirush, *Settlers, Liberty, and Empire: The Roots of Early American Political Theory, 1675-1775* (Cambridge: Cambridge University Press, 2011); Brian Steele, "The Literature of Revolution," in Kevin Hayes, ed., *The Cambridge History of Virginia Literature* (Cambridge: Cambridge University Press, 2015).

oblique fashion by thinking about 1776 through the lens of a literary text far removed from the events of 1776—a story by the Argentine writer Jorge Luis Borges—because I think Borges will help us think more clearly about the ways we read historical texts in general and events like 1776 in particular.

In defense of this approach, I'm quite certain that 1776 is big enough to handle multiple approaches to it. I don't think the Founders would tremble at such a project. Jefferson himself once wrote a beautiful letter to Robert Skipwith arguing that fiction is as effective and perhaps better as a teacher of ethical and moral lessons (about the real world, that is) than a shelf of treatises on morality. Not known as a great reader of fiction, Jefferson was, nevertheless, a huge fan of Laurence Sterne and, as it turns out, of Cervantes, whose *Don Quixote* he read on the passage to France as an aid to learning Spanish. Can we extrapolate a bit and assume that he might find fiction a not entirely unworthy way to approach or think through the founding moment?

* * *

To speak of legacies is to make an explicit appeal to values—or at least to the significance for us now, in the present, of some event or text or set of occurrences in the past (which, in turn, reveals a good deal about what we value now). And this is tricky because historians don't typically see such appeals as historical, or, rather, they insist on not mistaking "the coherence of a work or body of political writing, as political philosophy or as political theory" for "its character as a historical phenomenon," much less mistaking present use for historical event or intention.[6] Historians are, in theory, so committed to the recovery of *meaning* through deep contextualization that they can say little (or at least it is unnecessary and even anachronistic for them to

[6] J.G.A. Pocock, "Languages and Their Implications," in his *Politics, Language, and Time: Essays on Political Thought and History* (Chicago: University of Chicago Press, 1971) 6.

say much) about the present value or *significance* of those texts or events.

These are worthy commitments and help distinguish intellectual history as a discipline from philosophy or political theory. Historians don't think you can just read texts over and over, though they certainly do so as part of the effort to recover "the text as it bore meaning in the mind of the author or his contemporary reader."[7] What historians are going for, J.G.A. Pocock says, is "what *eigentlich* [actually] happened or—the special form which this takes in the history of thought—what *eigentlich* was meant."[8] And to understand what was meant, it is essential to explore the text in its larger context because we can derive the meanings of texts (broadly defined) only by "placing" them within what Quentin Skinner calls the "fields of meaning" within which they first entered the world.[9] To extract a text from and read it outside of the discursive formations within which it had meaning, within which it intended to speak, is a perfectly legitimate thing to do, but it is not, Pocock insists, historical inquiry. And that is because to do this damages the text or event and obscures its "original" meaning. For Pocock, only the "non-historical practitioner" can be less "concerned with what the author of a statement made in a remote past meant by it" than with "what" said practitioner "in his present can make it mean."[10] This kind of careful differentiation certainly preserves us in crucial ways from gross manipulation and abuse of history. Do what you want with a text, Pocock seems to say, just don't call it history unless you've done the work necessary to understanding "what *eigentlich* was meant." And if you have not, by no means preface your discussion of texts with the words, to take Pocock's example, "Hobbes said."[11]

---

[7] Ibid.

[8] Ibid., 7.

[9] Quentin Skinner, "Sir Geoffrey Elton and the Practice of History," *Transactions of the Royal Historical Society*, vol. 7 (1997): 301-316, at 302.

[10] Pocock, "Languages and their Implications," 7.

[11] Ibid., 8. Pocock suggests this preface instead: "if we repeat these words of Hobbes under given conditions, there ensue the following results." Which of

Insofar as historians situate texts and events in a time and place removed from the present, they play an important role in a republican polity as demythologizers. And to demythologize you must contextualize, understand texts and events on their own terms, allowing them to mean what they did at the time of their happening. All this said, nevertheless, this emphasis on deep contextualization, however essential to understanding something as complex as the American Revolution, also has a couple of other effects I consider to be less salutary—really, the defects of virtues—and to which political theorists and philosophers might be more attuned, I think.[12] One is that it tends to make historians *qua* historians less interested in the actual value of the texts for us today. Historians often move in the spirit of the classic image of the field anthropologist studying an exotic tribe: we should not presume an unjustified familiarity with the natives, and we want to come to understand how they think, not because that might shake us up and encourage us to live differently in the present—not because they have anything really to say to us, that is—but because it is simply worth knowing how people in that exotic culture live.[13] For historians, of course, the exotic culture is the past—which at least one histo-

---

course raises serious questions about the value of any reading forced to make this qualification.

[12] On the way of reading of texts associated with the humanities, and a distinguishing of this orientation from philosophy and political theory, see James Turner, *Philology: The Forgotten Origins of the Modern Humanities* (Princeton University Press, 2014).

[13] Though the "Cambridge School" has (perhaps understandably) been accused of being antiquarian in orientation, the charge is (though understandable) quite misleading and does not apply to the subtle formulations of Pocock and Skinner in particular however it may to other historians who have been influenced by their work. See Skinner's brilliant description of the value to the present of exploring—excavating, really—the past, in *Liberty Before Liberalism* (Cambridge: Cambridge University Press, 1998) chapter 3, esp. 112-118. It diminishes the complexity of his description to say that Skinner argues that knowing the past keeps us from becoming complaisant about the naturalness and superiority of our values. But this is certainly, I believe, within the spirit of the argument.

rian has explicitly called "a foreign country."[14] Historians committed to deeply contextualized readings of past events want to get at that thing and explain why it isn't ours in quite the ways we tend to think it might be, and why it cannot possibly have meant then everything we can do with it now. Again, this is essential practice and encourages us to pause lest we be too quick to assume familiarity, to overlook subtle transformations in the meaning of language and in the accumulations of lived experience over time. But contextualization, at the extreme end of its logic, renders historical events and ideas and texts dead: if texts and events of the past have meaning fully realized only in that past, then they can have little significance for us consistent with historical integrity.[15]

The other effect has been to turn historians into professional ironists: sadder, wiser, *superior* in comprehension to both those people in the past who couldn't possibly have understood themselves in the complex way we scholars can today, as well as to the poor schmucks who think they can establish some one-to-one correspondence between history and the present significance: that the founders, for ex-

---

[14] David Lowenthal, *The Past is a Foreign Country* (Cambridge: Cambridge University Press, 1986). The original line comes from a novel by L. P. Hartley. See James Turner, *Philology,* 395n.18.

[15] Skinner, "Hermeneutics and the Role of History," *New Literary History*, vol. 7 (Autumn 1975): 209-232, at 216. Skinner's most well-known statement of this methodology is "Meaning and Understanding in the History of Ideas," *History and Theory*, vol. 8 (1969): 3-53. Skinner has revised and significantly refined this essay in light of criticism in his *Visions of Politics: Regarding Method*, vol. 1 (Cambridge University Press, 1992) 57-89. Also see his ruminations (an advisedly chosen word) in an interview with *The Art of Theory* (http://www.artoftheory.com/quentin-skinner-on-meaning-and-method/). See, too, Pocock, "Introduction: The State of the Art," in *Virtue, Commerce, and History: Essays on Political Thought and History, Chiefly in the Eighteenth Century* (Cambridge University Press, 1985) 1-34. A helpful, if perhaps too critical and slightly misleading, introduction to this literature is David Harlan, *The Degradation of American History* (Chicago: University of Chicago Press, 1997) 3-31. I would like to acknowledge here, in appreciation, that Harlan first led me to Borges and that I consider this essay an extrapolation from and exploration of some of the questions he raises.

ample, can be trotted out and consulted as "timeless oracles" who can offer solutions to current problems.[16] I suppose that would include both political figures like Ted Cruz and Michele Bachmann as well as some prominent political theorists (of the type criticized by Pocock and Skinner, who preface remarks with "Hobbes says"). It might also include ordinary people on the streets who read *popularized* history and visit the National Archives to see the shrine to the Declaration and the Constitution.[17]

So, however valuable the historical approach described by Skinner and Pocock, I want to suggest that we are not quite free to treat 1776 in quite this way—to contextualize it away as "foreign" to our present or to be bemusedly ironic about it—precisely because we live still in the same political community, the nation, that was created in 1776, and the historical narratives we tell about it (which, remember, are not quite the same as the socio-historical process as it unfolded in 1776) are in fact and continue to be constitutive of that political community. They are inextricable from current politics precisely because they are carrying on the tradition inaugurated at the founding moment. This makes us—in a very real sense—*contemporaries* of the

---

[16] See Lloyd Kramer, "Literature, Criticism, and Historical Imagination: The Literary Challenge of Hayden White and Dominick LaCapra," in Lynn Hunt, ed., *The New Cultural History* (Berkeley: The University of California Press, 1989) 104-105. Kramer helpfully describes "ironic historians" as "analysts of the gap that separated past descriptions of the world from what was actually happening in the world as historians now understand it" (104). The quote about "timeless oracles" is from Richard Hofstadter, *The Progressive Historians* (London: Jonathan Cape, 1969). For a thoughtful and less arrogant way of talking about how historians should approach the problem that historical actors may be unaware of the fullness of their intentions (and certainly of all the potential consequences of their actions), see John Ashworth, "The Relationship Between Capitalism and Humanitarianism," in Thomas Bender, ed., *The Antislavery Debate: Capitalism and Abolitionism as a Problem in Historical Interpretation* (Berkeley, 1992) 180-199, esp., 182-184.

[17] For a good example see the introduction to Pauline Maier, *American Scripture: Making the Declaration of Independence* (New York: Vintage Books, 1997).

founding generation, and it means that we can't assume ourselves to be indifferent or utterly objective in our evaluation of it.[18]

For while such texts and events must be contextualized (as incredibly difficult as that project is), such texts and events also—as we so rightly recognize in this volume—have a legacy. They slip the boundaries of their language paradigm, the particular political culture in which they were birthed, and they speak to us. "Living events" like these, as Wolfgang Iser reminds us, "remain open." Or, as Frank Kermode notes, texts like the Declaration have "qualities not to be detected save at an appropriate moment in the future."[19] These events have legacies, afterlives. This is to say that I think the *significance* and not simply the *meaning* of historical texts and events are the province of historians, as long as we are careful to distinguish them from one another as honestly as we can. In other words, to turn Skinner and Pocock slightly around: if we want to understand the significance of a text or an event it is not sufficient to know what the authors intended or what it could have meant in the past. For an event like 1776 we need both.

I want to consider the legacy of 1776, especially of the Declaration of Independence, by turning to Borges. I do so not just because he is interesting, though he is that, but because his work (both in fiction and in his essays) is, I believe, essential—or at least very useful—for historians when they try to assess the significance of past events and texts.

Borges is a nearly uncategorizable writer who frequently disguised "his stories as essays" and in whose work the boundaries be-

---

[18] See reflections on this problem in Michel-Rolph Trouillot, *Silencing the Past: Power and the Production of History* (Boston: Beacon Press, 1995) chapter 1, esp. 16-24. Also see Brian Steele, "Thinking with Jefferson in the Age of Gatsby: Narratives of the Founding in American Political Discourse," *Amerikastudien*, vol. 61 (November 2016): 69-94.

[19] Iser, in "The Reading Process: A Phenomenological Approach," in David Richter, *The Critical Tradition: Classic Texts and Contemporary Trends*, Third Edition (New York: Bedford/St. Martin's, 2007) 1012; Frank Kermode, *Forms of Attention* (Chicago: University of Chicago Press, 2011) 75.

tween fiction and non-fiction are "notoriously blurred."[20] One of the finest examples of this is the wonderful story "Pierre Menard, Author of the *Quixote*," a brief memoir, by a friend, of the deceased writer Pierre Menard, who, we are told, left a body of work, almost exclusively non-fiction (along with some volumes of poetry).[21] This is, however, only the "*visible* work left" by Menard who, we are also told in the very first sentence, was a "novelist," though in the catalogue of his personal files there is not a single novel or a portion of any work of fiction.[22] But this *visible* work, listed, we are told, "in chronological order," is insignificant compared to "the subterranean, the interminably heroic, the peerless" and unfinished work, which turns out to be in the estimation of the narrator "perhaps the most significant of our time."[23] And what was this unfinished work? Precisely this: "The ninth and thirty-eighth chapters of the first part of *Don Quixote* and a fragment of chapter twenty-two."[24] Pierre Menard's life's work, in other words, was to write two chapters of the classic book by Cervantes. It is difficult for the reader to know at this point how to take the assertion. What a bewilderingly bizarre idea! Is Borges serious or is this just silly? The memorialist himself admits that it "seems an absurdity" and declares it to be his task, he tells us, to "justify" such a project as something fundamentally serious.[25]

So, if he's not simply transcribing the text, how does Menard go about writing it—arriving at the text? Menard had no interest in contemporary adaptations. The prospect of a "Don Quixote on Wall Street"—Menard simply "abhorred" with "all men of good taste." Such productions served either to feed "the plebeian pleasure of anachronism" or to "enthrall us with the elementary idea that all

[20] Eliot Weinberger, "A Note on This Edition," in Jorge Luis Borges, *Selected Non-Fictions*, ed., Weinberger (New York: Viking, 1999) xvi, xiv.

[21] Borges, *Labyrinths: Selected Stories and Other Writings*, ed., Donald A. Yates and James E. Irby (New York: New Directions, 1964) 36-44.

[22] Ibid., 36.

[23] Ibid., 38-9.

[24] Ibid., 39.

[25] Ibid.

epochs are the same or are different."[26] It is worth pausing here briefly to note that this is a description of a couple of the prime sins of the historical profession. Taken together, it seems, Borges (through this memorialist of Pierre Menard) is suggesting that all our most rigid efforts to catalogue or compartmentalize the past are doomed to some kind of failure.[27] Even the Cambridge School's careful excavation of texts is a kind of impossibility. Perhaps he is even suggesting—and this will be reinforced later in the story—that the historian must be in constant dialogue with an "autonomous past" which itself must be "allowed to question *our* recurring attempts to reduce it to order." "Every epoch," says intellectual historian Lloyd Kramer, "every important text, and every historical figure encompasses tendencies that defy and contradict the labels on which historiography depends."[28] Contexts themselves, upon which the distinction between meaning and significance turns, turn out themselves to be accessible to us at all, Dominick LaCapra reminds us, only via texts: "the past arrives in the form of texts and textualized remainders."[29]

In any case, Menard's plan was never "to compose another Quixote—which is easy—but *the Quixote itself*." Not to copy the *Quixote*, "*not a mechanical transcription of the original*," but just "a few pages which would coincide—word for word and line for line—with those of Miguel de Cervantes."[30]

The project, we are told, took him years of effort, sleepless nights, and "thousands of manuscript pages" (which he destroyed), all

---

[26] Ibid.

[27] It seems important to note that in both the stories, "On Exactitude in Science" in Jorge Luis Borges, *Collected Fictions*, trans. Andrew Hurley (Penguin Books 1998) 325, and "Funes the Memorious," in *Labyrinths*, 59-66, as well as the essay, "The Total Library" (1939), in *Selected Non-Fictions*, 214-216, Borges makes a crucially important case for the necessity of both categorization and reduction as well as interpretation.

[28] Kramer, "Literature, Criticism, and the Historical Imagination," 103.

[29] LaCapra quoted in Kramer, "Literature, Criticism, and the Historical Imagination," 115. See the helpful discussion on 114-117.

[30] "Pierre Menard," *Labyrinths*, 39.

for these few pages.[31] How to go about it? His first approach, our memorialist tells us, was simply to *become* Cervantes. How? "Know Spanish well, recover the Catholic faith, fight against the Moors or the Turk, forget the history of Europe between the years 1602 and 1918."[32] This project—in spite of its comic absurdity here—is not in all points unlike the prescription Pocock offers historians seeking to grasp the meaning of historical texts. First, "identify the 'language' or 'vocabulary' with and within which the author operated." Next, "show how it functioned paradigmatically to prescribe what he might say and how he might say it." It seems to boil down to an "empirical" investigation: these languages "are simply there" and "we get to know them," Pocock says, "by learning to speak them, to think in their patterns and styles until we know that we are speaking them and can predict in what directions speaking them is carrying us."[33] David Hollinger suggests that such a process would involve immersion in "the theoretical knowledge, literary and religious traditions, and other cultural resources that historians know to have been accessible to the most well-informed members of a given society at a given historical moment."[34] No simple task, it would seem. Yet Menard—fantastically, counterintuitively—discarded it as "too easy"![35] It is difficult to know what to make of such a claim except that Menard decided, says our narrator, that becoming "in the twentieth century, a popular novelist of the seventeenth" would be "a diminution" because "less arduous" and "less interesting" than it would be to "reach the

[31] Ibid.

[32] Ibid., 40. See also Walter Benjamin: "To historians who wish to relive an era, Fustel de Coulanges recommends that they blot out everything they know about the later course of history," in "Theses on the Philosophy of History," *Illuminations: Essays and Reflections*, ed. Hannah Arendt (New York: Random House, 1968) 256.

[33] Pocock, "Languages and Their Implications," 25-26.

[34] See Hollinger, "Historians and the Discourse of Intellectuals," in John Higham and Paul K. Conkin, eds., *New Directions in American Intellectual History* (Baltimore: The Johns Hopkins University Press, 1979) 55.

[35] "Pierre Menard," *Labyrinths*, 40.

Quixote through the experiences of Pierre Menard."[36] Cervantes had it easier because he could count on "chance."[37] In other words, Menard's task would be to "reconstruct" what was for Cervantes a "spontaneous" production.[38]

It was of course quite a "reasonable undertaking" for Cervantes "to compose the Quixote at the beginning of the seventeenth century."[39] It might even have been "necessary" and "unavoidable." But to do so in the twentieth century would be "almost impossible."[40] "It is not in vain that three hundred years have gone by," our narrator quotes Menard's commentary on his process, "filled with exceedingly complex events."[41] In other words, in the seventeenth century the Quixote was composed in its intellectual milieu, in its natural discourse. This is another way of saying that the intellectual historian's task of recovering that field of meaning is exceedingly complex. To be sure, Menard meticulously resists all temptation to embellish superficially in the manner of Flaubert's *Salammbo* (which elaborately fills in details left unclear by Polybius's original).[42] But despite this, his task's complexity is made that much more difficult by the event of "the Quixote itself."[43] The text itself, in other words, by the time Menard is working, has a history—a legacy, the result of its being interpreted and continually reconstructed (since, as Hans-Georg Gadamer points out, "even the naïve appropriation of tradition is a 'retelling'" rather

---

[36] Ibid.

[37] Ibid., 41.

[38] Ibid. A concept not unfamiliar to readers of Walter Benjamin, who once noted that: "The intention of the poet is spontaneous, primary, graphic; that of the translator is derivative, ultimate, ideational." Benjamin, "The Task of the Translator" (1923) in *Illuminations*, 76.

[39] "Pierre Menard," *Labyrinths*, 41.

[40] Ibid. See Borges's (critical) assessment of Richard Burton's translation of the *Nights*: "The basic problem," he says, was "how to entertain nineteenth-century gentlemen with the pulp fictions of the thirteenth century?" Borges, "The Translators of *The Thousand and One Nights*," in *Selected Non-Fictions*, 101.

[41] Ibid., 42.

[42] Ibid.

[43] Ibid., 39.

than a simple correspondence with the original).[44] However scrupulous Menard might be, the narrator suggests, he comes to learn that there no way for him to know the Quixote outside of the "event" of "the Quixote itself."

But here is the miracle: however insurmountable his task, Menard's Quixote turns out to be (counterintuitively?) "more subtle" than the original: "Cervantes' text and Menard's are verbally identical," the narrator tells us. "But the second is almost infinitely richer" and "more ambiguous."[45] The identical passage in Cervantes could never do the work that Menard's text is capable of in Menard's present precisely because it was not possible to mean in seventeenth-century Spain what Menard, "a contemporary of William James," might be understood to have intended by the same passage.[46] "History, the *mother* of truth!—the idea is staggering"[47] in Menard's *Quixote*, where in Cervantes's the same lines are "mere rhetorical praise of history" (though Cervantes, of course, had written identical words).[48] Cervantes, the narrator seems to say, could not possibly have meant what Menard could have—indeed, did—in his writing of the same passage, precisely because he could not be the beneficiary of the transformed world into which Menard himself would first arrive at the text, nor of the accumulated meanings acquired by the text itself as it had moved through generations of reading and interpretation and appropriation. This is why Menard's writing of the Quixote was a

---

[44] Hans-Georg Gadamer, *Truth and Method* (New York: Seabury Press, 1975) xxii.

[45] "Pierre Menard," *Labyrinths*, 42.

[46] Ibid., 43. Here is a kind of twisted endorsement of the Cambridge School's insistence that texts (however meticulously preserved by philologists, however "verbally identical") torn from the "fields of meaning" within which they emerged, cannot but be transformed by the present uses speakers of those same words make of them (Pocock couldn't say it better than Borges here, that the significance now cannot be *eigentlich* what was meant). But it is also an insistence that we cannot know them outside of our present, a suggestion that the space carved out by Pocock and Skinner is itself a kind of fiction.

[47] "Pierre Menard, Author of the *Quixote*," in *Collected Fictions*, 94

[48] "Pierre Menard," *Labyrinths*, 43.

lifetime's work. It is this very thing which makes Menard the *author* of the Quixote and not merely the re-writer or transcriber.

This difficulty—is it better to call it *possibility*?—travels both ways. If Cervantes could not possibly have meant what Menard might conceivably mean, it is likewise the case that Menard cannot fully enter into Cervantes's own intention (and he has the humility to understand this). This is why Borges tells us—in what may be the most significant line in the story—that "fame is a form of incomprehension."[49] In its own time, the *Quixote* was "above all, an entertaining book,"[50] now it is a work of art, and in our celebration of its fame as such we have unconsciously substituted significance for the present for what has in fact been lost: the intention with which it first entered the world (as well as what Benjamin called its "aura," because there is no longer a world in which it can *mean* as Cervantes intended).[51] We may think we understand what a text means, but we are in a sense blind both to what it could possibly have meant—which we might with intense effort be able to partially reconstruct—and also to the ways in which our reading of a text is always a participation in a re-writing of it, which on some level at least, cannot but take us ever farther away from the original. And Borges recognizes this: "There is no exercise of the intellect," he tells us, "which is not, in the final analysis, useless. A philosophical doctrine begins as a plausible description of the universe; with the passage of the years it becomes a mere chapter—if not a paragraph or a name—in the history of philosophy."[52] Note that the work of historians—secondary interpretative gloss—quickly becomes a primary source for later scholars, a cultural artifact of an era telling us more about the time of the historian perhaps than the past she purported to describe and explain.

---

[49] Ibid., 43.

[50] Ibid.

[51] Benjamin, "The Work of Art in the Age of Mechanical Reproduction," in *Illuminations*, 217-251. For subtle and profound (if problematic) reflections on this problem, also see Susan Sontag, *Against Interpretation* (New York: Farrar, Straus and Giroux, 1966) 3-14.

[52] "Pierre Menard," *Labyrinths*, 43.

But Borges I think does not leave us with quite so discouraging an ending. After all, what we give up in terms of getting back to the original meaning seems more than made up for by the revelations of the extraordinary richness of the rewriting. And this is, of course, a writer who once noted of a particular work, that "the original is unfaithful to the translation."[53] Is it possible for a translation to be superior to the original even though it succeeds it chronologically? Borges clearly *thinks* so. "Time, such a respected subversive, so famous for its demolitions and Italic ruins," he writes in another essay, "also constructs." "Time," is "Cervantes' friend," because it "has sagely revised his drafts."[54] This is obviously counterintuitive for most of us, and perhaps for historians in particular.

With "Pierre Menard," of course, we are not dealing with translation across languages, but over time.[55] And historians, as we have seen, are generally suspicious about the possibility of wrenching the meaning of the past undisturbed into the present. The historically-minded Max Weber was quick to distinguish "the spirit of the translators" from "the spirit of the original," claiming that the "present meaning" [of the word *Beruf*] "derives from the translations of the Bible."[56] The "present meaning," in other words, is a distortion emerging out of the present of the translators. Even Borges notes that translations "are a partial and precious documentation of the changes

---

[53] Borges, "On William Beckford's *Vathek*" (1943), *Selected Non-Fictions*, 239. Also see Borges, "The Homeric Versions" (1932), *Selected Non-Fictions*, 68: "To assume that every recombination of elements is necessarily inferior to its original form is to assume that draft nine is necessarily inferior to draft H – for there can only be drafts. The concept of the 'definitive text' corresponds only to religion *or exhaustion*;" and the interesting reflections on fidelity and license in Benjamin, "The Task of the Translator," in *Illuminations*, 77-78.

[54] Borges, "Literary Pleasure" (1927), in *Selected Non-Fictions*, 30.

[55] "There is no essential necessity to change languages; this intentional game of attention [the "long experimental game of chance played with omissions and emphases"] is possible within a single literature." Borges, "The Homeric Versions," 68.

[56] Weber, *The Protestant Ethic and the Spirit of Capitalism*, ed. Peter Baehr and Gordon C. Wells (New York: Penguin, 2002) 28.

the text suffers."[57] Pocock, remarkably sanguine about the ability of historians to become sufficiently immersed in the conceptual worlds and language systems of the past, is nevertheless even more straightforwardly hostile to the prospect of any clear coincidence between an "author's use of his words" and "his modern interpreter's use of them." Any "communication between author and interpreter... necessarily entails an element of translation and consequently of *traduttore traditore*."[58]

This is not necessarily at odds with Borges's conclusion in "Pierre Menard," though Borges is not interested in prosecuting traitors. Borges knows that Menard's work is extraordinarily different (it is by no means the same work, all appearances to the contrary). And despite his apparently cavalier attitude about translation, Borges insists that his view is neither "desperation [n]or nihilism." He certainly has no "wish to foment negligence."[59] He is quite aware of the "careless" anachronism of—to take his example—a translator's placing "the adjective *romantic* in the bearded mouth of a twelfth-century Muslim."[60] However, he never dismisses Menard's work as distortion or as harmful to Cervantes. And remember, Menard's project was a life's work, hardly "careless," demanding, rather, in the extreme. But Borges also describes the commonplace insistence upon "the inferiority of translations" as itself a "superstition... coined by the well-known Italian adage" [*traduttore traditore*] and "the result of absentmindedness."[61] For Borges, it is clear that translation is both an act of reverence (that which demands to be translated is that which is worthy of translation[62]), and also an act of preservation, even as it is inevitably—

---

[57] Borges, "The Homeric Versions," *Selected Non-Fictions*, 68.

[58] Pocock, "Languages and Their Implications," 7.

[59] Borges, "The Superstitious Ethics of the Reader" (1931), in *Selected Non-Fictions*, 54.

[60] "The Translators of *The Thousand and One Nights*" (1934-1936), in *Selected Non-Fictions*, 95.

[61] Borges, "The Homeric Versions," 68.

[62] And it must be, as Benjamin notes, "transmissible." See "Unpacking my Library" in *Illuminations,* 59-67.

as it is in the case of Pierre Menard—a re-writing of the original. And although we cannot even see clearly enough to parse out the "previous" writing from the "final" draft (in the palimpsest that becomes Menard's text)—the accumulated meanings acquired by the text in the course of its experience of interpretation (what Gadamer calls the *accretions* of the text)—we are the beneficiaries of readings that keep the text itself alive into the present. In this sense at least, Borges's assertions track with Walter Benjamin's sense that "a translation issues from the original" but "not so much from its life as from its afterlife." And it is the translation that "marks their stage of continued life."[63] The familiarity of Cervantes's *Quixote* allows us to pass over it without noticing. It becomes a fixed ruin of sorts. For "every image of the past that is not recognized by the present as one of its own concerns threatens to disappear irretrievably."[64] What Menard (and presumably each succeeding generation of Menards) does is force the text upon us again—though, significantly, only in fragments—so that its power and significance becomes manifest in the present, in the *Jetztzeit*, as Benjamin put it: "the time filled by the presence of the now."[65]

This point is further illuminated by another fascinating passage from Borges's essay on translations of the *Thousand and One Nights*, in which Borges wrestles with the "common knowledge" that certain nineteenth-century translators—Antoine Galland and Edward Lane, to be exact—"disinfected the *Nights*," by removing passages that might offend Victorian sensibilities. For all of Lane's firsthand experience in the Middle East (and its language paradigms), Borges writes, "neither the high Egyptian nights nor the black and opulent coffee with cardamom seed nor the frequent literary discussions with the Doctors of the Law nor the venerable muslin turban nor the meals eaten with his fingers made him forget his British reticence"

---

[63] Benjamin, "The Task of the Translator," in *Illuminations*, 71.
[64] Benjamin, "Theses on the Philosophy of History, in *Illuminations*, 255.
[65] Ibid., 261.

which turned his "exceedingly erudite version of the *Nights*" into "a mere encyclopedia of evasion."

But, counterintuitively, Borges disputes the claims of Galland and Lane's "detractors" who "argue that this process destroys or wounds the good-hearted naiveté of the original." "They are," Borges pronounces, "in error." Why? Because the original stories are "not obscene"—a focus on those passages or even a fastidious translation of them would miss the point. It is the "impassioned and sad" emphasis on "death for love" and the "atmosphere of magic" that emerge from the stories as translated and transform "the timidities of Galland and Lane" into "*the restoration of a primal text.*" I take this to mean that these corrections and omissions—which Borges earlier lampoons at length and with great good humor—in fact have removed what would have been distracting to "Victorian" sensibilities so that those readers could have access to, strange to say, the original. "An evasion of the original's erotic opportunities is not an unpardonable sin in the sight of the Lord," Borges writes, "when the primary aim is to emphasize the atmosphere of magic," which Borges suggests is the essential spirit of the stories. The *Nights*, through this process which detractors have dismissed as butchery, have been restored so that modern readers can experience them as the "repertory of marvels" they were when they first emerged in the world. Borges even goes so far as to say that Arab readers are "less fortunate than we" precisely because they are already so "well acquainted with the men, mores, talismans, deserts, and demons that the tales *reveal* to us."[66] This mirrors the way Cervantes's *Quixote*, in the very familiarity of its fame, has become incomprehensible.

Translation, in other words, is what keeps texts alive. Or to put it negatively, translation is what preserves them from death, from becoming mere lifeless chronicle. If, for Borges's narrator, alteration is the inevitable price a work pays for staying alive, it is also clear that, as with Menard's Quixote, the very transformation can potentially

[66] "The Translators of *The Thousand and One Nights*," in *Selected Non-Fictions*, 94-96. Emphasis added.

both exceed in power and illuminate or realize more fully the original. As for Benjamin, so with Borges, the "fame" of a work of art becomes manifest in the "potentially eternal afterlife" where "the life of the originals attains in [translations] to its ever-renewed latest and most abundant flowering." Originals live on in the translation, but only in the altered form of re-writing: "no translation," Benjamin insists, "would be possible if in its ultimate essence it strove for likeness to the original. For in its afterlife—which could not be called that if it were not a transformation and a renewal of something living—the original undergoes a change." Texts that remain alive in the imagination of later generations inevitably undergo "constant changes in meaning in the subjectivity of posterity" (just as neuroscientists tell us that with every memory we make subtle adjustments or calibrations that fit the memory into the altered state of our lives; this is not pathological but the opposite—essential to making our way through life). And this means for both Benjamin and for Borges, not a diminution but an insurance of continuing life. Benjamin likens it to birth: translation being the literary form "charged with the special mission of watching over the maturing process of the original language and the birth pangs of its own."[67] Borges sees this process as the source of "heterogeneous and even contradictory richness."[68] The richness emerges out of "the commerce between" the past and the present, between the seventeenth and nineteenth centuries even within a single literary (or, as we might suggest, political) tradition. It is the in-

[67] Benjamin, "The Task of the Translator," in *Illuminations*, 71-73. See Borges's skepticism of claims to a "'literal and complete' version of a passage composed in the thirteenth century," in "The Translators of *The Thousand and One Nights*," 103. Here, note, his critique is not that Mardrus is not a faithful translator but of such an assertion of completeness, literalness, which Borges would consider a missing of the point.

[68] Borges, "The Homeric Versions," 70-71. On this fundamental difficulty, see also Borges, "Shakespeare's Memory" in *Collected Fictions*, 508-515. Not that Borges is, as one would expect, ever entirely straightforward about it. Consider the labyrinthine passage in "The Homeric Versions," 74, and see "Translators of *The Thousand and One Nights*," 95.

corporation of the present into the past and vice versa that constitutes that tradition and perpetuates it.[69]

What has all of this to do with the legacy of 1776? Quite a lot. We can offer deeply rich, highly contextualized readings of that event—that is what historians do, and many do it quite well. But historians know better perhaps than others that today's interpretation of 1776 becomes tomorrow's cultural artifact of the era in which the interpretation was written (historiography itself is a kind of palimpsest). This is not to say that these readings are unhelpful, only that they are destined to be remembered less perhaps for what they tell us about 1776 than what they tell us about our tradition of interpreting 1776 and about what 1776 has meant to successive generations of Americans.

But this is also why I said at the outset that the most significant thing that happened in 1776 was the founding of a nation, the inauguration of a tradition, and the creation of an interpretative community. Without a community within which they continue to have meaning, texts and events lose their relevance. We can continue to have a conversation about perennial questions raised in 1776 only within a particular intellectual and cultural community and tradition that considers them to be relevant, perennial.[70]

In her essay in this volume, Diana Schaub asks us to consider the significance of Lincoln's "four score and seven years ago." The question of whether there is such a thing as a life-span for a political community was one the founding generation would generally have answered *yes*. And Lincoln raised the question explicitly in the Gettysburg Address: the war itself, he said, was a question about whether "any nation so conceived and so dedicated could long endure." It was a matter of the life or death of republican government itself, whether it would live or "perish from the earth." It was in this sense about the continuation of the founding moment in 1776. And Lincoln had a

[69] Borges, "The Translators of *The Thousand and One Nights*," 108.

[70] For a reflection on this idea see Paul Rahe, *Republics Ancient and Modern: Classical Republicanism and the American Revolution* (Chapel Hill: The University of North Carolina Press, 1992) 45-46.

profound sense, as did many of the founders, that the continuation of the project was not inevitable, but must be actively preserved.[71]

The fragility of interpretative communities is nowhere more compellingly (and tragically) illustrated than in Richard Wilbur's poem, "To the Etruscan Poets," which describes the few fragments we have of the Etruscan language—now untranslated or untranslatable. The texts exist. These poets speak, but there is no longer any community of remembrance within which their utterance has meaning. They left their verse "Like still fresh tracks across a field of snow/ Not reckoning that all could melt and go."[72] One cannot help thinking of Machiavelli's sense that republics that have long life are those whose orders and institutions have the capacity for self-renewal, that without this capacity for self-renewal republics "cannot continue to exist," and that the "mode of renewing them is… to lead them back toward their beginnings."[73]

Sheldon Wolin calls the tradition into which we have emerged a "birthright," and it's an interesting description (in his specific argument it is to be distinguished from contract), not least because birthrights are inherently messy things because fathers are both wise and they are foolish; they have good benevolent intentions and they have ulterior interests; they bequeath benefits and encumbrances.[74] Since they are messy, they are continually contestable; and since they are living, they are never closed to rewriting, just as legacies are always possible to compound or to squander. This makes them dangerous,

---

[71] Lincoln, "Address to the Young Men's Lyceum of Springfield: The Perpetuation of Our Political Institutions" (1832), in *Abraham Lincoln: Speeches and Writings, 1832-1858*, ed., Don E. Fehrenbacher (New York: Library of America, 1989) 28-36.

[72] Wilbur, *Collected Poems, 1943-2004* (New York: Houghton Mifflin, 2004) 130.

[73] Machiavelli, *Discourses on Livy*, Book 3, chap.1. The first quotation is from *The Prince and the Discourses*, trans. Luigi Ricci (New York: The Modern Library, 1950) 397; the second is from *Discourses on Livy*, ed. and trans., Harvey Mansfield and Nathan Tarcov (Chicago: University of Chicago Press, 1996) 209.

[74] Wolin, *The Presence of the Past: Essays on the State and the Constitution* (Baltimore: The Johns Hopkins University Press, 1989).

because they can always go either way (for example: we have a civic ideal of citizenship but we also have an ethnic history and a record of parsing out the benefits of citizenship on the basis of ascriptive characteristics. Which will be the more American? We think we know at any one moment, but at another, the question is re-opened.)[75] Aristotle wondered whether it was possible to judge or fully evaluate a man's life until he was dead—until the story was over. Until then, his character and meaning could still potentially go several ways.[76] So, as Lincoln put it, the meaning of the founding moment must be "constantly labored for, constantly approximated," just as Pierre Menard labored much of his working life—tearing up thousands of manuscript pages—to finally write those two and one half chapters of the *Quixote*. One day we too (collectively) may be remembered as having written a phrase or two of the Declaration of Independence. Certainly Lincoln always will be so remembered. This is possible as long as the political community within which this text retains salience lives and continues to remember and validate its authority.

We return, then, to 1776. The question raised by the following essays, about whether Lincoln was right about the founding—that the nation was created in the hope and expectation that slavery was in "the course of ultimate extinction" and that the founders understood this as consistent with the Declaration's spirit—continues to be controversial. The founding fathers left us a mixed bag on slavery and there is an argument to be made that Stephen Douglas was right about the founders not intending to include blacks in the equality of "all men." But remember, to understand the significance of a text it is not sufficient to know what was intended. Lincoln's reading of the founding—which is not by any means unpersuasive as history—

---

[75] See Rogers Smith, *Civic Ideals* (New Haven: Yale University Press, 1997); Steele, "Inventing Un-America," *Journal of American Studies* (2012): 881-902. And no one understands better or drives this home more clearly than Roth. See *The Plot Against America* (New York: Houghton Mifflin, 2004).

[76] Aristotle, *Nicomachean Ethics*, trans., Terence Irwin (Indianapolis: Hackett, 1999) Book 1, Chapter 10, p.13.

certainly *became* right in 1865 (or one might say 1863),[77] just as the independence that was declared in 1776 became real retroactively once the war was over. So there is a sense in which we're not getting back to the founding moment so much as re-writing it—or rather, to paraphrase Benjamin, our fidelity to origins is possible only because we have the license to re-write those origins.[78] Of course, both Benjamin and Borges understand that there must be something essential in the original that can emerge into the present. As Borges puts it: "the page that becomes immortal can traverse the fire of typographical errors, approximate translations, and inattentive or erroneous readings without losing its soul in the process." This is not true of just any text: "One cannot with impunity alter any line fabricated by Góngora," for example. "But *Don Quixote* wins posthumous battles against his translators and survives each and every careless version."[79] This is also Lincoln's (and Jefferson's) essential insight about the Declaration, about 1776: that the truths asserted there, because eternal, would travel well through and against the potential distortions of time.

As with Borges, founders like Jefferson wanted us to revere 1776 not as a dead record from the "musty" past, but as a living birthright that would continually force us to think about whether we were living up to the values articulated there and perfecting our ability to do so, making "periodical repairs" so that it might be "handed on... from generation to generation, to the end of time."[80] Each translation would allow the Declaration to remain alive in the present. Birthrights of this sort open in us a capacity for shame as well as pride and, in fact, the most successful American reformers have always appealed to the founding as aspiration: from the free black community in the north who almost immediately saw radical potential in the Declara-

[77] See the careful treatment in Don E. Fehrenbacher, *The Slaveholding Republic: An Account of the United States Government's Relations to Slavery*, completed and edited by Ward M. McAfee (Oxford: Oxford University Press, 2001).

[78] Benjamin, "Task of the Translator," in *Illuminations*, 77-78.

[79] "The Superstitious Ethics of the Reader," in *Selected Non-Fictions*, 54.

[80] Jefferson to Samuel Kercheval, July 12, 1816, in *Jefferson: Writings*, ed. Merrill D. Peterson (New York: Library of America, 1984) 1404.

tion and asserted claims for racial equality on the basis of its language; to the women's rights advocates at Seneca Falls in 1848; to Martin Luther King, Jr., who called upon America to live out into the present the "true meaning of its [original] creed."[81] And, perhaps especially, this applies to Lincoln (1776's Pierre Menard?) who always described as continuity what was in fact *also* a profound social and political transformation. Ending slavery demanded a social revolution, over 600,000 lives, and a government confiscation of property the likes of which the world would not see again, perhaps, until the twentieth century revolutions.[82] But the Declaration, in Lincoln's reading of it, allowed the nation to make the transition sound more or less seamless. We have always described even our most radical social transformations as a kind of natural or logical fulfillment of the original meanings that themselves justify and validate—might we even say *anticipate*?—those very transformations.

In the wake of the Kansas-Nebraska Act, Lincoln sardonically noted that "the fourth of July has not quite dwindled away; it is still a great day—*for burning fire-crackers!!!*" Lincoln had identified in the 1850s a threat to what he considered the American tradition. It was, as he increasingly recognized, what Benjamin would call "a moment of danger," danger to "the content of the tradition."[83] Lincoln's 1855 note of despair about a holiday increasingly devoid of meaning, a celebration of the original without any confidence about its significance in the present, is worth reading against the almost total collapse of any celebration of the Fourth of July in the South by the end of the Civil War. The holiday had become too closely associated with

---

[81] Mia Bay, "'See Your Declaration Americans!!' Abolitionism, Americanism, and the Revolutionary Tradition in Free Black Politics," in *Americanism: New Perspectives on the History of an Ideal*, ed., Michel Kazin and Joseph McCartin (Chapel Hill: University of North Carolina Press, 2006) 25-53; Stephen Kantrowitz, *More Than Freedom: Fighting for Black Citizenship in a White Republic, 1829-1899* (New York: Penguin Books, 2012); Steele, *Thomas Jefferson and American Nationhood* (Cambridge: Cambridge University Press, 2014) 302-304.

[82] See James McPherson, *Abraham Lincoln and the Second American Revolution* (New York: Oxford University Press, 1991).

[83] Benjamin, "Theses on the Philosophy of History," in *Illuminations*, 255.

emancipation and black equality for white southerners to any longer take part in it. Mary Chestnut put the story of the Civil War in a nutshell when she penned this entry into her Diary: "Black 4th of July – 1865."[84] The meaning of the event, still in contestation in 1855, had become clarified by 1865. In some fundamental sense, the Declaration had been re-written in the interim, even though it remained, as with Menard's Quixote, "verbally identical" to the original.

It all boiled down, in this case, as Lincoln himself noted, to a dispute over definitions of the same words. Hitherto, he wrote, the world has not "had a good definition of the word liberty" and, shockingly, even "the American people, just now," he wrote, "are much in want of one." Everyone is for liberty, "but in using the same *word* we do not all mean the same *thing*." "The shepherd drives the wolf from the sheep's throat, for which the sheep thanks the shepherd as a *liberator*, while the wolf denounces him for the same act as the destroyer of liberty, especially as the sheep was a black one. Plainly," Lincoln wrote, "the sheep and the wolf are not agreed upon a definition of the word liberty." With emancipation, Americans had "been doing something to define liberty." And by 1864, Lincoln asserted, "the wolf's dictionary, has been repudiated."[85] Or, as Benjamin put it in words that seem hardly irrelevant to Lincoln's description: "In every era the attempt must be made anew to wrest tradition away from a conformism that is about to overpower it. The Messiah comes not only as the redeemer, he comes as the subduer of Antichrist."[86]

If the "principles of '76," as Jefferson once wrote, would "forever form a point of union round which we," Americans "shall learn to

[84] Paul Quigley, "Independence Day Dilemmas in the American South, 1848-1865," *Journal of Southern History*, vol. 75 (May 2009): 263.

[85] Address to Sanitary Fair, Baltimore, April 18, 1864, in *Lincoln: Speeches and Writings, 1859-1865*, ed., Don E. Fehrenbacher (New York: Library of America, 1989) 589-590.

[86] Benjamin, "Theses on the Philosophy of History," in *Illuminations*, 255.

rally & to recognize one another," what are those principles?[87] What did the founders mean and how ought we tend that "mysterious fire" (Borges), that "sacred fire" (Jefferson), into our present? We continue to wrestle with this and have done so since the moment of the founding. As Robert Frost put it so nicely: Jefferson's "hard mystery" will "trouble us a thousand years." "Each age will have to reconsider it."[88] We can think with these texts but we have to think for ourselves with them. The fathers often asked questions that are similar to ours, but their answers cannot be precisely ours. And, as James Read has demonstrated, there is no single founder's answer to any question.[89] The relationship between power and liberty remains salient for us as a question to this day, but Jefferson, Wilson, Hamilton, and Madison each had quite different answers to it (and even theirs were of necessity sometimes ambiguous—see, for example, *Federalist* 37). Our answers must be different from all of theirs because in many fundamental senses we live in a different world—a world that presents us even with questions they did not have, even as we continue to live in the political community they made. A slavish devotion to the founders is in fact as antithetical to the Revolutionary spirit as British Redcoats. And for all of this we have Jefferson's imprimatur: "laws and institutions," he said, "must go hand in hand with the progress of the human mind. As that becomes more developed, more enlightened, as new discoveries are made, new truths disclosed, and manners and opinions change with the change of circumstances, institutions must advance also, and keep pace with the times. We might as well require a man to wear still the coat which fitted him when a boy as civilized

---

[87] Jefferson to Fayetteville Republican Citizens, March 17, 1801. In *The Papers of Thomas Jefferson*, ed. Julian P. Boyd, vol. 33 (Princeton University Press, 1950) 319.

[88] Frost, "The Black Cottage," in *Collected Poems, Prose, & Plays*, eds. Richard Poirier and Mark Richardson (New York: Library of America, 1995) 60.

[89] Read, *Power versus Liberty: Madison, Hamilton, Wilson, and Jefferson* (Charlottesville: University of Virginia Press, 2000).

society to remain ever under the regimen of their barbarous ancestors."[90]

Borges, who, again, bore no undue reverence for originals as such, nevertheless understood translation as a perpetuation of, or bearing an essential continuity with, the original. In his "Ode Composed in 1966," Borges noted that the nation was an unfolding into the present, "a continuous act." "No one is the homeland," he wrote, but we in the present should all,

> Be worthy of that ancient oath
> Which those gentlemen swore—
> To be something they didn't know, to be Argentines;
> To be what they would be by virtue
> Of the oath taken in the old house.
> We are the future of those men,
> The justification of those dead.
> Our duty is the glorious burden
> Bequeathed to our shadow by those shadows;
> It is ours to save.
>
> No one is the homeland – it is all of us.
> May that clear, mysterious fire burn
> Without ceasing, in my breast and yours.[91]

It is precisely this sense—that we are our ancestors' posterity—that connects our translation with the original. In this sense, the original meaning rests with our continuing to locate its significance in the present. As Aristotle suggested, "even if someone has lived in blessedness until old age, and has died appropriately, many fluctuations of his descendants' fortunes *may still happen to him*." And it would be "absurd," he wrote, "if the condition of descendants did not affect

[90] TJ to Samuel Kercheval, July 12, 1816, in *Jefferson: Writings*, 1401.

[91] Trans. W.S. Merwin, *Jorge Luis Borges: Selected Poems, 1923-1967*, ed., Norman Thomas Di Giovanni (London: Delacorte Press, 1972) 225-227.

their ancestors at all."[92] This of course makes the work of posterity imperative, not to ossify the founding but to tend its living "mysterious fire" into the present and thereby redeem the past.[93] When it comes to texts like 1776, each present generation is essential to the task of preservation and perpetuation. "Our duty is the glorious burden… it is ours to save."

The point is not to become the founders and thoughtlessly recapitulate the founding texts, but to be us and think with the meaning of 1776 in the *Jetztzeit*. Every now is eternal and, as Benjamin puts it, "each moment" the past "has lived becomes a *citation à l'ordre du jour*—and that day is Judgment Day."[94] Paul Tillich describes this as the moment in which "what has true and final being" will be separated "from what is merely transitory and empty of true being."[95] Such thinking through and with the significance of historical events in the present is not unfaithful but the only way 1776 can remain alive. And remember, as Pierre Menard's memorialist insisted, this was the immensely more difficult task. But we can think *with* them about matters that remain salient within the community they founded, which is why their own fame continues—why we continue to care so much about them and what they said and did. As the writer of Hebrews put it: they without us cannot be made perfect. Is that another way of saying that the "original is unfaithful to the translation," that the original can be perfected by translation into the present?

But let us also never forget that fame is also, as Borges insisted, a form of incomprehension. For that problem, we'll continue to need historians as well as political and literary theorists, and, dare I add, writers of fiction.

---

[92] *Nicomachean Ethics*, Book 1, Chapter 10, p.13. Emphasis added.

[93] See Benjamin, "Goethe's Elective Affinities," in *Walter Benjamin: Selected Writings*, volume 1, 1913-1926, ed., ed., Marcus Bullock and Michael W. Jennings (Cambridge, MA: Harvard University Press, 1996) 297-299.

[94] Benjamin, "Theses on the Philosophy of History," 254.

[95] Tillich, "Forgetting and Being Forgotten," *The Eternal Now* (New York: Scribner, 1963) 35.

7

"THE PUBLIC MIND SHALL REST": LINCOLN, PUBLIC OPINION, POLITICAL PARTIES, AND THE EXTINCTION OF SLAVERY

James H. Read

In his June 16, 1858 "House Divided" speech, Abraham Lincoln predicted that "Either the *opponents* of slavery, will arrest the further spread of it, and place it where the public mind shall rest in the belief that it is in course of ultimate extinction; or its *advocates* will push it forward, till it become alike lawful in *all* the states, *old* as well as *new*—*North* as well as *South.*" Lincoln then asked in alarm, "Have we no *tendency* to the latter condition?"[1]

The most obvious message of this passage, and the one that drew the most attention at the time, was Lincoln's claim that neutrality was impossible: the status of slavery in the United States would ultimately have to be decided one way or the other. Stephen Douglas, Lincoln's opponent in the 1858 U.S. Senate race, criticized Lincoln's "House Divided" speech as a call for "a war of the North against the South."[2] South Carolina's December 24, 1860 Declaration of the Causes of Secession denounced a president-elect who had publicly declared that the United States "cannot endure permanently half slave, half free." In South Carolina's view, this meant that Lincoln

---

[1] Abraham Lincoln, "House Divided Speech," Springfield, Illinois, June 16, 1858. Don E. Fehrenbacher, ed., *Abraham Lincoln: Speeches and Writings, 1832-1858* (New York: Library of American, 1989) 426.

[2] Stephen Douglas, Speech in Chicago, July 9, 1858. Robert W. Johannsen, ed., *The Lincoln-Douglas Debates* (New York: Oxford University Press, 1965) 29.

and the Republican Party intended "a war...waged against slavery until it shall cease throughout the United States."[3]

Lincoln himself denied that the House Divided speech expressed any intention "to bring about a war between the free and slave states." His purpose instead was to set in motion the ultimate extinction of slavery by "putting the seal of legislation *against its spread.*" Once that point was gained—which Lincoln considered difficult enough, given the enormous political momentum toward "the *perpetuation and nationalization of slavery*"—the actual extinction of slavery could proceed gradually, according to a time scale whose upper limit, at least in those states where the institution was most deeply entrenched, might be as long as a century.[4]

That is not how it happened, of course. The lower South seceded from the Union before Lincoln took office. Slavery was stamped out by military force in a horrific war, and its abolition legitimized by a constitutional amendment made possible only by the war's outcome. Some historians believe that peaceful abolition of slavery was impossible under the circumstances of 19th Century America.[5]

It is impossible conclusively to answer the counterfactual question whether slavery could have been peacefully abolished in the United States. But my aim in this essay is to think through the challenge of abolishing slavery gradually and peacefully as it looked to Lincoln before the slave states' secession and the shots fired at Fort Sumter. If the course of events demonstrated that Lincoln was overly

---

[3] State of South Carolina, "Declaration of the Immediate Causes which Induce and Justify the Secession of South Carolina from the Federal Union," December 24, 1860. Web posting from The Avalon Project: Documents in Law, History, and Diplomacy (http://avalon.law.yale.edu/19th_century/csa_scarsec.asp).

[4] Lincoln, First Joint Debate, Ottowa, Illinois, August 21, 1858. Johannsen, ed., *The Lincoln-Douglas Debates*, 54-55. Emphasis in original.

[5] For a recent example see James L. Huston, who writes that the only imaginable paths by which civil war could have been avoided in 1860-61 would have meant "slavery's continued existence—probably until the Great Depression." "Did the Tug Have to Come? A Critique of the New Revisionism of the Secession Winter," *Civil War History*, 62:3 (September 2016): 283.

optimistic, he was not delusional. The problem with Lincoln's plans for ultimate abolition, from many secessionists' point of view, was not that they were unrealistic, but that they were too realistic. Leading secessionists in the lower South pressed for immediate secession, before Lincoln could take office, because they believed that slavery might indeed be abolished through the kind of long, slow squeeze that Lincoln and the Republicans planned. Pre-emptive secession was designed to forestall this possibility before it could take hold.[6]

What exactly did Lincoln mean when he argued that the crisis would be reached and passed when "the public mind" shall once again "rest" in the conviction that slavery was in course of ultimate extinction? The verb "to rest" is puzzling and ambiguous in this context. If by "resting" Lincoln meant a kind of relaxed and passive political attitude—i.e., as soon as we make a few symbolic anti-slavery gestures and publicly reaffirm the Framers' hopes that it will someday disappear, then the slavery crisis is resolved and we can turn our attention to other issues—his "House Divided" formula would be morally and politically empty. For it would have done little actually to set slavery "in course of ultimate extinction." On this interpretation, Lincoln's exalted antislavery rhetoric would have been no more than an election-winning strategy, unaccompanied by actual plans for abolishing slavery, as some historians charge.[7]

---

[6] I agree with Huston, "Did the Tug Have to Come?" that it was not Lincoln's resistance to compromise between November 1860 and April 1861 that prevented the peaceful extinction of slavery, but the refusal by slaveholders of the lower South to accept *any* negotiated resolution of the sectional conflict unless it perpetuated slavery. Where the interpretation I offer below differs from Huston's view that slavery could only be abolished by warfare, is in the greater emphasis I place on slave state leaders' fear that the tide of events would soon turn against them, and make peaceful abolition a real possibility unless they acted immediately.

[7] See for example Michael F. Holt, who writes that the absence of any substantive issues separating Lincoln and the Republicans from Stephen Douglas's popular sovereignty platform drove Lincoln to employ "ever more extreme rhetoric to perpetuate fear of a Slave Power conspiracy...Lincoln desperately needed an issue to draw a distinction between himself and Douglas...To establish that distinction, he argued that black slavery was immoral, and should be placed on

Moreover the notion of an American public passively "resting" in the belief that slavery was on the way out is difficult to reconcile with Lincoln's own description of the political dynamics of the slavery crisis. Later in the "House Divided" speech, Lincoln worried that "We shall *lie down* pleasantly dreaming that the people of *Missouri* are on the verge of making their State *free*; and we shall *awake* to the *reality*, instead, that the *Supreme* Court has made *Illinois* a *slave* State."[8] Thus Lincoln clearly warned opponents of slavery against "resting" in the sense of "pleasantly dreaming" that slavery would disappear without determined political action. If the corner should be turned *in favor* of the full nationalization of slavery—which Lincoln described as a clear present "tendency"—he did not imagine that proslavery forces would simply "rest" from that point forward. Instead of relaxing their efforts, the advocates of slavery would "push it forward, till [slavery] become alike lawful in *all* the states, *old* as well as *new*." The whole import of the "House Divided" metaphor was that on a matter such as slavery, stasis was impossible: either one moved forward or backward. It would follow, therefore, that *opponents* of slavery likewise could not relax their efforts until slavery had been abolished in all the states, old as well as new. For otherwise the momentum would soon turn again in favor of slavery.

Thus by "resting" Lincoln could not have meant relaxation. Instead, public opinion on slavery would need to "rest" in opposition to slavery in the dynamic sense that a body, once set in motion, tends to stay in motion. I will argue here that Lincoln's purposes in the House Divided speech, and his many similar public statements of the late 1850s through his 1860 election, were first, *to fix public opinion* against the perpetuation of slavery; second, *to reverse the political tendency* toward the nationalization of slavery; and third, *to initiate policies designed to abolish slavery peacefully, democratically, and constitutionally*. Few historians would dispute that Lincoln had the first two goals

the road to 'ultimate extinction.'" Holt, *The Political Crisis of the 1850s* (New York: Wiley, 1978) 209-210.

[8] Lincoln, "House Divided" speech, June 16, 1858. Fehrenbacher, ed., *Lincoln: Speeches and Writings, 1832-1858*, 432.

in mind. I will suggest that he intended all three, and saw them as practically interconnected.

How did Lincoln imagine that these three interconnected goals could be peacefully, democratically, and constitutionally realized? At least one essential part of the answer is: through the creation of a major political party (the Republican Party) publicly committed to those goals; capable of winning the support of a majority of American voters in the North, Midwest, and West; and functioning to legitimize antislavery speech and electioneering even in southern states where Republican candidates were extremely unlikely to win office.

Among his other gifts and accomplishments, Abraham Lincoln was a party-builder. He had played an important role in organizing the Whig party in Illinois during the late 1830s and early 1840s, and once again in building a Republican party in Illinois and nationally during the late 1850s. He did not regard party labors as distasteful, as merely playing the role of a "hack politician."[9] Instead he regarded party work as an important calling and essential to democracy.[10]

The creation and endurance of the Republican Party was from Lincoln's perspective essential to the peaceful and democratic extinction of slavery for several reasons. First, the creation of the Republican Party gave millions of Americans who considered slavery to be morally wrong the opportunity, for the first time in American political history, to actually *vote* for a major political party committed to the ultimate abolition of slavery. Lincoln believed that the vast major-

[9] Harry V. Jaffa, *Crisis of the House Divided: An Interpretation of the Issues in the Lincoln-Douglas Debates*, 50th anniversary edition (Chicago: University of Chicago Press, 2009) 185. Jaffa focuses in the book on Lincoln's political philosophy, but appears uninterested in Lincoln's party-building as an application of that philosophy.

[10] See for instance Lincoln's praise of Henry Clay in terms that would equally apply to Lincoln himself: "…the man who is of neither party, is not – cannot be – of any consequence. Mr. Clay, therefore, was of a party." Lincoln, "Eulogy on Henry Clay," July 6, 1852. Fehrenbacher, ed., *Lincoln: Speeches and Writings, 1832-1858*, 265.

ity of white non-slaveholders were at least latently anti-slavery.[11] But an enormous and difficult leap was necessary to convert this generalized antislavery sentiment into a personal commitment strong enough to determine one's vote amid a host of other important competing issues. The Republican Party made it possible for northern white citizens to vote against slavery without "throwing their vote away" on an abolitionist candidate who could not win.

Moreover, the very existence of a major national party with a large, durable electoral base and publicly committed to the ultimate extinction of slavery would significantly reshape American public opinion—and not only among those who voted for that party. Lincoln remarked in his First Debate with Stephen Douglas (whom he accused of teaching public opinion *not to care* about whether slavery was right or wrong): "In this and like communities, public sentiment is everything. With public sentiment, nothing can fail; without it, nothing can succeed. Consequently he who moulds public sentiment goes deeper than he who enacts statutes or pronounces decisions. He makes statutes and decisions possible or impossible to be executed."[12] Lincoln's observations on the power of public opinion are typically—and correctly—taken as a statement about the crucial role of statesmanship in a democracy and about his own self-understanding as a statesman.[13]

---

[11] For example, Lincoln remarked in 1854 that, though there were some like Stephen Douglas who had "no very vivid impression that the negro is a human," Lincoln himself was certain that "the great mass of mankind...consider slavery a great moral wrong; and their feeling against it, is not evanescent, but eternal." Lincoln, Speech on Kansas-Nebraska Act, October 16, 1854. In Fehrenbacher, ed., *Abraham Lincoln: Speeches and Writings, 1832-1858*, 346.

[12] Lincoln, Reply to Douglas, Ottawa Debate, August 21, 1858. Fehrenbacher, ed., *Lincoln: Speeches and Writings, 1832-1858*, 524-525.

[13] For example, Harry V. Jaffa emphasizes Lincoln's remarks on the role played by democratic statesmen in shaping citizens' views about the morality of slavery, but Jaffa does not highlight the role of *political parties* as well as statesmen in shaping moral opinion. Jaffa, *Crisis of the House Divided*, 267-271 and 308-310.

What has been less emphasized by scholars is the way in which Lincoln's statement applies equally to political parties as molders of public opinion. Political parties do not just shape public opinion among their supporters. They also reconfigure public opinion among voters who support an opposing party, and among those who do not affiliate with any party. Political parties do not act in isolation from one another but collectively produce what is typically described as "a party system."[14] At least in a peaceful and functional democracy, there is often a kind of tacit cooperation among competing major parties: though they take contrasting positions on many major issues, they implicitly agree on *what issues ought to be debated and decided.* During the 1830s and 1840s when the Jacksonian Democrats fiercely competed with the Whig party over banking, currency, public land policy, and many other economic questions, the two parties worked in tandem to sideline the slavery question, in part because they recognized how explosive it was.[15] In that sense it was both major parties, not just Stephen Douglas, that deliberately moulded public opinion "not to care" about slavery. Indeed, anti-slavery politics was considered so divisive and union-threatening that from 1836 to 1844 leaders in both parties cooperated—with diminishing success—to muzzle public discussion of slavery in Congress.[16]

In that sense the formation of the Republican Party, however moderate its antislavery stance compared to the abolitionists, was a

---

[14] There is a large literature in both political science and history on party systems in general and American party systems in particular. Significant works here include Richard Hofstadter, *The Idea of a Party System: The Rise of Legitimate Opposition in the United States, 1780-1840* (Berkeley: University of Chicago Press, 1970); and William Nisbet Chambers and Walter Dean Burnham, eds., *The American Party Systems: Stages of Political Development* (New York: Oxford University Press, 1975).

[15] See for example Joel H. Silbey, *Party over Section: The Rough and Ready Presidential Election of 1848* (Lawrence, KS: University Press of Kansas, 2009); and Silbey, *The Partisan Imperative: The Dynamics of American Politics Before the Civil War* (New York: Oxford University Press, 1987).

[16] See William Lee Miller, *Arguing About Slavery: John Quincy Adams and the Great Battle in the United States Congress* (New York: Vintage, 1998).

radical development. Slave state leaders had spent decades endeavoring to keep antislavery speech off the public agenda altogether: out of the halls of Congress, out of the mails, even out of northern states, where slaveholders demanded that abolitionist societies be suppressed. Until the formation of the Republican Party, explicitly antislavery political parties (like the Liberty Party) could be dismissed as marginal.[17] With the Republican Party, openly antislavery political speech entered the political mainstream, and upon Lincoln's election would be for the first time publicly voiced by a President of the United States. If states of the lower South had allowed Lincoln to take office—instead of seceding before he could take office—they would have tacitly accepted the legitimacy of a type of public political speech they had hitherto treated as beyond the pale. For many slaveholders, it hardly mattered that Lincoln and the Republicans were not radical abolitionists demanding the immediate destruction of slavery; what mattered was that, like the abolitionists, Republicans publicly denounced slavery as deeply unjust. Moreover, as candidates of a major party, Republicans were in a position to broadcast these moral denunciations in parts of the country where radical abolitionists had not been permitted to set foot. In that way, among others, the formation of the Republicans as a major party would significantly recalibrate American public opinion on slavery, even if the party's actual electoral success was negligible in the slaveholding states.

Therefore one answer to the question, "How did Lincoln believe that slavery could be peacefully, gradually, and democratically extinguished?" is: through the formation of a major political party whose status *as a legitimate party* had been tacitly conceded by its opponents, a party which would thus be in a position over the course of several decades to publicly advocate for the containment and ultimate extinction of slavery, and which would be openly rewarded by millions of

[17] For extended discussion of the Liberty Party, see Richard H. Sewell, *Ballots for Freedom: Antislavery Politics in the United States, 1837-1860* (New York: W.W. Norton, 1980).

voters for doing so. No such party had ever before existed in the United States.

The theme of this volume is "1776," the year that the American colonies declared their independence from the British Empire and famously declared that "All men are created equal." The Declaration of Independence goes on to claim that, because of this natural equality, governments must derive their just powers from "the consent of the governed."

But what if "the governed" are themselves deeply divided—as they were in Lincoln's day, and also so in our own? A pessimist might conclude that government by consent—and practically speaking, by election results—is sufficient for deciding ordinary questions during ordinary times, but incapable of resolving very difficult problems in very polarized times. The 1850s were such a time. So is our own.

If the Framers of the U.S. Constitution, the members of every Congress elected between 1788 and 1860, and the U.S. Supreme Court had failed to resolve the slavery question, why should anyone expect a political party to fare any better? Perhaps there was no peaceful, democratic way to abolish slavery in the United States. But I am moved by Lincoln's faith that a constitutionally-governed electoral process, characterized by competition among political parties that recognize one another as legitimate and agree to respect the results of elections, was capable of peacefully resolving even a problem as fatefully divisive as slavery.

* * *

Lincoln and other Republicans articulated a variety of scenarios for the peaceful extinction of slavery over an extended timeline, without violating any express provision of the Constitution. There is an excellent recent book on the subject, *The Scorpion's Sting* by James Oakes (2015).[18] The Republican strategy was to abolish slavery through con-

[18] James Oakes, *The Scorpion's Sting: Antislavery and the Coming of the Civil War* (New York: W.W. Norton, 2015).

tainment and slow suffocation. Slavery, the argument went, was inherently aggressive and expansive. If it did not continually find new territories in which to expand, it would contract and ultimately die. Slave state leaders themselves frequently voiced this view. "We must expand or perish," Robert Toombs insisted during the Georgia Legislature's November 1860 secession debate.[19] Thus neither Republicans nor secessionists took the dismissive view that the Republican platform was merely a symbolic gesture devoid of practical significance, a dispute about "an imaginary Negro in an impossible place."[20] On the contrary, Republicans as well as secessionists assumed that halting the expansion of slavery was only the first step to its eventual abolition everywhere on American soil.

Lincoln and the Republicans conceded that Congress could not constitutionally abolish slavery in the states where it already existed. But they argued that Congress could constitutionally prohibit slavery in federal territories not yet states, because Congress had constitutional power under Article IV, Section 3 to "make all needful Rules and Regulations" for the territories. Lincoln believed that a newly-settled territory whose political institutions were formed without the stain of slavery, such that its inhabitants could make decisions about the future of slavery "uninfluenced by the actual presence of the institution among them," would be unlikely to introduce it upon attaining statehood.[21] As more and more free territories entered the Union as free states, the slave states, as a bloc, would lose the rough political equality they had long enjoyed in the Union—especially their veto power in the Senate. Thus keeping slavery out of the territories in the

---

[19] Robert Toombs Secessionist Speech, November 13, 1860. In William W. Freehling and Craig M. Simpson, eds, *Secession Debated: Georgia's Showdown in 1860* (New York: Oxford University Press, 1992) 40.

[20] The original phrase comes from James G. Blaine, *Twenty Years of Congress from Lincoln to Garfield*, Vol. 1, (Norwich: Henry Hill, 1884) 272. The phrase has been frequently repeated in the works of historians who endorse the thesis that the Republican platform of 1860 had no practical significance except to help Republicans win elections in northern states.

[21] Lincoln, from the Second Joint Debate with Douglas, Freeport, August 27, 1858. Johannsen, ed., *The Lincoln-Douglas Debates*, 78.

short term would over the long term magnify the free states' future political power to enact antislavery measures of other kinds. Secessionists were fully aware of this prospect.

The Constitution also gave Congress the exclusive power to legislate "in all cases whatsoever" in the District of Columbia, which (in Republicans' view) meant that Congress could legitimately abolish slavery there. Slaves constituted a relatively small proportion of the District's population, but because of its status as the national Capital and Congress's direct role in legislation for the district, every public action affecting slavery there took on enormous significance.[22] In his debates with Douglas, Lincoln denied that he was "pledged" to abolish slavery in the District of Columbia, but immediately followed by proposing several specific guidelines for doing exactly that. The first was "that the abolition should be gradual." Second, Lincoln added, "it should be on a vote of the majority of qualified voters in the District"; Lincoln did not consider such a referendum constitutionally obligatory, but believed it politically prudent and likely to succeed as long as all of the District's eligible voters—not just its slaveholder minority—were permitted to participate. Finally, Lincoln stipulated "that compensation should be made to unwilling owners," which suggests that he rested abolition of slavery in the District upon Congress's power to take private property for "public use," conditional upon paying "just compensation" to property owners as provided in the Fifth Amendment.[23]

---

[22] See Don E. Fehrenbacher's chapter "Slavery in the National Capital" from Fehrenbacher, *The Slaveholding Republic: An Account of the United States Government's Relations to Slavery* (New York: Oxford University Press, 2001) 49-88.

[23] Lincoln, from the Second Joint Debate with Douglas, Freeport, August 27, 1858. Johannsen, ed., *The Lincoln-Douglas Debates*, 78. For discussion of Congressman Lincoln's 1849 introduction of a "hopeless" bill to gradually abolish slavery in the District of Columbia, see Fehrenbacher, *The Slaveholding Republic*, 78, 82. Lincoln's remarks on the subject in the Lincoln-Douglas debates indicate that in 1858 he did not consider the prospect hopeless. In December 1860, in the face of the secession of the lower South in response to his election, Lincoln appears to have retreated, at least temporarily, from his proposal to abolish slavery

In the exchange cited above from the Lincoln-Douglas debates, Lincoln's proposal for gradual abolition applied directly only to abolition in the District of Columbia; the antebellum Constitution vested Congress with no equivalent authority over state legislation on matters related to slavery. Nevertheless, what Lincoln said in 1858 about abolition in the District provides clues about how he may have envisioned the long-term extinction of slavery on the wider national stage. His words suggest, first of all, that wherever he believed Congress *did* have legitimate power to act with respect to slavery, Lincoln supported using those powers to their fullest constitutional extent, with the aim of ultimately abolishing slavery, not just halting its expansion. Second, the referendum component of the D.C. proposal shows Lincoln's confidence that under the right political circumstances, even in a slaveholding jurisdiction, a majority of white voters (though almost certainly not a majority of slaveholders) could be persuaded to support a plan of gradual, compensated emancipation. Finally, Lincoln's D.C. proposal underscores his assumption that the peaceful and gradual abolition of slavery was a legitimate public purpose for which Congress could constitutionally appropriate funds, and also promote in other ways, as long as such actions respected the regular constitutional checks and obligations, such as compensating property owners for public use.

As late as 1862, amid the very different circumstances of the war, Lincoln still voiced the hope that slavery might be peacefully abolished through compensated emancipation, framed as an expenditure of public funds for achieving a public good.[24] Lincoln's immediate aim in proposing a compensated emancipation plan in late 1862 was to persuade the border slave states (Maryland, Kentucky, Missouri), which had not seceded and thus were not subject to the soon-to-be-issued Emancipation Proclamation, to set an example by will-

in the District (Fehrenbacher, *The Slaveholding Republic*, 77), though not from his commitment to prevent the spread of slavery to new territories.

[24] Lincoln, "Annual Message to Congress," December 1, 1862. Don E. Fehrenbacher, ed., *Abraham Lincoln: Speeches and Writings, 1859-1865* (New York: Library of America, 1989) 403-413.

ingly agreeing to compensated emancipation; such a precedent in turn, Lincoln hoped, would persuade at least some seceding states willingly to return to the Union, and thus "shorten the war," rather than hold out to the end and have emancipation imposed by military force.[25]

If Lincoln had publicly proposed such a plan before the war began it would have appeared shockingly radical, though it was in many respects the logical extension of Lincoln's "ultimate extinction" principle in the House Divided speech. By late 1862, after 20 months of intense warfare, the plan was too conservative for the radicals in his party, while the border slave states Lincoln hoped to enlist continued to oppose emancipation in any form. The increasingly lethal war continued for another two and a half years. Under the Thirteenth Amendment (1865), which Lincoln successfully shepherded through Congress, slavery was abolished everywhere in the United States without compensation.

Because Lincoln's compensated emancipation proposal went nowhere in 1862, it might appear a mere historical curiosity occasioned by a particular and transient moment in the war. It is more significant, I would argue, because of what it reveals about the peaceful and democratic path to ultimate extinction Lincoln advocated before he took office.

Among other things, under the 1862 proposal Congress would have been authorized—though not obligated—to provide funds for colonization.[26] But Lincoln did not make colonization of former slaves a *precondition* of emancipation, as Thomas Jefferson and many other advocates of colonization did.[27] Just as with Lincoln's 1849 District of Columbia proposal, under the 1862 national proposal compensated emancipation would proceed with or without colonization.

---

[25] Lincoln, "Annual Message to Congress," December 1, 1862. Fehrenbacher, ed., *Abraham Lincoln: Speeches and Writings, 1859-1865*, 411.

[26] Ibid., 412.

[27] Thomas Jefferson, *Notes on the State of Virginia,* Query XIV. Merrill D. Peterson, ed., *Thomas Jefferson: Writings* (New York: Library of America, 1984) 264.

No individual would be "colonized" without his or her consent. And even as he indicated his personal support for colonization, Lincoln answered at length the objection that "free colored persons remaining in the country...would injure, and displace white labor and white laborers"—an objection which Lincoln characterizes as "largely imaginary, if not sometimes malicious."[28] Though Lincoln unquestionably became more sympathetic to the rights of free blacks over the course of the war, even before the war he had signaled his willingness, if not exactly enthusiasm, to accept a large, permanent free black labor force in the United States as a consequence of his party's antislavery policies. In a Cincinnati speech in 1859, Lincoln publicly responded to the "black labor drives out white labor" objection in terms very similar to what he said as president in defense of his 1862 compensated emancipation proposal. Black *slave* labor hurts free white labor, Lincoln acknowledged; but he insisted there was no necessary conflict between *free* black labor and free white labor. On the contrary, in the United States, Lincoln argued, "there is room enough for us all to be free."[29] For Lincoln in the 1850s, what was morally and politically *essential* was that slavery be actively placed on the road to extinction. Colonization was one option among others, not a requirement.

By December 1862 Lincoln probably recognized that abolition on a mass scale would only come through armed force. Nevertheless he used the occasion to point out that more peaceful paths to the extinction of slavery were still imaginable.

* * *

Neither in his 1858 U.S. Senate campaign, nor in the 1860 presidential contest, did Lincoln campaign as an individual with his own personal image and "message," as has become standard practice today. Lincoln campaigned in 1860, not only as a candidate for President of

---

[28] Lincoln, "Annual Message to Congress," December 1, 1862. Fehrenbacher, ed., *Abraham Lincoln: Speeches and Writings, 1859-1865*, 412.

[29] Lincoln, Speech at Cincinnati, September 17, 1859. Fehrenbacher, ed., *Abraham Lincoln: Speeches and Writings, 1859-1865*, 68.

the United States, but also as head of a recently-formed political party committed to halting the expansion of slavery and ultimately extinguishing it, peacefully and constitutionally, over some gradual timeline. Those who voted for Lincoln, those who voted against him, and those who threatened to secede if he became president all knew that, if voters elected him, they were at the same time legitimizing the Republican Party and probably ensuring its long-term future. Lincoln himself was 52 years old when he was inaugurated as President. He would not have lived long enough to implement the ultimate extinction of slavery according to his own projected timeline. What mattered most was what the Republican Party stood for, and what action it would take, over a timeline extending beyond Lincoln's presidency and life span.

Moreover, if the seceding states had returned peacefully to the Union as Lincoln had urged them to do, and the Democratic Party mended the deep internal divisions that had ensured Lincoln's election in 1860, then the most that Lincoln and his party could have hoped for in his first term would have been halting the further expansion of slavery. Given the long winning streak that proslavery forces had enjoyed during the 1850s, halting and reversing this political momentum would have been a difficult and significant accomplishment for a first-term Republican president. Nearly every antislavery step beyond that first one depended as much on what other Republican leaders thought and did, in both the short and long term, as on Lincoln's own individual actions and views.

For this reason it is helpful to widen our perspective and describe the full range of Republican scenarios for the ultimate extinction of slavery. Some of these proposals were more radical than what Lincoln himself publicly endorsed. Lincoln's own views generally fell in the center of the Republican spectrum—probably not by accident but by design, for as a party-builder Lincoln worked to ensure that the more radical as well as the more conservative elements of the Republican coalition stayed on board.[30] What most distinguished Lincoln from the more radical members of his party was not any major difference in his scenarios for the ultimate extinction of slavery, but his more careful attention to establishing the wider democratic and constitutional legitimacy of the "cordon of freedom" policy upon which Republicans of all stripes agreed.

In contrast to proslavery leaders, who argued that slavery was a national institution to be protected everywhere the American flag flew and restrictions on slavery merely local, all Republicans—Lincoln included—insisted upon the reverse: that freedom was national and slavery local.[31] All Republicans, including Lincoln, conceded that the antebellum Constitution prevented the federal government from abolishing slavery in the states where it currently existed. But once the principle was established that slavery was legitimized *only* where state law specifically authorized it, then a whole range of policies designed to weaken and ultimately destroy slavery through a long slow squeeze became imaginable. All of the following positions (drawn in part from Oakes's useful summary in *The Scorpion's Sting*)[32] were advocated by at least some Republicans, and many of them by Lincoln himself.

> • Prohibiting slavery in all U.S. territories not yet states, based on Congress's constitutionally authorized power "to make all needful Rules and Regulations respecting the Territory or other Property belonging to the United States." All Republicans, from the most radical to the most conservative, endorsed this position.
>
> • Restricting or prohibiting slavery on U.S. military bases, including those located within the boundaries of slave states.

---

[30] For Lincoln's role as a mediator between conservative and radical factions within the Republican coalition, see William E. Gienapp, *The Origins of the Republican Party* (New York: Oxford University Press, 1987) 294.

[31] For extended discussion of how the "Freedom National" principle shaped policy from the beginning of Lincoln's presidency, see James Oakes, *Freedom National: The Destruction of Slavery in the United States, 1861-1865* (New York: W.W. Norton, 2012).

[32] Oakes, *The Scorpion's Sting*, 30-32.

• Using the U.S. Navy to protect freedom on the high seas, and effectively suppress the coastal slave trade.

• Abolition of slavery in the District of Columbia, which as the national capital conveyed symbolic messages of enormous importance with respect to slavery. (The slave trade in the District of Columbia had already been abolished as part of the 1850 Compromise.)

• Restricting, perhaps even prohibiting, the *interstate* slave trade, on the basis of Congress's Article I Section 8 power to regulate commerce "among the several states."

• Refusal to employ the power of the federal government to assist in recapturing fugitive slaves—in other words, repealing the Fugitive Slave Act of 1850—and instead leaving such enforcement merely local, which meant that it would be weak or nonexistent in northern states.

• Refusal to admit any new slave states into the Union.

• Ultimately amending the Constitution to restrict or abolish slavery even in the states where it had long existed. For if no new slave territories or slave states were admitted into the Union, and if some border states like Maryland and Kentucky decided to cut loose from an increasingly troublesome and unprofitable institution, the free states would ultimately reach the three-fourths threshold necessary to amend the Constitution. As Oakes describes this scenario: "the number of free states would grow steadily and the number of slave states inexorably decline, shifting the balance of power in national politics from slavery to freedom. All it would take was a shift from slavery to freedom in half a dozen states to make an abolition amendment feasible."[33]

As for this final and most radical of the Republican proposals: Lincoln himself never publicly advocated an abolition amendment of this kind. On the contrary, as he said in his August 21, 1858 debate with Stephen Douglas and repeated in his First Inaugural Address of March 4, 1861, "I have no purpose, directly or indirectly, to interfere with the institution of slavery in the States where it exists. I believe I

[33] Oakes, *The Scorpion's Sting,* 33-34.

have no lawful right to do so, and I have no inclination to do so."[34] Nevertheless everyone on both sides of the slavery contest understood that the chances for a future amendment of this kind would go up significantly as soon as Lincoln and the Republicans blocked the flow of new slave states into the Union. Georgia secessionist Thomas L. Benning, in his speech of November 19, 1860, argued that the western territories would ultimately form the basis for twenty new states, all of which would be free states if Republicans restricted the expansion of slavery. Meanwhile Delaware, Maryland, and Kentucky would in time join the ranks of free states. "When that time comes, and indeed long before that time comes, the North—the Black Republican party...will have it in its power... to amend the Constitution, and take what power it pleases upon the subject of slavery."[35] Lincoln himself would no longer be in office, and probably deceased, by the time an amendment of this kind became possible, but by restricting the expansion of slavery he would have put into place the first essential step; over time his "Black Republican party" would finish the job.

On many of the other Republican proposals listed above, Lincoln kept his options open: on the one hand, he denied that he was "pledged" to do many of these things, but neither did he promise *not* to do them. In his Second Debate with Douglas (Freeport, August 27, 1858), in response to the latter's interrogatories, Lincoln denied that he was "pledged" to the abolition of slavery in the District of Columbia—but then insisted that Congress had full power to do so, and laid out the specific manner (summarized above) in which he hoped abolition here would occur and thus "sweep from our Capital that foul blot upon our nation."[36]

Likewise Lincoln stated that "I do not stand pledged to the prohibition of the slave-trade between the different States."[37] But neither

---

[34] Johannsen, ed., *The Lincoln-Douglas Debates,* 52; Lincoln, First Inaugural Address, Fehrenbacher, ed., *Abraham Lincoln: Speeches and Writings, 1859-1865*, 215.

[35] Freehling and Simpson, eds., *Secession Debated*, 118-119.

[36] Johannsen, ed., *The Lincoln-Douglas Debates,* 76-78.

[37] Ibid., 76.

did he pledge *not* to restrict the interstate slave trade. Nor does he appear to have doubted that restricting the interstate slave trade lay within the constitutional powers of Congress. Slave state leaders considered legislation of this kind an imminent possibility under a Republican-controlled federal government. Georgia secessionist Thomas R.R. Cobb included, as a reason for immediate secession from the Union, the fact that "The inter-State Slave Trade is within the letter of the Constitution"; Lincoln and the Republicans could target it immediately, without waiting for a constitutional amendment specifically authorizing them to do so.[38]

Lincoln likewise denied that he stood "pledged against the admission of any more slave States into the Union." Here he made his thinking clear: he would be very glad never to admit another slave state; and he considered it unlikely that the people of a newly-formed state would introduce slavery upon statehood "if slavery shall be kept out of the Territories during the territorial existence" so that its people would be "uninfluenced by the actual presence of the institution among them." Should, however, the people of a free territory do something so "extraordinary" as to "adopt a slave Constitution" at the moment of statehood, Lincoln would consider himself and his party obliged to admit that state into the Union.[39] Lincoln was in effect betting that prohibition of slavery at the territorial stage would effectively ensure that Republicans never had to face such a vote.

Lincoln's stance here, it is worth emphasizing, would have permitted him to vote against the admission of Cuba as a new slave state, upon which slave state leaders had their eyes, with Stephen Douglas's active encouragement.[40] For neither Cuba, nor any other territories in the southward-expanding slave empire that southerners demanded in

---

[38] Freehling and Simpson, eds., *Secession Debated*, 15.

[39] Johannsen, ed., *The Lincoln-Douglas Debates*, 76-78.

[40] For Douglas's support for slave-state demands to annex Cuba as a new slave state, see Robert W. Johannsen, *Stephen A. Douglas* (New York: Oxford University Press, 1973) 147, 326-327, 528-529, 683, 692. For Douglas's own public endorsement of Cuban annexation in the Lincoln-Douglas debates of 1858, see Johannsen, ed., *The Lincoln-Douglas Debates*, 130.

compensation for being shut out of Kansas and Nebraska, would have been free of slavery during the pre-statehood stage.

Lincoln was not among those Republicans calling for a full repeal of the Fugitive Slave Act. "I do not now, nor ever did, stand in favor of the unconditional repeal of the Fugitive Slave Act."[41] He considered return of fugitive slaves a clearly-expressed constitutional obligation, even though many northerners had to "crucify their feelings" in order to fulfill it.[42] He also recognized during the secession crisis that it was futile to insist that slave states respect their constitutional obligations unless free states did so also. Yet even here Lincoln added qualifications designed to undermine the long-term viability of slavery. In his First Inaugural Address, after affirming his respect for the constitutional obligation to return fugitive slaves, Lincoln immediately added that "any law upon this subject" ought to include "all the safeguards of liberty known in civilized and humane jurisprudence, so that a free man be not, in any case, surrendered as a slave"; and to ensure that "The citizens of each State shall be entitled to all privileges and immunities of citizens in the several States."[43]

Lincoln, in other words, signaled that any Fugitive Slave law he could support would have to provide that persons suspected of being fugitive slaves enjoy the right to a fair trial, including the presumption of innocence and the right to testify in their own defense; and that persons of African descent could indeed be citizens of the United States—which slave state leaders denied—and thus protected by the Constitution's privileges and immunities clause. These commitments stood in stark contrast to the actual provisions of the Fugitive Slave Act of 1850, which as David Potter observes, "left all free negroes with inadequate safeguards against claims that they were slaves, and it

---

[41] Lincoln, from the Second Joint Debate with Douglas, Freeport, August 27, 1858. Johannsen, ed., *The Lincoln-Douglas Debates*, 76.

[42] Lincoln to Joshua F. Speed, August 24, 1855. Lincoln, from the Second Joint Debate with Douglas, Freeport, August 27, 1858. Johannsen, ed., *The Lincoln-Douglas Debates*, 361.

[43] Lincoln, First Inaugural Address, in Fehrenbacher, ed., *Abraham Lincoln: Speeches and Writings, 1859-1865*, 216-217.

exposed them to the danger of kidnapping."[44] Lincoln's proposed reforms of fugitive slave law also undermined slave state legal practice. Most slave states prohibited slaves from testifying in court in any form, even on occasions when such testimony would have been to a slave holder's advantage, because this would have contradicted the presumption that, legally, slaves counted as property rather than persons.

The "cordon of freedom" that Lincoln and other Republicans envisioned would not have quickly extinguished the institution of slavery. But once enacted, such measures would have almost immediately transformed slavery from a very profitable into an increasingly unprofitable institution. The value of slave property, for example—by far the greatest economic asset in the southern economy—would begin to fall immediately as soon as it became less portable and more difficult to sell. Turning slavery from an economic benefit into an economic burden would, Republicans believed, be a crucially important step in putting slavery "in course of ultimate extinction," as Lincoln put it in the House Divided speech.

In comparing what Lincoln himself said on the theme of peaceful abolition with the positions staked out by other Republican leaders and spokesmen, the differences one finds are not dramatic. Lincoln appears more inclined than some other Republicans to keep his tactical options open and his timing flexible. Moreover, Lincoln understood better than many other antislavery leaders how enormously difficult even the first step would be—firmly halting the expansion of slavery. For that reason he would have considered it politically counterproductive to stake out firm public positions on even more explosive questions (like restricting the interstate slave trade) before it was necessary to do so. But Lincoln's overall strategy for extinguishing slavery through a slow, firm, irreversible territorial squeeze fits comfortably within the broad channel of Republican thinking that Oakes describes in *The Scorpion's Sting*.

---

[44] David M. Potter, *The Impending Crisis, 1848-1861* (New York: Harper, 1976) 131.

* * *

What does distinguish Lincoln from most other Republicans was the greater effort he put into arguing for *the political legitimacy* of the Republican Party and its commitment to the peaceful extinction of slavery. In surveying Republicans' various public and private statements before the war (including those catalogued in *The Scorpion's Sting*), one is struck by how little thought many Republicans put into the question: why would slave state leaders permit *any* of these policies to go into effect, rather than secede and risk civil war?

The tone of many Republican statements from the late 1850s instead suggests confidence that, once the party achieved a governing majority at the national level, it would have sufficient power to impose its antislavery policies, and there would be little that slave states could do to stop this. For, many Republicans argued, slave state leaders knew that if they seceded and forced a war, Republicans would then use all of the war powers authorized by international law to attack slavery much more directly and effectively than they could during peacetime, when subject to the regular constitutional restraints. Antislavery radicals, Oakes observes, "assumed that the South would never secede because that would mean war and with war came military emancipation." Even as late as December 1860, Republicans found it "hard to believe that the slave states would reject the alternative of peaceful, gradual abolition in favor of a war that promised swift, bloody military emancipation."[45]

Yet it soon became clear that slave state leaders were in fact willing to accept civil war rather than allow slavery to be subjected to the long slow territorial squeeze envisioned by Republicans, even if such a war carried some risk of destroying slavery itself. Whether Lincoln himself was as naïve as other Republicans about the prospect of secession and civil war may be debated (I would suggest he was not), but this would be a theme for another essay. What is clear is that Lin-

[45] Oakes, *The Scorpion's Sting*, 18, 38.

coln—more than most other Republicans—appealed to slave state leaders' own commitment to constitutional democracy, rather than assume they would tolerate the imposition of Republican policies simply because they had no alternative.

To secede and resort to arms because one does not like the results of a constitutionally fair election sets a precedent which, as Lincoln argued in his First Inaugural Address, would destroy popular government at its core.[46] Though in the end Lincoln was not able to stem the tide of secession, his concerns about the precedent set by pre-emptive secession were echoed by some southern leaders whose views on slavery itself were worlds apart from those of Lincoln and his party.

In South Carolina, the first state to secede, the vote was unanimous; there was no debate. But in Georgia, secession was seriously debated and the vote was relatively close; if Georgia had voted against secession, its momentum might have stalled and the events of Lincoln's presidency taken a different course. In the Georgia secession debate, Alexander Stephens (who later became vice-President of the Confederacy) argued that Lincoln's election by itself did not justify secession. To secede from the Union, Stephens said, "because a man has been constitutionally elected, puts us in the wrong...The result was different from what we wished, but the election has been constitutionally held." Stephens made clear that he *was* willing to secede if Lincoln, once in office, began putting his slavery-restrictionist agenda into effect. But, he argued, Lincoln was unlikely to get Congress to support his antislavery policies, which would be hemmed in by a whole array of constitutional checks.[47] Stephens (who exchanged private letters with Lincoln during the secession crisis) knew that Lin-

---

[46] Lincoln, First Inaugural Address, Fehrenbacher, ed., *Abraham Lincoln: Speeches and Writings, 1859-1865*, 220.

[47] Alexander H. Stephens's Unionist Speech, November 14, 1860. Freehling and Simpson, eds., *Secession Debated*, 55-56.

coln was not John Brown and would not attempt forcible abolition through unconstitutional means.[48]

The advocates of immediate secession in the Georgia debate replied that, even if Lincoln committed no overtly aggressive act against slavery, his election threatened to turn Northern public opinion against slavery. "Delay is dangerous," Thomas R. R. Cobb warned, "because it demoralizes our position—takes away from our cause its justice in the eyes of the world." Moreover, even if Lincoln's antislavery agenda were blocked in Congress, he would still exercise the power of appointment. That would mean sending Republican appointees into the South as postmasters and customs collectors and military officers. This would "open our territory to the emissaries of the North," Cobb argued.[49] In short, delay was dangerous because if the slave states permitted Lincoln to take office without resistance, then the Republican Party and its antislavery agenda would acquire legitimacy and the tide of public opinion would have turned against slavery.

Robert Toombs, another Georgia advocate of immediate secession, emphasized the way in which Lincoln's election legitimized decades of antislavery speech "by Abolition societies, by publications made by them, by the public press, through the pulpit and their own legislative halls." Lincoln's election represented "the indorsement, by the non-slaveholding States, of all those acts of aggression upon our rights by all these States, legislatures, governors, judges, and people."[50] From this perspective it almost did not matter what actual antislavery policies Lincoln would be able to enact once he took office;

[48] Lincoln to Alexander H. Stephens, December 22, 1860. Fehrenbacher, ed., *Abraham Lincoln: Speeches and Writings, 1859-1865*, 194. For Stephens's reply, see Stephens to Abraham Lincoln, December 30, 1860. Alexander H. Stephens, *A Constitutional View of the Late War Between the States*, vol. II (Philadelphia: National Publishing Company, 1870) 267-270.

[49] Thomas R. R. Cobb's Secessionist Speech, November 12, 1860. Freehling and Simpson, eds., *Secession Debated*, 27.

[50] Robert Toombs Secessionist Speech, November 13, 1860. Freehling and Simpson, eds., *Secession Debated*, 44-45.

that his election legitimated and further encouraged antislavery speech was reason enough for pre-emptive secession.

Beneath such denunciations of Lincoln lay a broadly accurate reading of his long-range intentions. Toombs and Cobb, no less than Stephens, knew that Lincoln was not John Brown. They knew Lincoln aimed at a gradual, procedurally legal extinction of slavery over a long time frame. Their words and actions betray their suspicion that Lincoln and his party might be able to pull this off if not immediately and forcefully resisted.

Lincoln, for his part, fully understood what was at stake in the matter of southerners conceding or refusing his party's legitimacy. He knew that neither he nor his party could bring slave state leaders around to the view that slavery was a moral and political evil—at least not in the foreseeable future. But in the period leading up to the 1860 election, Lincoln did hope to convince slave state leaders to accept the Republicans as a "normal" political party and to confine their opposition to regular political methods. (Lincoln's efforts along this line suggest that he did *not* dismiss the danger of secession and war.) In his Cooper Institute Address of February 1860, Lincoln addressed one section of his speech directly to the South: "When you speak of us Republicans, you do so only to denounce us as reptiles...You will grant a hearing to pirates or murderers, but nothing like it to 'Black Republicans.'"[51] Lincoln knew he would not change their minds on slavery. He asked only to be "granted a hearing." That was a minimal but crucially important request, because it meant legitimizing a kind of antislavery speech whose suppression slave state leaders had been demanding for decades.[52]

[51] Lincoln, "Address at Cooper Institute," New York City, February 27, 1860. Fehrenbacher, ed., *Abraham Lincoln: Speeches and Writings, 1859-1865*, 120.

[52] For recent discussion of how fully committed slave states of the lower South were to suppressing abolitionist agitation everywhere in the United States, and the role this played in the willingness of both North and South to make war rather than compromise, see Huston, "Did the Tug Have to Come?"

Lincoln went on to observe that, to southerners, proving that Republicans would leave slavery alone where it currently existed was apparently not enough to calm their fears. "What will satisfy them?" Lincoln asks. "This, and this only: cease to call slavery *wrong*, and join them in calling it *right*. And this must be done thoroughly—done in *acts* as well as in *words*...Silence will not be tolerated—we must place ourselves avowedly with them...The whole atmosphere must be disinfected from all taint of opposition to slavery, before they will cease to believe that all their troubles proceed from us."[53]

In the Cooper Institute Address, Lincoln also responded to the charge that Republicans were a sectional party, and therefore illegitimate, because "our party has no existence in your section—gets no votes in your section." If the sectionalism charge meant only that Republican candidates have received no votes in the South, Lincoln replied, then it would cease to be true as soon as the party did begin receiving some votes in the South, "for we shall get votes in your section this very year."[54] He did not pretend that Republican Party candidates were likely to *win* anywhere in the South. But receiving even a handful of votes in some slave states would weaken the sectionalism charge and help establish the party's legitimacy.

As it turned out, though Lincoln was kept off the ballot in all the slave states of the lower South, he did receive 1929 votes in Virginia, 2294 votes in Maryland, 1364 votes in Kentucky, 17,028 in Missouri, and 3822 votes in Delaware, all of which were slaveholding states in 1860. These vote totals, though small, would have provided a foothold for future party expansion in the upper South if secession and war had not intervened. Daniel Crofts observes that "Once Lincoln was elected, secessionists persistently accused him of planning to build an antislavery party in the upper South"—which of course was exactly what Lincoln hoped to do. In Tennessee, where Lincoln had

---

[53] Lincoln, "Address at Cooper Institute," New York City, February 27, 1860. Fehrenbacher, ed., *Abraham Lincoln: Speeches and Writings, 1859-1865*, 128-129.

[54] Lincoln, "Address at Cooper Institute," in Fehrenbacher, ed., *Abraham Lincoln: Speeches and Writings, 1859-1865*, 120-121.

been kept off the ballot in 1860, advocates of secession warned that Lincoln and William Seward (who became Lincoln's Secretary of State) would employ "postmasterships, mail agencies and government contracts" to successfully build an antislavery party in the upper South; by 1864, "a 'Black Republican ticket' would be 'openly run in Tennessee.'"[55] Though secessionists characterized Lincoln and his party as illegitimate because they had no presence in slaveholding states, their even greater fear was precisely that Lincoln and his party would establish and expand their presence in the region over time. Lincoln hoped—and secessionists feared—that the Republican Party would eventually win the support of non-slaveholding southern whites who resented the power and privilege of the slaveholding elite.

To return to Lincoln's House Divided speech and its emphasis on the public mind "resting" in the conviction that slavery was in course of ultimate extinction: I would suggest Lincoln believed that if the Republican Party and its elected officials were accepted as legitimate by the South—treated as a normal political party entitled to exercise the regular constitutional powers vested in the offices the party had won, and to express their views publicly everywhere in the United States—then the crucial corner would be turned and slavery *would* be placed in course of ultimate extinction, through one path or another, though this would still require enormous and sustained effort over a long period of time.

I would also suggest that advocates of pre-emptive secession fully understood Lincoln's strategy, judged that it had a realistic chance of success, and decided it must not be permitted a beachhead. For they feared that, once this point was conceded, time lay on the Republicans' side. This helps us understand why the states of the lower South seceded when they did—before Lincoln could even take office; how they justified the act; and why they were willing to run such enormous risks when the *immediate* threat to slavery was comparatively small.

---

[55] Daniel W. Crofts, *Reluctant Secessionists: Upper South Unionists in the Secession Crisis* (Chapel Hill: University of North Carolina Press, 1989) 93-94.

* * *

In conclusion, I want to return to the question I posed at the beginning of the essay. How, in Lincoln's view, would it have been possible to abolish slavery peacefully, democratically, and constitutionally?

Such an accomplishment required, in the near term, reversing the strong trend toward the full nationalization of slavery. That depended in turn on the formation of a political party publicly committed to the ultimate extinction of slavery. Such a party would give antislavery opinion a clear voice by providing it with a clear vote. Once the party was accepted as legitimate, even by those strongly opposed to its platform, the battle was already half won, and the public mind could "rest" in the belief that slavery was on the road to ultimate extinction. That party's first step once in office would be to halt the continued expansion of slavery. Over time, as that party acquired an enduring national majority, consolidating its support in the North and building a following in the upper South, it would begin implementing the various "cordon of freedom" measures (described above) designed to subject slavery to a long slow squeeze, to make it unprofitable, progressively to reduce its political clout, and ultimately to abolish it through peaceful, constitutional, and democratic means. Lincoln himself would no longer be president by this point, and perhaps deceased, but he saw his task as taking that first crucial step.

Lincoln was clearly right about the possibility of creating such a party, capable of winning elections and shaping public opinion. He was clearly mistaken in his hope that the party's election victories would be recognized as legitimate by the South. In that respect his strategy for a peaceful, gradual, democratic abolition of slavery failed. But it is important clearly to understand *why* it failed. The strategy was in no sense unrealistic. On the contrary, slave state leaders feared that once Lincoln was recognized as a legitimately elected president, and his party a legitimate party, the policy of abolition through a long, slow, nonviolent squeeze stood a real chance of success.

The theme of this volume is "1776," the year that American colonists severed their ties with the British Empire. Many of the secessionists of 1860-1861 invoked 1776 as a precedent. But there are important differences between the two cases. The American colonists were entirely unrepresented in the British Parliament. The slave states of the American South were fully represented in the United States Government—indeed overrepresented because of the notorious three-fifths clause. The American colonists broke with Britain after "a long train of abuses," including military occupation, the closure of the Port of Boston in a cruel act of collective punishment, and several pitched battles. The slave states of the lower South seceded before Abraham Lincoln could take office.

Finally, the American colonists justified their act to the world in the name of the universal natural rights of mankind. The slave states of the American South steered clear of any such justification, and rightly so. For if they could invoke the natural rights of human beings to defend their secession from the Union, their own slaves could have likewise invoked natural rights to "secede" from those who held them in bondage, and take up arms in defense of their own liberty. This in fact they did by joining the Union Army in large numbers during the Civil War, thereby earning Lincoln's deep respect.

But Lincoln's first hope had been to abolish slavery and redeem the natural rights of humankind through peaceful democratic means. Peaceful abolition of slavery did not become impossible in the United States because a democratic majority was incapable of the long-term commitment that such an accomplishment required. It failed because a slaveholding minority chose to secede and make war rather than permit the majority to attempt anything of the kind.

8

LINCOLN AND THE DAUGHTERS OF DRED SCOTT: A REFLECTION ON THE DECLARATION OF INDEPENDENCE

Diana Schaub

"Four score and seven years ago:" those words alone might serve to justify an essay on Lincoln in a volume devoted to 1776. Since that first clause of the Gettysburg Address refers to the year of the nation's birth, Lincoln could have begun his speech by saying "In 1776, our fathers brought forth on this continent, a new nation, conceived in Liberty, and dedicated to the proposition that all men are created equal." Or, he could have said, "Through the Declaration of Independence, our fathers brought forth on this continent, a new nation, conceived in Liberty, and dedicated to the proposition that all men are created equal."

Instead, he made his audience and all subsequent readers do a fair bit of arithmetic in order to puzzle out the date. For those not familiar with old English terms of measurement—like a bushel and a peck, or an ell and a dram—a "score" is a period of 20 years. "Four score" (4 times 20) "and seven" (plus seven) equals 87 years. Lincoln's Gettysburg Address was delivered in 1863; subtracting 87 from that date takes you back to 1776. It is often said that Lincoln must have chosen his opening phrase because it sounded more poetic than the alternatives, but I must say it's an odd form of poetry that requires so many mathematical operations, from multiplication to addition to subtraction.

The phrase "four score and seven" does, of course, evoke the beautiful language and cadence of the King James Bible. Lincoln's audience would have been familiar with the 90th Psalm which numbered the human lifespan at "threescore and ten," or at most, "fourscore." Many of them would also have known that the reason given for why the life of man is so "soon cut off" is that we spend our days in "labor and sorrow," consumed by God's wrath. By thus alluding to Scripture's harsh verdict on the lifespan of sinners, Lincoln forces us to wonder whether there are similar limits on the lifespan of mankind's political collectives. The nation, at fourscore and seven, is now just beyond the furthest term of an individual life. Moreover, as the audience well knows, and Lincoln soon acknowledges, the nation is engaged in a terrible civil war—a war that might cause the nation to perish.

But before he even gets to any mention of the war, in this opening paragraph which seems to be a purely admiring description of the achievement of the Founding Fathers, Lincoln is able to strike a darker note—a note of inevitable, and perhaps incipient, death—through this phrase "fourscore and seven."[1] In the ears of Americans, "1776" always has a hopeful and joyous ring to it; even though it is a date from the past, it looks forward; it smiles on the future. By contrast, "fourscore and seven years ago" has a somber resonance—it hints at the passing away of "the days of our years." So, yes, it is poetic, but not in the sense of a flowery fancying-up of ordinary speech; rather, like all genuine poetry, it imbues language with more complex and multilayered meanings—meanings that work upon and move the audience whether they are aware of it or not.

One final observation about the word "score." In its oldest denotation, it describes an activity that can be traced all the way back to the Paleolithic era, when numerical records were kept by scoring, which is to say cutting or notching, a piece of ivory, or bone, or wood. The scored item, sometimes called a tally stick, was employed as a mnemonic device—a way of keeping track of the passage of time (or

---

[1] In his 1859 address at the Wisconsin fair, Lincoln had considered whether national existence must pass away [*Abraham Lincoln: His Speeches and Writings*, ed. Roy P. Basler (Cambridge, MA: Da Capo Press, 2001) 504]. See also the Lyceum Address where he speaks of the nation existing "to the last" or until "the last trump" (*Lincoln*, 85).

other quantities) that stretched beyond the verge of human memory. So, we might say that Lincoln begins the Gettysburg Address by presenting the nation's tally stick or scorecard.[2] Again, it is highly significant that the nation's scorecard has just exceeded the scorecard of any individual.[3] Because no one in his audience, at that moment in 1863, could have been a participant in the events of 1776, American citizens were in need of new, more permanent, less flesh-bound forms of remembrance. Lincoln had been aware of this need since his Lyceum Address in 1838, when he noted that the veterans of the Revolution had nearly all "gone to rest," and with them had gone the "living history" of "the scenes of the revolution."[4] In effect, what Lincoln does in the first paragraph of the Gettysburg Address is carve a solid and enduring substitute. He condenses the meaning of the Declaration into one sentence. His formulation of what happened in 1776 is lapidary—a sentence that can be scored into memory.

This immortal sentence is a culmination of reflections on the Declaration in which Lincoln had been intensively engaged for the past decade at least. After the authors themselves (and maybe more than the authors themselves), Lincoln is the greatest expositor and disciple of the Declaration. Speaking from Independence Hall in Philadelphia, on the birthday of George Washington no less, President-elect Lincoln made a striking claim. He said that he had "never had a feeling politically that did not spring from the sentiments embodied in the Declaration of Independence."[5] Beginning with his eu-

---

[2] Lincoln had done something similar in the second sentence of his Lyceum Address, although there he sets the nation's existence within two larger horizons, the natural one of the earth's existence and the historical/religious one of Christianity: "In the great journal of things happening under the sun, we, the American People, find our account running, under date of the nineteenth century of the Christian era" (*Lincoln*, 76).

[3] Lincoln, a baseball fan, might have been familiar with the recent invention of the box score in 1859.

[4] "The Perpetuation of Our Political Institutions: Address before the Young Men's Lyceum of Springfield, Illinois January 27, 1838," in *Lincoln*, 84.

[5] "Address in Independence Hall, Philadelphia, February 22, 1861" in *Lincoln*, 577.

logy of Henry Clay in 1852, Lincoln had been not only appealing to the Declaration, but presenting interpretations of it in nearly every major speech, as well as in letters, even developing further arguments on scraps of paper (possibly for future use). Sustained treatments of the Declaration can be found in his Peoria Address of 1854, his Kalamazoo Address of 1856, his speech on the *Dred Scott* decision in 1857, and then the great rush of speeches during the senatorial campaign against Stephen Douglas in 1858, including not only the seven Lincoln-Douglas debates, but also major speeches in Chicago and Springfield.[6] In fact, the only major speeches during the decade of the 1850s that don't center on the Declaration are the House Divided speech and the address at Cooper Union. Because the House Divided speech was given at the Republican nominating convention, Lincoln did not need to convince his audience "to re-adopt the Declaration"—indeed, the maintenance of its principles was the first item in the Republican Party platforms of 1856 and 1860.[7] As for Cooper Union, it

---

[6] See the following Declaration-themed passages in *Lincoln*: 276 (Clay eulogy); 291, 303-4, 314-15 (Peoria Address); 331 (letter to George Robertson); 336 (letter to Joshua Speed); 342 (Kalamazoo 1856); 358-63 (Dred Scott, 1857); 400 ff (Chicago 1858); 422-23 (Springfield 1858); 445, 460 (Lincoln-Douglas debates); 478-79 (letter to J. N. Brown); 488-9 (letter to H. L. Pierce and Others); 513 (fragment on the Constitution and the Union); 577 (Philadelphia 1860); 709 (Response to a Serenade, 1863); 734 (Gettysburg 1863).

[7]This was not just a pro forma statement. Surveying Republican platforms in the 19th century, only those of 1856, 1860, 1868, and 1876 reference the Declaration. There is then a 100 year gap until the platform of 1976 mentions it (in a call to celebrate the bicentennial). [There are echoes in 1932 on black rights and 1956 on rights from the Creator.] The platform of 1996 concludes with an explicit re-affirmation of the truths of the Declaration. Beginning in 2000, the Republican platform has invoked the Declaration in the context of a call for a right-to-life amendment.

On the other side, Democratic platforms from 1840-1856 mention the Declaration but only in the context of immigration policy. (The Declaration is mentioned again in 1884, but with a shift against immigration.) Neither of the two platforms adopted by the splintered Democrats in 1860 makes any mention of the Declaration. After that, the Democratic platforms of 1900 and 1976 re-affirm the truths of the Declaration. The others make no explicit mention of the document, although there are echoes of its language in 1956 and 1960 through

presents an exclusively Constitution-based argument, setting forth with lawyerly precision the constitutional status of federal control over slavery in the territories, based on exhaustive research into the voting records of the Founding generation.[8]

Fittingly, after delivering the Gettysburg Address, Lincoln makes no further statements about the Declaration. His thought had achieved its final form. Moreover, the dedication to "a new birth of freedom," with which the Gettysburg Address concludes, marks a decisive moment, the beginning we might say of a new scorecard, a card that has been scored with the blood sacrifice of "these honored dead."[9] The scenes of the Civil War will rival in American memory the scenes of the Revolution, just as the sentences of Lincoln rival those of Jefferson.

This doesn't mean that the Declaration has been superseded. Far from it. After all, it was by returning to the Declaration—and by delineating "the practices, and policy, which harmonize with it"[10]—that Lincoln was able to meet the challenge posed by slavery. Often today, the persistence of slavery into the 19th century is viewed as a reason for disparaging the Founders. Lincoln, however, did not think they were to blame for the worsening situation, which he attributed rather to the failures of subsequent generations, beginning around the 1830s. Lincoln, in fact, credited the Founding generation with having contained slavery—a feat they achieved despite the extreme weakness of federal power under both the Articles of Confederation and the Constitution. As he put it, they "hemmed it in to the narrowest limits

references to equal rights and the rights of man. Additionally, the Democrats frequently invoke the name of the Declaration's primary author, Thomas Jefferson, and the Republicans do the same for its greatest defender, Abraham Lincoln.

[8] Given in New York City, the speech was designed to convince the snooty East Coast Republicans that Lincoln was not a clownish frontiersman.

[9] Think too of the grim accounting that Lincoln says a just God may exact: a continuation of the war until "every drop of blood drawn with the lash, shall be paid by another drawn with the sword" ("Second Inaugural Address, March 4, 1865," in *Lincoln*, 793).

[10] "Peoria," in *Lincoln*, 315.

of necessity."[11] They also forthrightly condemned slavery as a moral and political evil. Lincoln saw his own policy as faithful to the Founders' intentions. By banning slavery from the territories and keeping slavery quarantined in the existing slave states, slavery could be put back on the path toward eventual extinction—which was the path on which he believed the Founders had originally placed it.

All Men are Created Equal

After this fairly elaborate stage-setting, I would like to focus on one speech of Lincoln's—his June 1857 speech in response to the infamous *Dred Scott* decision. This speech contains one of his clearest explanations of what he believed the Founders meant in declaring that "all men are created equal." After exploring this central passage, I will then look at three other moments in the speech that show Lincoln applying the Declaration, in very concrete but somewhat surprising ways. What I find fascinating is that all three of these passages involve women. Out of all Lincoln's speeches, his *Dred Scott* speech is unique for its density of female references.

Lincoln's main purpose in this speech was to correct a dangerous misreading of the Declaration put forth by his Democratic political opponents, in particular Roger Taney (chief justice of the Supreme Court and author of the *Dred Scott* ruling) and Stephen Douglas (the leading Democrat in the Senate and Lincoln's longtime rival who had delivered his own speech in support of the *Dred Scott* decision just two weeks earlier).

Lincoln's generation, no less than our own, struggled to make sense of the stark contrast between the Declaration's ringing endorsement of mankind's natural equality and the ongoing existence of chattel slavery. No one wanted to denounce the Founders as hypocrites. One way to rescue the Founders from the charge that they said one thing, and did another, was to simply read blacks out of the Declaration. That is what both Taney and Douglas did. They argued that "all men" really meant "all white men." Here's Douglas:

---

[11] Ibid., 313.

> Can any sane man believe that the signers of the declaration of independence...intended to **place** the negro race on an equal footing with the white race? If such had been their purpose would they not have abolished slavery and converted every negro into a citizen on the day on which they put forth the Declaration of Independence?...
>
> No one can vindicate the character, motives, and conduct of the signers,...except upon the hypothesis that they referred to the white race alone, and not to the African, when they declared all men to have been created equal—that they were speaking of British subjects on this continent being equal to British subjects born and residing in Great Britain.[12] [emphasis added]

Lincoln rejected this exclusionary, white-supremacist interpretation as nonsensical—he said it did "obvious violence to the plain, unmistakable language of the Declaration."[13] He reiterated the original, expansive, and inclusive reading of the Declaration. At the same time, he honestly acknowledged the distance between the Founders' theoretical principles and their political practice. He didn't think that the gap between words and deeds made them hypocrites, however. He emphasized the insuperable obstacles the Founders faced in trying to reform unjust practices. He reminded his audience that democratic statesmen—constrained as they always are by tradition and public opinion—are not free to "place" folks, whether black or white, instantly on a footing of full equality. That limitation does not mean that the words of the Declaration are empty platitudes. Properly understood, they vitalize and guide political life.

Here is the central passage from Lincoln's speech:

> I think the authors of that notable instrument intended to include *all* men, but they did not intend to declare all men equal *in all respects.* They did not mean to say all were equal in color, size, intellect, moral developments, or social capacity. They defined with tol-

[12] "Remarks of the Hon. Stephen A. Douglas, on Kansas, Utah, and The Dred Scott Decision, delivered at Springfield, Illinois, June 12th, 1857." Chicago: Printed at the Daily Times Book and Job Office, 1857, p. 8.

[13] "Dred Scott," in *Lincoln*, 360.

> erable distinctness, in what respects they did consider all men created equal—equal in "certain inalienable rights, among which are life, liberty, and the pursuit of happiness." This they said, and this meant. They did not mean to assert the obvious untruth, that all were then actually enjoying that equality, nor yet, that they were about to confer it immediately upon them. In fact they had no power to confer such a boon. They meant simply to declare the *right*, so that the *enforcement* of it might follow as fast as circumstances should permit. They meant to set up a standard maxim for free society, which could be familiar to all, and revered by all; constantly look to, constantly labored for, and even though never perfectly attained, constantly approximated, and thereby constantly spreading and deepening its influence, and augmenting the happiness and value of life to all people of all colors everywhere.[14]

According to Lincoln, human beings are equal, but they aren't equal "every which way."[15] They are equal only in a highly specific way. Before specifying that way, however, Lincoln first details some of the manifold ways in which humans are unlike one another: he says they are not the same in "color, size, intellect, moral developments, or social capacity." That is an intriguing list. It begins with two visible natural differences: color and size. If we think about how contemporary society approaches human difference, the first two categories that spring to mind are probably "race and gender." Lincoln's categories may have some connection to those, but they are definitely not identical to them.

Let us consider color first. Given that Lincoln's dispute with Taney and Douglas concerned the Founding era's view of black people, it isn't surprising that Lincoln begins by acknowledging a difference that presents itself to all eyes. Human beings don't look the

---

[14] Ibid., 360-61.

[15] See "Harrison Bergeron," by Kurt Vonnegut, Jr. in *What So Proudly We Hail: The American Soul in Story, Speech, and Song*, ed., Amy A. Kass, Leon R. Kass, and Diana Schaub (Wilimington, Delaware: ISI Books, 2011) 90. Vonnegut's story provides a dystopic vision of a United States in which "Nobody was smarter than anybody else. Nobody was better looking than anybody else. Nobody was stronger or quicker than anybody else."

same; they come in different colors. In the speech that Stephen Douglas had given, he spoke repeatedly of the "African race," and "other inferior races"; he also spoke of the "superior" "white race." Lincoln, by contrast, rarely even uttered the term "race." Instead of dividing human beings into fixed categories, Lincoln presents the difference between blacks and whites as a purely superficial difference of skin tone. Moreover, in other writings, he points out that skin tone is not actually binary (black and white) but a matter of degree (lighter and darker). Thus, he warns slaveholders that if they regard whiteness as a title to mastery, they can't escape the logical conclusion that they themselves should be enslaved to the first person who comes along with paler skin than their own.[16] By speaking of color rather than race, Lincoln suggests the existence of a spectrum of infinite gradations. Although he highlights the visible difference of color among human beings, he hints at its individual rather than class character. He bridges the racial divide with a rainbow, such that by the end of this passage he is able to envision "all people of all colors everywhere" enjoying the benefits of "free society."

What about size—the next element in the list? Whereas an individual's "color" remains constant, "size" changes dramatically over the lifecycle. Each of us starts as an extraordinarily tiny, indeed embryonic, being, only gradually attaining our mature form. Even in adulthood, weight (unlike height) is notoriously subject to fluctuation. Differences in size are not purely individual since they can be correlated with certain category differences. For instance, adults are generally larger than children; males, on average, are larger and stronger than females. However, mostly what we see is an array of individual differences from short to tall and light to heavy. Size, like color, is spread along a continuum. Built upon these two properties, the visible spectacle of humanity is astonishingly varied. What we experience is not sameness, but diversity.

The next (and central) item on Lincoln's list is "intellect." He has moved from external to internal differences among human beings.

[16] "Fragment on Slavery," in *Lincoln*, 58.

He has also moved from qualities that are given by nature to a quality that is more complex inasmuch as intellect has long been thought to have both natural and acquired components. Differences with respect to intellect can also be a very significant driver of economic and social inequality. We know that Lincoln's overall aim in this passage is to define and defend the self-evident truth of equality. What we note is that equality, in the sense intended by the Declaration, can be vigorously upheld while at the same time one can admit that there is a range of intellect among human beings, a range that presumably entails differences in degree of intellect (from dumb to brilliant) as well as differences in type of intellect (as, for instance, verbal as compared to spatial abilities). We know how dangerous it can be when people make assumptions about intellect on the basis of other categories, like race. Lincoln lessens the likelihood of that by refusing to employ race as a category, instead treating all these differences as individual in nature.

The fourth item on the list is "moral developments." The phrase is interesting, since it suggests that good morals must be instilled. Even if there is such a thing as a conscience or an inborn moral compass, it requires support and development. Because of the effects of early habituation on our moral formation, institutions like the family, the church, and the political order itself can profoundly influence, if not determine, the degree of one's moral development. Unfortunately, these institutional influences can sometimes be harmful. Thus, the long-continued existence of an unjust practice like slaveholding might compromise one's moral development. Slaveholding had the power to corrupt family life, religious faith, and fidelity to the principles of republican self-government. Certainly, Lincoln believed that many Americans had already veered off "into the hateful paths of despotism."[17] It turns out that human differences are not simply individual in nature; rather, those differences can assume intractable social and political shapes which can imperil the achievement of justice.

---

[17] "Dred Scott," in *Lincoln*, 361.

The final item on Lincoln's list is "social capacity." What, one wonders, is this? Lincoln seems to say that human beings differ in their ability or power or fitness for social interaction. We know, of course, that there are introverts and extroverts. Extremely shy individuals might find it hard to participate in social activities, while extremely overbearing individuals might find themselves less than welcome at social gatherings. We also know that some forms of social disability are so extreme as to be considered "antisocial" pathologies. Whatever the range of individual possibilities, we might also wonder whether the notion of "social capacity" implies that human beings are by nature social creatures. Aristotle famously argued that we are not only social, or gregarious, by nature, but political as well, by which he meant that we are justice-seeking beings who must live in political community in order to achieve our highest flourishing.[18] Of course, other political theorists, especially those we term "modern," have argued, contrarily, that human beings are originally asocial or apolitical, exclusively concerned with their own individual self-preservation. Such atomized individuals might be driven into political association out of desperation but they are not drawn there by the higher longings of their souls.

Lincoln's suggestive phrase, "social capacity," does not tell us how he viewed this matter, other than that he thought human beings manifested some degree of difference with respect to social capacity. It may also be that social capacity refers less to natural gifts or sensibilities and more to inherited or acquired social standing. As Aristotle admitted, virtue itself requires a certain amount of "equipment"—goods of the world, such as wealth and friends, that allow virtue a field of exercise. Clearly, one's power and influence in society are affected by access to and possession of the externals. Thus, Lincoln's category of "social capacity" may point to structural and systematic matters of class and caste, both economic and political. We note also that the previous category of "moral developments" might have some bearing on this ultimate quality of "social capacity." So, for instance, a

[18] Aristotle, *Politics*, book 1, chapter 2.

people with a long history of living under the rule of law—and with the moral developments to match—might be more ready for the rigorous demands of self-government as compared to a people who have suffered under generations of tyrannical rule or a people who have grown used to ruling over others tyrannically. Neither slavery nor mastery prepares one for the self-restraint at the moral heart of "government of the people, by the people, for the people."[19]

A little reflection on Lincoln's list shows how carefully constructed it is—ascending from simpler, physical differences to more complex, multi-dimensional differences—and how it aims to be comprehensive, capturing the tremendous variety of humanity: in appearance, and faculties, in character and circumstance. The list also hints at a difficult question: what account, if any, must be taken of these inequalities in a just political system?

Having acknowledged the scope of differences among men, Lincoln returns to the matter of our essential similarity. What is the precise respect in which human beings are alike? Lincoln quotes directly from the Declaration: we possess "inalienable rights," which is to say, rights that belong to us by virtue of the kind of creature we are. According to Lincoln, there should be no confusion about the meaning of equality. Equality isn't some vague generality. On the contrary, the Declaration offers a definition of its central concept. Equality means equality with respect to natural rights.

None of the significant differences among human beings, which Lincoln went to the trouble of listing, invalidates the equal entitlement to "life, liberty, and the pursuit of happiness." Lincoln's verdict echoes that of the Declaration's main author. In a letter to the French abolitionist Henri Grégoire, Thomas Jefferson insisted that intellectual differences were irrelevant to the truth of equal rights: "Because Sir Isaac Newton was superior to others in understanding, he was not

[19] "Address at Gettysburg, Pennsylvania," November 19, 1863, in *Lincoln*, 417.

therefore lord of the person or property of others."[20] Rights are not contingent on anything but membership in what Lincoln calls the "human family." This phrase is a direct riposte to Stephen Douglas, who had insisted that "our fathers did not regard the negro race as any kin to them."[21]

Lincoln's next step in his analysis of the Declaration is crucial to his moral vindication of the Revolutionary generation. He considers again what the authors did not intend to say. While they were deadly serious about the truth of human equality, they knew full well that not all were, as Lincoln puts it, "actually enjoying that equality." Indeed, by their assessment, they themselves were not enjoying equal rights; that, after all, is why they wrote the Declaration: to present to the world the evidence of their oppression as justification for their independence from Great Britain.

By focusing on what the Founders did not mean to say, Lincoln reminds his audience of how insecure rights are and how often they are violated. Indeed, most people in most times and most places have not enjoyed the equality to which they are entitled. What did the authors of the Declaration propose to do about this nearly universal disrespect for the rights of man? According to Lincoln, "they had no power" to set the world "immediately" to rights. Remember, at the time, it was pretty unclear whether the colonists would have sufficient power to reclaim their own usurped rights, much less anyone else's. It would take eight years of war against the British Empire to achieve "the separate and equal Station to which the Laws of Nature and of Nature's God entitle them."[22]

Having dashed any utopian hopes about perfect equality, Lincoln concludes with two ringing sentences stating what the Founders did mean. They declared "the *right*," and by doing so generated the expectation that "the *enforcement*" would follow as soon as possible,

---

[20] Thomas Jefferson, "To Henri Grégoire," February 25, 1809, in *The Portable Thomas Jefferson*, ed. Merrill D. Peterson (New York: Viking Penguin, 1975) 517.

[21] Douglas, "Remarks," 11.

[22] Declaration of Independence, first paragraph.

which is to say, as speedily as prudence permits. Whereas the declaration of right is universal and absolute, the enforcement of right is dependent on circumstances. To take the case of black slavery: by the premises of the Declaration, it is undeniable that black persons possessed a natural right to liberty that was being wrongfully denied by the laws and practices of the colonists. The rectification of that injustice was neither quick nor easy. As it turned out, it required a Civil War, followed by the 13th,14th, and 15th Amendments to the Constitution, and a long, torturous process of societal reconstruction stretching over the next century and into our own.

But what must be stressed is Lincoln's conviction that the declaration of right in 1776 was itself epoch-making. It established a lodestar—or what Lincoln calls a "standard maxim"—guiding incremental improvement, or at least shining the torch of reason on oppression. Without that clearly articulated standard, there would be no inherent pressure for reform. This is a truly new thing: a government that has within itself a principle of self-correction. Fidelity to the origins—indeed, fidelity to the point of reverence—becomes the engine of perpetual progress.[23] According to Lincoln, the spread of equal liberty is not limited to the United States. The Declaration of Independence is global in its reach, not because the United States will impose regime change by force, but because awareness of the foundations of free society moves men longingly towards it. Knowledge of the truth ("familiar to all") produces attachment to the truth ("revered by all") which in turn produces action on behalf of the truth ("constantly labored for").

What About Women?

To see how women fit into Lincoln's interpretation of the Declaration, we might start by reviewing what is generally known on the topic of Lincoln and women. We know he was awkward around women; that he waffled terribly before he finally carried through on

[23] Lincoln's attaches great significance to "reverence" beginning with his Lyceum Address in 1838.

his engagement to Mary Todd; and that she proved a difficult wife.[24] We know of his sensitivity to the suffering of women who lost loved ones during the Civil War. Think of his inexpressibly touching letter to Mrs. Bixby, a mother who lost five sons in battle, or his call to care for the war widows in his Second Inaugural. Finally, we know that Lincoln supported at least a qualified vote for women as early as 1836 and that, late in 1860, he grew his beard in response to the suggestion of an eleven year old girl, Miss Grace Bedell.[25] What is less commonly noted about her suggestion is that it hinged on a claim about the indirect political power of women. In her letter, Miss Bedell writes: "All the ladies like whiskers and they would tease their husbands to vote for you and then you would be President."[26] Whether simply to oblige Miss Bedell or in the belief that facial hair might indeed garner him a few more votes, Lincoln acted on the advice of his girlish political consultant.

While Lincoln was not what one would call "a ladies man," it seems that he did follow the famous advice of Abigail Adams to "Remember the ladies." Nowhere is this more powerfully on display than in the *Dred Scott* speech. In the opening paragraphs, before outlining his response to the controversial Supreme Court decision, Lincoln makes some brief remarks about the situation in the territory of Utah, where the Mormons were taking up arms against the U.S. government. Lincoln does not spend much time on the practical question of what to do about the Mormon Rebellion.[27] Instead, he deftly shifts

---

[24] See the nuanced portrait in Lord Charnwood's classic account, *Abraham Lincoln: A Biography* (Lanham, MD: Madison Books, 1996) 61-69.

[25] "Announcement of Political Views in *Sangamo Journal*. June 13, 1836," in *Lincoln*, 58 and "Letter to Miss Grace Bedell October 19, 1860," in *Lincoln*, 561-62.

[26] Ibid., 562.

[27] Lincoln's opponent, Stephen Douglas, had come out in favor of strong measures, revoking Utah's territorial status, in effect denying the residents of Utah the "popular sovereignty" which was the centerpiece of Douglas's policy for the territories. Lincoln skewered Douglas for his hypocrisy, claiming that his readiness to abandon popular sovereignty for Utah proved that the real, but unavowed, purpose of "pop sov" was to benefit slavery.

the discussion to the underlying moral question of polygamy. At the time, plural marriage was part of the religious doctrine of the Church of Jesus Christ of Latter-Day Saints. It is estimated that one-third of Mormon women were in polygamous marriages.

The Republican platform of 1856 had linked polygamy and slavery, denouncing them as "twin relics of barbarism" and calling upon Congress to prohibit both practices in the territories. It's worth noting that the main reason polygamy was considered barbarous was because it involved the subordination of women to the patriarchal authority of men. Furthermore, because family structure and political structure are linked, sexual despotism in the household was regarded as the handmaiden of despotic theocratic rule. Look today at the status of women in Islam to confirm that domestic matters are not unconnected with the fate of political liberty.

Lincoln tries to force his political opponent, Stephen Douglas, to take a position on the morality or immorality of polygamy—something Douglas had absolutely refused to do on the subject of slavery, where he professed not to care whether voters in the territories embraced or rejected slavery. According to his doctrine of popular sovereignty, residents of the territories had a sacred right to decide all matters for themselves on the basis of local majority rule. Lincoln is testing the limits of Douglas's view that majorities—majorities composed of white males—can do whatever they like (whether it be to keep a stable of black men as slave labor or a stable of white women as sex slaves). He is trying to puncture Douglas's stance of non-judgmentalism or moral neutrality. While Douglas can perhaps get away with saying he doesn't care one way or the other about slavery, since the nation was about evenly split on that issue, he can't adopt that strategy with respect to Mormon polygamy, since it had triggered vehement public outrage. Remember, the reason the Mormons were all the way out in the Utah desert was because they had been chased out of every other place they had tried to settle.

After pressuring Douglas on the polygamy issue (and making a few barbed remarks about the situation in Kansas), Lincoln arrives at his main topic: his objections to the *Dred Scott* decision. Quite surprisingly, this discussion turns out to involve yet another controversial form of sexual union. Just about the only thing that Stephen Douglas did express moral disapproval of was any kind of intimate mixing between the races. When Republicans insisted that slavery was wrong and that all human beings had a natural right to liberty, Douglas argued that must mean that Republicans endorsed full social and political equality for blacks. Or, as he summarized it: if the Declaration of Independence applies to the "African race," that would "authorize negroes to marry white women on an equality with white men."[28] Douglas did all he could to stoke white fear—which is to say the white male fear—of miscegenation, the fear that a daughter of theirs would bring home a negro, the "Guess Who's Coming to Dinner" kind of fear. Female supporters of Douglas even embroidered their dresses with the slogan "White Men or None."[29]

Given the inflamed state of public opinion, Lincoln had to deny that intermarriage was the endpoint of his anti-slavery position. He does so in a most interesting way. Here's what he says:

> Now I protest against that counterfeit logic which concludes that, because I do not want a black woman for a *slave* I must necessarily want her for a *wife*. I need not have her for either, I can just leave her alone. In some respects she certainly is not my equal; but in her natural right to eat the bread she earns with her own hands without asking leave of any one else, she is my equal, and the equal of all others.[30]

Note that Lincoln avoids any mention of the black man/white woman pairing that is the surefire trigger for white outrage. Instead he speaks of a black woman, and then shows the illogic of Douglas's claim by making himself the illustrative example. Lincoln hates slavery and yet does not seek a black wife. By personalizing the issue, Lincoln man-

[28] Douglas, "Remarks," 8.

[29] Allen C. Guelzo, *Lincoln and Douglas: The Debates that Defined America* (NY: Simon & Schuster, 2008) 186 and 219. Taney too had made much of the criminalization of miscegenation, arguing that it showed the Founders could not have meant to include blacks in the Declaration's "all men."

[30] "Dred Scott," in *Lincoln*, 360.

ages to deny that he is any kind of advocate for amalgamation; but he does so without giving any credence to the overheated fears of the white racial imagination. His example skirts all those nasty stereotypes about predatory black men. Instead, in a deft rhetorical move, he turns his disavowal of race mixing into an endorsement of the essential equality and independence of women.

Speaking of this hypothetical black woman, Lincoln says he need not "have her" as either a slave or a wife. He can just let her be, allow her to go about her business as a self-determining agent. I am reminded of the great black leader, Frederick Douglass, who said:

> What I ask for the Negro is not benevolence, not pity, not sympathy, but simply *justice.* The American people have always been anxious to know what they shall do with us....I have had but one answer from the beginning. Do nothing with us? Your doing with us has already played the mischief with us. Do nothing with us! ... All I ask is, give [the Negro] a chance to stand on his own legs! Let him alone! If you see him on his way to school, let him alone, don't disturb him! If you see him going to the dinner-table at a hotel, let him go! If you see him going to the ballot-box, let him alone, don't disturb him! If you see him going into a work-shop, just let him alone,—your interference is doing him a positive injury.[31]

Lincoln's statement embodies this same liberal attitude—liberal in the authentic sense of leaving individuals free to exercise their talents and pursue their interests.

I suspect that contemporary listeners might be put off by Lincoln saying that this woman is in some respects not his equal. I must say I am not at all bothered by that, since I do not regard myself (or indeed anyone I've ever met) as Lincoln's equal, except, of course, in the respect he mentions: that of having an equal natural right to enjoy the fruits of one's own labor.

Having accorded this black woman equal respect, Lincoln moves immediately to his consideration of the meaning of the Declaration's

---

[31] Frederick Douglass, "What the Black Man Wants." (http://teachingamericanhistory.org/library/document/what-the-black-man-wants/).

equality clause—the passage we have already discussed at some length. Nothing could be clearer than that for Lincoln, "all men" includes not only black men, but all women as well, since his leading example of a person entitled to natural rights is a black woman.[32]

The third and final passage about women in this speech comes directly after Lincoln has finished his commentary on the individual rights doctrine of the Declaration. Since Stephen Douglas is frightening whites in the free states away from their belief in individual rights by hinting that black freedom would endanger the purity of white womanhood, Lincoln returns once more to this matter of race mixing. This is an admission of sorts that his earlier disavowal, being limited to a description of his own desires and behavior, did not fully meet the case. The issue is not whether Lincoln must himself engage in the ultimate social mixing, but whether someone with his views must allow others to do so. His initial response is to say: "agreed for once—a thousand times agreed. There are white men enough to marry all the white women, and black men enough to marry all the black women; and so let them be married."[33] Lincoln cheerfully, even humorously, acknowledges that folks tend to stick to their own when it comes to marriage; his ready agreement has the effect of defusing Douglas's attempt to stir up racial chauvinism.

And then, Lincoln's argument takes a bold turn. Citing the available census statistics on the number and residence of mixed race individuals, Lincoln proves that the real cause of amalgamation—this thing that Douglas is so horrified by—is slavery. The problem isn't marriage between whites and free black people. The problem is the

---

[32] Steven Spielberg's *Lincoln* has a lovely scene between Lincoln and Mrs. Keckley that nicely captures Lincoln's attitude:

> I…I don't know you, Mrs. Keckley. Any of you. You're…familiar to me, as all people are. Unaccommodated, poor, bare, forked creatures such as we all are. You have a right to expect what I expect, and likely our expectations are not incomprehensible to each other. I assume I'll get used to you. But what you are to the nation, what'll become of you once slavery's day is done, I don't know.

[33] "Dred Scott," in *Lincoln*, 363.

rape of black women by white masters. Lincoln is well aware that slavery violates not only the right to the fruits of one's labor but the right to the integrity of one's body. He points out that where freedom exists, and especially where civic equality exists, mixed race unions are very rare. New Hampshire, "the State," he says, "which goes the farthest toward equality between the races," has the fewest mulattoes.[34] This is a classic instance of Lincoln's brilliant redirection. He has taken the white fear of race mixing and shown how it ought to lead those who have that fear to endorse not only black freedom but civic equality (or at least a greater degree of civic equality).

Today, interracial marriage is no longer controversial. That welcome change can make it difficult for us to appreciate the strategy behind Lincoln's language. We expect all good people to be ostentatiously anti-racist. While I truly believe that Lincoln himself is quite free of racial prejudice, he does not make a big show of being morally outraged by racist views. He knows that attacking the core beliefs of one's audience doesn't generally win any friends or any votes. Instead, through his cool, numerical analysis, Lincoln tries to persuade even racial bigots that they ought to rethink their policy preferences. He is willing to exploit white chauvinism in order to further the anti-slavery cause.

The final step in his argument involves a shift in tone. It is as if he has now prepared his audience to hear a higher type of appeal. Lincoln reminds us that the *Dred Scott* case, in which the slave Dred Scott was suing for his freedom, involved not just a black man, but "his wife and two daughters." With respect to this black family, Lincoln says, "We desired the court to have held that they were citizens so far at least as to entitle them to a hearing as to whether they were free or not; and then, also, that they were in fact and in law really free." Why did Lincoln care about Dred Scott, his wife, and two daughters? What was at stake? Here's what Lincoln says: "Could we have had our way, the chances of these black girls ever mixing their blood with that of white people, would have been diminished at least

[34] Ibid.

to the extent that it could not have been without their consent."[35] Lincoln enshrines the notion of consent, not only in the public, political realm, but in the private, sexual realm. Lincoln is not outraged by race mixing, but by the violent and non-consensual aspect of such mixing as occurs, inevitably, under slavery.[36]

Lincoln contrasts his policy favoring black freedom with the effects of Douglas's endorsement of the *Dred Scott* decision: "But Judge Douglas," he says, "is delighted to have them decided to be slaves, and not human enough to have a hearing . . . and thus left subject to the forced concubinage of their masters, and liable to become the mothers of mulattoes in spite of themselves."[37] This is a profoundly empathetic statement. Lincoln has managed to move his listeners from Douglas's horror at the thought of "the mixing of blood by the white and black races" to sympathy for the daughters of Dred Scott now sent back to the real horrors of slavery. In place of those bigoted caricatures of black men, he encourages his male listeners to put themselves in the shoes of Dred Scott, the father of vulnerable daughters—daughters he will be powerless to protect from the depredations of the slave system.

The argument has come full circle. Lincoln knows his audience is repelled by polygamy. He has now shown that American slavery, at least for women, is often a form of polygamy, the worst kind of polygamy, "forced concubinage." While not making any accusation against Dred Scott's master, Lincoln nonetheless indicates that "a per centage of masters . . . are inclined to exercise this particular power which they hold over their female slaves."[38]

---

[35] Ibid., 364.

[36] It is true that Lincoln swears to stand by the laws banning mixed-race marriages in the Charleston debate. Once again, though, he plays that endorsement for a joke, vowing to uphold the miscegenation statutes for the sake of "Judge Douglas and his friends" who "seem to be in great apprehension that they might [marry negroes], if there were no law to keep them from it," suggesting further that Douglas be kept in the Illinois State Legislature (and out of the U.S. Senate) so that he can fight any attempt to repeal the restraining order against his runaway desires.

[37] "Dred Scott," in *Lincoln*, 364.

[38] Ibid.

At the very close of his speech, Lincoln sums up the three planks of the Republican position: "that the negro is a man, that his bondage is cruelly wrong, and that the field of his oppression ought not to be enlarged."[39] All three derive from his understanding of the Declaration. Throughout the decade of the 1850s, Lincoln used his oratorical powers to revive the American faith in human equality. Uniquely in this speech, he sought to strengthen the anti-slavery sentiments of his audience—sentiments that Lincoln believed lay at the very foundation of our sense of justice—by his subtle focus on the fate of women. Lincoln manages to expand our human sympathies without sacrificing analytic rigor and without descending into either overt emotionalism or demagogic appeals to anger (as so many of the abolitionist orators did). By studying Lincoln's speeches, we learn of the Declaration's timeless power, the ever-present need to understand it rightly, and, not least, the possibility of persuasive political speech that enlightens and ennobles its listeners. If only our nation could be blessed with the likes of Lincoln again.

---

[39] Ibid., 365.

INDEX